Teenage Pregnancy and Your Parenthood

Teenage Pregnancy and Young Parenthood provides a comprehensive, unparalleled insight into the UK Government's highly successful Teenage Pregnancy Strategy (TPS) for England, which reduced the under-18 pregnancy rate by well over 50 per cent, and considers how the lessons from this policy can be applied internationally.

This important book captures and shares the lessons from the TPS for future governments and policy makers, and documents the details of implementing a long-term strategy with its innovative approach to policy issues. After providing the rationale for prioritising teenage pregnancy, the book demonstrates evidence for what is effective, both in helping young people avoid unplanned pregnancy and in improving outcomes for young parents. The TPS is analysed against the World Health Organization's key actions for effective scale-up of adolescent sexual and reproductive health programmes, to offer an important contribution to international understanding of this global public health challenge.

Advocating a 'whole systems' multi-agency approach, this book translates evidence into clear action, and combines theory and practice with illustrative case studies to demonstrate how to implement policy successfully. It is valuable reading for policy makers and practitioners dealing with young people's health, as well as undergraduate and postgraduate students in the fields of psychology, health studies, social work, youth work, education, social policy, sociology and related disciplines.

Alison Hadley OBE is the Director of the Teenage Pregnancy Knowledge Exchange at the University of Bedfordshire and Teenage Pregnancy Advisor to Public Health England. She previously led the implementation of the Labour government's Teenage Pregnancy Strategy for England.

Roger Ingham is Professor of Health and Community Psychology at the Centre for Sexual Health Research at the University of Southampton and was research advisor on the strategy's Independent Advisory Group.

Venkatraman Chandra-Mouli works on Adolescent Sexual and Reproductive Health in the World Health Organization's Department of Reproductive Health and Research.

Adolescence and Society

Series Editor: John C. Coleman
Department of Education, University of Oxford

In the 20 years since it began, this series has published some of the key texts in the field of adolescent studies. The series has covered a very wide range of subjects, almost all of them being of central concern to students, researchers, and practitioners. A mark of its success is that several books have gone to second and third editions, illustrating their popularity and reputation.

The primary aim of the series is to make accessible to the widest possible readership important and topical evidence relating to adolescent development. Much of this material is published in relatively inaccessible professional journals, and the objective of the books has been to summarise, review, and place in context current work in the field so as to interest and engage both an undergraduate and a professional audience.

The intention of the authors is to raise the profile of adolescent studies among professionals and in institutions of higher education. By publishing relatively short, readable books on topics of current interest relating to youth and society, the series makes people more aware of the relevance of the subject of adolescence to a wide range of social concerns. The books do not put forward any one theoretical viewpoint. The authors outline the most prominent theories in the field and include a balanced and critical assessment of each. While some books may have a clinical or applied slant, the majority concentrate on normal development.

The readership rests primarily in two major areas: the undergraduate market, particularly in the fields of psychology, sociology, and education, and the professional training market, with particular emphasis on social work, clinical and educational psychology, counselling, youth work, nursing, and teacher training.

Also in this series:

Teenage Pregnancy and Young Parenthood

Effective Policy and Practice

Alison Hadley

with Roger Ingham
in collaboration with
Venkatraman Chandra-Mouli

Routledge
Taylor & Francis Group

LONDON AND NEW YORK

First published 2018
by Routledge
2 Park Square, Milton Park, Abingdon, Oxon OX14 4RN

and by Routledge
711 Third Avenue, New York, NY 10017

Routledge is an imprint of the Taylor & Francis Group, an informa business

© 2018 Chapters 1 and 2 Roger Ingham
© 2018 All other chapters Alison Hadley

The right of Alison Hadley and Roger Ingham to be identified as authors of
this work has been asserted by them in accordance with sections 77 and 78
of the Copyright, Designs and Patents Act 1988.

All rights reserved. No part of this book may be reprinted or
reproduced or utilised in any form or by any electronic, mechanical,
or other means, now known or hereafter invented, including photocopying
and recording, or in any information storage or retrieval system,
without permission in writing from the publishers.

Trademark notice: Product or corporate names may be trademarks
or registered trademarks, and are used only for identification
and explanation without intent to infringe.

British Library Cataloguing in Publication Data
A catalogue record for this book is available from the British Library

Library of Congress Cataloging in Publication Data
A catalog record for this book has been requested

ISBN: 978-1-138-69954-0 (hbk)
ISBN: 978-1-138-69956-4 (pbk)
ISBN: 978-1-315-51661-5 (ebk)

Typeset in Bembo and Gill Sans
by Florence Production Ltd, Stoodleigh, Devon, UK

For Jamie, George and Lorna

Contents

Foreword

*Ian Askew, Director, Reproductive Health
and Research, WHO*

An outstanding initiative that has made one country proud; an initiative
that could well be emulated by other countries around the world.

Almost a fifth of the world's population comprises adolescents aged 10 to 19
years. Adolescence is characterised by significant developments – physical,
hormonal, mental, emotional, sexual – during the transition from being a child
to an adult. Equally important are the changes in the type and nature of the
person's relationships with their parents, family, friends, community and society.
These changes make adolescents a distinct population group, with needs and
concerns that are different from those of both younger children and adults.
They are also diverse in terms of their stages of development and life circumstances, and have different and changing needs. The importance for all governments to actively focus on addressing the particular needs of their adolescents
if their countries are to achieve the Sustainable Development Goals (SDGs) by
2030 has been widely recognised and prioritised.

Several global initiatives have been launched to provide guidance and
support for these endeavours. Most notably, in 2015, the United Nations
Secretary-General launched the Global Strategy for Women's, Children's and
Adolescents' Health, highlighting the critical importance of including adolescents 'because they are central to everything we want to achieve, and to the
overall success of the 2030 Agenda. By helping adolescents to realise their rights
to health, well-being, education and full and equal participation in society, we
are equipping them to attain their full potential as adults.'[1] The World Health
Assembly in 2016 requested that the World Health Organization develop a
*Global Accelerated Action for the Health of Adolescents (AA-HA!) Implementation
Guidance* to support countries in planning, implementing and monitoring a
response in line with the Global Strategy. Published in 2017, this toolkit
provides detailed guidance based on different needs, country-specific objective
and target setting, the selection of information and service delivery strategies
with proven effectiveness, approaches for monitoring and evaluation, and
research priorities.

This book focuses on one challenging aspect of adolescence that is common to all countries – teenage pregnancy. For some societies, for a teenage girl to have one or more pregnancies before she turns 20 is not only normal, it is desirable – although only if it occurs within marriage. Indeed, this was the situation in England less than a hundred years ago. However, the overwhelming body of evidence from the past three decades, and from all regions of the world, highlights how early pregnancy can be a cause and consequence of inter-generational disadvantage and inequality, which extends in some countries to significantly higher rates of maternal and infant mortality.

Global trends towards greater enrolment and completion of secondary and tertiary education, increasing economic opportunities for young women, improved autonomy in decision making, and later marriage mean that an unplanned teenage pregnancy can also be a severe constraint on achieving one's life goals. Consequently, from several perspectives – health and wellbeing, economic development, individual rights, social norms – preventing teenage pregnancies is not only an individual concern, but for many governments it has become an increasingly high priority. As is becoming increasingly apparent, however, designing and implementing programmes that effectively reduce teenage pregnancies is proving extremely challenging for several reasons.

First and foremost, teenage pregnancies in most countries are characterised by inequality – an unwanted pregnancy is more likely to occur among dis-advantaged and disenfranchised teenagers and those living in vulnerable situations; furthermore, it is frequently intergenerational, with daughters of young mothers becoming young mothers themselves. Second, teenage pregnancy is a nationwide problem, and as such requires a nationwide response that can be effective at scale and also among economically, socially and ethnically diverse populations. Third, it is not a problem that is ever going to be 'solved' once and for all; the reasons for teenage pregnancies, and the societal perceptions of them, will continually evolve, and so a government programme needs to be both sustainable and sufficiently robust to adapt to changing social norms and political ideologies. Fourth, evidence shows that simply promoting particular moral positions and delivering piecemeal inter-ventions, such as providing information and education, or making available contraceptive methods, are not enough. The reasons for teenage pregnancies are multi-factorial, and so any efforts by governments and their partners must involve multiple sectors, ministries and departments, working together collaboratively and in coordination. Adolescent sexuality and pregnancy cannot be addressed separately from other aspects of an adolescent's life, including their living conditions, family relationships, education and/or employment, social networks, and use of alcohol and drugs, among others.

Many programmes to address teenage pregnancy have been developed and tested in numerous countries, but very few have provided lessons that can be adapted by others. Most have been too small in scope, poorly resourced and with no expectation of being implemented at scale or sustained indefinitely.

Importantly, many have been poorly designed, without reference to a theory of change, to the needs of diverse populations of adolescents and/or to the context in which they are implemented. The majority have also been poorly monitored, with unrealistic expectations of immediate impact.

The programme implemented in England described in this book was none of these; indeed, its primary attributes are the polar opposites. The demonstrated success in achieving goals, and in sustaining implementation over a long period of time and at scale – as well as through a change of political government – illustrates that this is a highly credible example for many others, including low- and middle-income countries. While specific elements of the strategy may need adapting to other contexts, the real lessons are in the broad principles that can guide the design and implementation of similar programmes around the world:[2] creating and maximising the opportunity for concerted and collaborative action; developing an evidence-based strategy with agreed-upon local and national targets; establishing the structures and working mechanisms for effective strategy implementation; tailoring strategy actions to reflect the findings of progress reviews; and embedding the strategy in wider government programmes. Key to its success were maintaining government leadership through the strategy and a dogged commitment to achieving the strategy's aims, even when early results were disappointing. Subsequently, considerable progress has been made, with rates continuing to decline and some new policy developments. Indeed, in March 2017, the UK government announced its decision to make relationships education compulsory from age 4 and relationships and sex education compulsory from age 11 in all schools by 2019. This was in recognition of the need for government to ensure all children and young people are equipped to develop healthy and safe relationships in the increasingly complex twenty-first-century world of the internet and social media. However, there is still more to be done to ensure that the gains made during and after the strategy are sustained into the future.

As an organisation fully committed to ensuring the sexual and reproductive health and rights of all adolescents everywhere, the World Health Organization is very pleased to have been involved with documenting and analysing the extraordinary story of England's Teenage Pregnancy Strategy. We will continue to share widely the lessons learned throughout our networks, and especially through the new AA-HA! Guidance, so that governments and adolescents the world over can benefit from this unique yet replicable experience.

Notes

1   Every Woman Every Child. 2015. *The Global Strategy for Women's, Children's and Adolescents' Health (2016–2030): Survive, Thrive, Transform*. New York: United Nations, page 5.
2   Hadley, A., Ingham R. and Chandra-Mouli V. Implementing the United Kingdom's ten year teenage pregnancy strategy for England (1999–2010): How was this done and what did it achieve? *Reproductive Health* (2016) 13:139.

Acknowledgements

I have so many people to thank for their help with this book. Firstly, John Coleman, OBE, the series editor, who believed this book was important to write, and my two collaborating authors, Professor Roger Ingham from the University of Southampton and Dr Venkatraman Chandra-Mouli from the World Health Organization: Roger for his expertise on the evidence and providing such helpful advice on the other chapters, and Chandra for his invaluable international perspective, and his enthusiasm and encouragement to share England's success more widely. Special thanks also to Anne Colquhoun, Alice Crutwell, Kerry Clarke, Stephen Clarke, Gill Frances, OBE, Alexa Gainsbury, Jo Nichols, Kate Quail, Gail Teasdale and Anne Tierney for their generosity in reading and commenting on some of the chapters.

Huge thanks too to those who helped with case studies to illustrate what the teenage pregnancy strategy meant in practice, or quotes to show what the journey of implementation felt like: Antoinese Akuffo, Mya Bhoodram, Carol Bowery, Jess Burns, Sue Burchill, Luke Carter, Mitch Denny, Lucy Emmerson, Laura Hamzig, Laura Hannah, Katie Herbert, Rhiannon Holder, MBE, Geoff Holliday, Sue Jablonskas, Marie Jarrett, Adrian Kelly, Lesley Kerr-Edwards, Catherine Kirk, Carmen Lau Clayton, Karen Lawrenson, Jane Lees, Nursal Livatlayi, Etty Martin, Jenny McLeish, Anna Martinez, Tom McLaren, John May, Saira Mumtaz, Caroline Palmer, Sue Pettigrew, Alison Poxon, Liza Scanlon, Naomi Sheppard, Vicki Smith, Louise Sweeney, Kate Thurland and Stephanie Whitehead. Much gratitude also to the contributors of the international case studies: Uwem and Adenike Esiet (Nigeria), Julio Pacca (Mozambique), Aparajita Gogoi (India), Qadeer Baig (Pakistan) and Galina Lesco (Moldova).

And lastly, although they didn't directly contribute to the book, I'd like to thank all those who worked on the strategy over its long journey. The Teenage Pregnancy Unit – particularly Cathy Hamlyn – the first head of the Unit, Karen Turner, Ruth Stanier, Jane Rumble, Jude Williams and Rob Greig in the early years and Marcus Bell, Robert Drake, Angela Edwards, Karen Gregory, Rob Macpherson, Laurence Russ, Dilwyn Sheers and Michelle Warne who helped to champion the strategy through its second phase; the regional coordinators who provided the essential intermediate layer between the TPU and local areas and provided expert support; the Teenage Pregnancy National Support Team whose bespoke advice helped accelerate progress in areas that were struggling; the independent advisory group who always balanced challenge with encouragement and support, and played a crucial role in maintaining the strategy's priority; the national and local politicians and senior leaders who maintained a commitment to the strategy and believed change could happen, often in the face of strong opposition; and finally all the brilliant and dedicated local teenage pregnancy coordinators who, in collaboration with their partner agencies and frontline practitioners, made the implementation of the strategy possible.

Introduction

It was seeing the reality of young parents' lives when I was working as a health visitor in London that first sparked my interest in teenage pregnancy. Their predominant experience was isolation, poor housing and no support to continue their education or think about their future.

Most hadn't planned their pregnancy. Their choice had been denied by poor or absent sex and relationships education (SRE), no discussion at home and fears about asking for contraception. The minority who had chosen pregnancy were often entering parenthood with a burden of disadvantage; wanting to do things differently from their own experience, but with little help, many were struggling to cope. Young fathers seemed invisible to services and their involvement and support needs rarely considered.

Watching the fragility of their lives crystallised for me the fundamental importance of information, support and reproductive rights in giving young people control over their life choices. It set me on a career journey for the next thirty years.

Working first as a nurse at Brook, the UK's leading young people's sexual health charity, I saw again the consequences of neglected needs. Young people pressured into having sex they didn't want, or unable to enjoy the pleasures of exploring sex because of pregnancy fears. Young people who trusted to luck to protect them, rather than risk asking for contraception and being met with judgemental staff. Perhaps most memorable was seeing a 15-year-old girl who had been taken to her family doctor by her mother because she had missed two periods, but denied any possibility of pregnancy because her mother was in the room and didn't know her daughter was having sex. The absence of periods was put down to exam stress and her pregnancy continued until she eventually came to Brook at 25 weeks' gestation. Too late for an abortion, her life had been fundamentally changed by the doctor's failure to give her a moment of confidentiality.

Later in the 1980s, and fuelled with such compelling evidence that change was needed, I moved from frontline practitioner to a role of policy and advocacy at national Brook. The 1980s were a challenging decade, marked by cuts in contraceptive clinics, a conservative approach to sex education, a legal challenge to the right of under-16s to confidential contraceptive advice and a rise in youth unemployment. As young people in some other Western European countries experienced declining levels of pregnancy, England's teenage pregnancy rates were steadily increasing. Every year as data were published, Brook called for government to take responsibility for equipping young people with the knowledge and skills they need to prevent unintended pregnancy and look after their sexual health.

In 1992, the Conservative government acknowledged the need for some action in their Health of the Nation strategy. This resulted in a welcome increase in young people's services, notably Brook. But teenage pregnancy was still viewed as solely a health issue, with the strategy not involving other services, having no structures for implementation and paying no attention to young parents.

The window of opportunity for change finally came with the election of the Labour government in 1997. Responding to the strong advocacy from NGOs, teenage pregnancy was prioritised in the government's new focus on reducing social exclusion and inequalities. A ten-year strategy was developed, involving all government departments, addressing the underlying causes of England's high rates and connecting to all aspects of young people's lives. The goal was ambitious – to halve the under-18 conception rate and bring it closer to the levels of our Western European neighbours – but also to provide high-quality support for young people who chose early parenthood. Most importantly, the long timescale recognised that change would take time.

This was a chance not to be missed, so in 2000 I left Brook to join the strategy's new Teenage Pregnancy Unit, a team under the initial steward-ship of Cathy Hamlyn, which blended the skills of civil servants with external specialists. It was a big step to move from an NGO into government, and to shift from the role of vocal advocate to civil servant working to ministers. But this was a once in a lifetime opportunity to channel my years of advocacy into delivering England's first ever comprehensive and evidence-based strategy, and be part of the journey of change.

Implementing the strategy over the following twelve years was an all-consuming but wonderful experience, working with fantastic colleagues in the Unit, regionally and locally. It was a huge programme of work needing dogged persistence in maintaining the priority and continually making the case for why teenage pregnancy was relevant to other government programmes. There were challenges from a vocal minority about improving sex education, and confused media messages blaming teenage mothers but complaining if younger teenagers were given easier access to contraception. Perhaps most difficult was that early progress was slow, and the press was very quick to declare the strategy a failure.

I still remember the nervousness in the Unit and in local areas as we opened the e-mails from the independent national statistics office to see each new set of data! When rates were slow to decline there was a lot to do to maintain morale, and to reassure ministers to hold their nerve. But having an evidence-based strategy, advice from respected experts and overwhelming support from NGOs and professional organisations helped anchor the belief that the actions local areas were taking – improving SRE, the expansion of services, youth-friendly practitioners and committed senior leaders – would in the end reap rewards.

That belief was consolidated by the mid-course review, which made it clear that in areas that were implementing all aspects of the strategy, rates were coming down. It was a light-bulb moment for some senior leaders to see that high rates were not an intractable part of English life, if the right actions were taken and young people were given choices. This was a milestone for the strategy and galvanised the redoubling of effort in the second phase. Aided by a hugely committed team of ministers – notably the Children's Minister Beverley Hughes and Secretary of State Ed Balls, and the health minister Caroline Flint – the downward trend accelerated rapidly from 2007.

In 2010, following thirteen years of continuous Labour administration, a coalition government was elected. After a further couple of years in the Teenage Pregnancy Unit I left government to establish the Teenage Pregnancy Knowledge Exchange at the University of Bedfordshire – to provide a continued national source of expertise and keep local leads connected as networks were dismantled. The key aim was to maintain the priority and the powerful momentum that had been established. Keeping the focus was important – the 50 per cent reduction goal of the strategy wasn't reached until 2014. I am very grateful to the university for recognising the value of the work, the importance of translating evidence into policy and practice, and the relevance to their students, many of whom will be the frontline practitioners of the future.

As England's progress finally began to be reported by the media (including some of the previously fervent critics!) and discussed in conferences, others became interested in the strategy. Particularly the World Health Organization (WHO), which was looking for examples of nationally led, scaled-up and effective programmes on adolescent sexual and reproductive health. WHO saw, as Ian Askew highlights in his foreword, how lessons from England could be applied elsewhere, and together we distilled the ingredients of success to inform international guidance. Most recently, Thailand has adopted much of the England model in their new ten-year strategy to address high teenage birth rates.

So, as the journey continues, eighteen years after the strategy was launched, it felt important to bring together much of this experience in a book, which has three key aims. First, to capture and share the lessons for current and future governments, policy makers, commissioners and frontline practitioners – to ensure progress continues in England and to contribute to developments internationally. Second, to document the detail of a long-term strategy and its innovative approach to addressing complex policy issues. Government and organisational memory can sometimes be frighteningly short! Brilliant policies, which were carefully developed and implemented, are often quickly forgotten with changes of government, and energy wasted in working out 'new' approaches. Third, to pay tribute to the many wonderful people involved in the strategy, nationally, regionally and locally – although only a tiny fraction of their work is captured here. The following chapters inevitably and rightly focus on policy and the process of implementation, but behind each strand of work were committed and passionate individuals, determined to bring about change and make a real difference to young people's lives.

The first two chapters focus on research and evidence, and are written by Professor Roger Ingham, the research adviser on the Strategy's Independent Advisory Group and a long-time champion of young people's reproductive rights. **Chapter 1** considers different ways of understanding the term 'teenage pregnancy' and provides an overview of relevant research. Drawing on literature mainly from the UK and USA, issues discussed include why teenage pregnancy is of concern, the international, regional and local variations in rates, who is more likely to become pregnant and the likely outcomes, and the research challenges in understanding the causes and consequences of early pregnancy. **Chapter 2** explores some of the evidence of what contributes towards helping young people avoid unplanned conceptions – in particular the essential contribution of high-quality sex and relationships education and access to effective contraception – but highlights that there is no easy answer to such a complex issue. The chapter concludes that the solution rests with a whole systems approach, with different agencies contributing what they can, and with the interests of young people at the centre. This was the approach of the England strategy and seems to be what encapsulates the situation in those countries that have adapted well to the changing circumstances of young people and society in general.

The next two chapters describe the journey of implementing the Labour government's ten-year strategy. **Chapter 3** sets out the rationale for prioritising teenage pregnancy, the analysis of why England had such high rates, the development of an evidence-based action plan and the structures that were necessary for implementing a multi-agency, long-term programme. This is followed by an overview of the first phase of implementation from 1999 to 2005, describing specific actions of the strategy and how they were integrated into wider government programmes. **Chapter 4** describes the second phase of the strategy's implementation, starting with the mid-course review, which confirmed the ten key factors for an effective strategy, the subsequent actions and ministerial involvement to accelerate progress, the strengthened focus on reaching young people most at risk, and the final push to improve sex and relationships education and young people's access to effective contraception. The chapter discusses how the priority was maintained over such a long period, and the importance of integrating teenage pregnancy into mainstream programmes to help sustain progress following the end of the strategy.

Chapter 5 focuses in more detail on how the national strategy was implemented in local areas: how the ten key factors confirmed in the mid-course review were translated into action to create the necessary whole systems approach. The contribution of the ten factors is described with reference to the supporting national actions. Each is illustrated by local case studies, chosen from a mix of urban and rural areas which significantly reduced their under-18 conception rates. The vast majority of the case studies were originally supported through the teenage pregnancy grant, but subsequently secured funding from mainstream resources. Each section concludes with the key principles for successful implementation. These are drawn from the mid-course review, subsequent learning over the ten years of the programme and consultation with experienced teenage pregnancy coordinators who led local implementation. The principles deliberately do not refer to England-specific policies or structures, so that they can be applied in a range of national, cultural, policy and commissioning contexts.

Chapter 6 focuses on the actions the strategy took to support teenage mothers and young fathers. The support programme was implemented through the same national, regional and local structures as described in Chapters 3 and 4. This chapter describes the factors that may contribute to poorer outcomes for some young parents and their children, along with the evidence for the effectiveness of coordinated support, drawn from evaluations of the *Sure Start Plus* and *Family Nurse Partnership* programmes, specialist education support, funded childcare to enable young parents to return to education or training and models of supported housing to reduce isolation and exclusion. Case studies from local areas and quotes from teenage mothers and young fathers illustrate different aspects of the support programme. The chapter concludes with a recommended multi-agency care pathway for pregnant teenagers and young parents, from maternity services through to postnatal and early years support, the principles of which can be applied in a range of settings.

Chapter 7 is written in collaboration with Dr Chandra-Mouli from the World Health Organization, who first saw the transferability of the strategy and has championed England's success internationally. It discusses the key success factors of the England strategy, some of the challenges faced and elements that could (and should) have been done differently, and how the learning can be applied in other country contexts. To provide a consistent framework, the factors are described under the WHO five key actions for national adolescent sexual and reproductive health programmes: placing adolescent sexual and reproductive health on the national agenda; planning for scale-up from the start; managing scale-up effectively and efficiently; building support while anticipating and addressing opposition; and promoting and safeguarding sustainability. These actions were identified in a global consultation on the lessons learned from the first generation of scaled-up programmes, to which England contributed. Five case studies – from Nigeria, India, Mozambique, Pakistan and Moldova – illustrate how the actions can be applied in widely differing settings. Finally, the chapter summarises the next steps for addressing teenage pregnancy in the global context, capitalising on what is described as a 'never before' moment in adolescent health with the 2015 United Nations Global Strategy for Women's, Children's and Adolescents' Health and WHO's new *Global Accelerated Action for the Health of Adolescents (AA-HA!) Implementation Guidance*.

I end the book with a short epilogue, reminding us that the long, complex and sometimes tortuous journey of the teenage pregnancy strategy was in the end all about making a difference to young people's lives. Although there is still much to do to ensure all young people are able to make well-informed choices and that young parents have the support they need to fulfil their ambitions, without feeling stigma or judgement, much has changed for the better. I hope the quotes I end with give a small flavour of how young people have benefited, but also illustrate the passion and dedication of all those who have worked on the strategy for so long. The Labour government deserves the credit for developing, prioritising and resourcing the strategy over such a long period. As one journalist pointed out when reflecting on the strategy's success, which was reported after Labour left office – 'good government often goes unnoticed and unrewarded' (Hardman, 2016). But it was the leadership and collaborative effort of many hundreds of committed individuals who made it a success.

Chapter 1

Variation in teenage conception rates

1.1 Background

1.1.1 What is teenage pregnancy?

Although the phrase 'teenage pregnancy' is widely used and may sound straightforward, there is some confusion in the media and elsewhere as to what is actually covered. Strictly speaking, it should refer to a conception that occurs while a woman is still a teenager; that is, prior to her 20th birthday. However, such a definition would include births that occur up to about 20 years and 8 to 9 months of age, as well as abortions that take place either before the 20th birthday or some time afterwards. Such refined data are simply not readily available in the vast majority of countries.

Data on abortions by age are not routinely available in many countries. This is sometimes due to its illegality, the stigma attached to the process or a relative lack of concern among the official statistical authorities or the public health departments. In all of these countries, abortions among residents still occur, through women travelling to another country for the purpose of obtaining one, or by obtaining medication for early medical abortion from the internet, or through unofficial, and often unsafe, provision. These cases do not appear in routine official statistics.

What is important to clarify is how the phrase 'teenage pregnancy' is operationalised in practice. As mentioned above, strictly speaking it should cover all teen ages. However, countries use different age bands for various reasons, even within the UK.[1] In England, the main policy concern has focused on conceptions that occur under the age of 18, the statutory age for participation in education and training, with an additional focus on young women who conceive before 16, the legal age of sexual consent. Delaying conceptions in the later teenage years is generally regarded as a lower priority, partly as they occur, in theory, after the young woman has completed her statutory education, but also because, as age increases, higher numbers are within marriage, which is assumed to reflect a stable relationship.

The England strategy, which is described in this book, set a target to halve conceptions among under-18s and establish a downward trend in conceptions among under-16s. What were of interest were the rates, not the absolute numbers, since an increase in age-specific population sizes will affect the actual numbers of cases. That said, calculating the rates based on the whole under-18 population would be misleading, mainly because most of the people captured within this group are not of reproductive age.

So, the pragmatic approach adopted in the UK for many years has been to use the age range 15 to 17 years as the denominator to calculate under-18 rates, and the age range 13 to 15 years to calculate under-16 rates. Data on conceptions are compiled by combining information from registrations of births and notifications of legal abortions. Estimates are made for each birth and abortion as to the likely date of conception, and that date is linked to the age of the woman at the time. All such events that are estimated to have occurred between her 15th birthday and the day before her 18th birthday are counted as a case (for under-18 conceptions) and the overall numbers are linked to the annual population size estimates of that age group to calculate rates. As an example, 60 conceptions among 2,000 women aged 15 to 17 years would be a rate of 30; 80 conceptions among 4,000 women aged 15 to 17 years would be a rate of 20. Clearly, some estimates regarding the actual dates of events are needed for these calculations, but the assumption is that these inbuilt errors are consistent and so do not seriously affect data comparisons over time or place. Miscarriages are disregarded for the calculation of these rates, partly because their occurrence is assumed to be comparable across areas (so not affecting comparative analyses) but also because some occur without a woman's knowledge or do not require clinical intervention, and so are not included in any official hospital data.

A further figure that is of relevance is the proportion of those conceptions that do occur that end in abortion. This is important if the policy concern is more directed towards births that occur to young women, as opposed to conceptions *per se*. Out of every 100 conceptions a certain proportion will end in termination – this is called the *abortion proportion* (or *abortion ratio*).

These definitional distinctions are important since, among the various approaches to understanding the area of early conceptions, comparing data from different areas enables lessons to be learned as to how policy can be directed in more fruitful ways. For example, when the monitoring data for the England strategy showed that, within the overall reduction in conceptions, there was a steeper decline in births compared with abortions, additional investment was made in improving young people's access to, and uptake of, contraception. It is to some of these comparative data that focus is now directed.

1.1.2 International comparisons in teenage birth rates

Some of the earliest national comparative data analyses involved researchers from the Guttmacher Institute in the USA who collected data from 37 industrialised countries in the mid-1980s; the data included teenage *birth* rates (not *conception* rates due to unavailability of abortion data in many countries) alongside a range of other indices that were thought could be related. These included the Gini coefficient (an index of income distribution within countries), levels of sex and relationships education in schools and the degree of openness regarding sexual issues, including, for example, television advertising of contraception. In summary, they reported that countries with lower birth rates were characterised by a smaller gap between rich and poor, as well as having more 'open' cultures regarding sexual issues (Jones *et al.*, 1985; 1986). A replication of this approach many years later focused on a smaller number of countries (five) in Europe and obtained very similar results (Darroch *et al.*, 2001).

What had sparked these concerns in the USA was the country's very high birth rate compared with other rich nations. UNICEF carried out a similar comparative analysis in 2001, comparing data from 28 OECD countries (UNICEF, 2001). They pointed to the very wide range in teenage (under-20s) birth rates, with South Korea and Japan at one extreme (with around 3 per thousand), through Switzerland (5.5), the Netherlands (6.2) and Sweden (6.5) to the UK at 30.8 and the USA at 52.1. The proportions of these women who were married at the time varied from 86 per cent in Japan to 2 per cent in Iceland and about 10 per cent in the UK, although no data are presented on cohabitation rates.

In attempting to account for these wide variations, the UNICEF report noted that there had been a general decline in teenage motherhood in most countries (probably linked to the increase in average age at marriage) but also large increases in sexual activity among young people. They argued that countries that have successfully reduced rates of teenage births are characterised by, among other features, 'rising levels of education, more career choice for women, more effective contraception, and changing preferences' (p. 2) and 'the widespread rejection of traditional sexual codes' (p. 8). They also point out that, despite the general reduction over time in teenage birth rates, the perception of this being a problem in society has increased. In highlighting commonalities between countries in that birth rates are higher in the poorer areas, the authors proposed that rates can be understood in terms of both *means* and *motivation* to avoid early pregnancy. The *means* involves the availability of contraception and sex and relationships education that enables young people to make informed and mutually respectful choices; on the other hand, the expectation of inclusion in the benefits from education, employment and economic opportunities provides *motivation* to delay parenthood. It was this principle that underpinned the England strategy and the reason for its close links with other government programmes aimed at increasing educational attainment and narrowing inequalities of opportunity.

1.1.3 Regional variations in under-18 conception rates

As well as national variations, there are quite substantial regional variations in conception and birth rates within countries; here, the focus is on the situation in England.

In 1998 (the baseline year for the strategy), there were 41,089 conceptions to women aged under 18, with an overall rate per thousand of 46.6; using the government regions, the rates ranged from 66.7 in Inner London to 37.8 in the South East (Office for National Statistics, 2017a). At the local government level, rates ranged from 87.2 to 16.9. At the lower geographical level of electoral wards (averaged over three years to avoid large year-by-year fluctuations due to small numbers), the rates for 2001 to 2003 ranged from 213.0 to 6.4.

Variation between countries, and regions within countries, indicates that research exploring why such variations occur will be fruitful, and should point towards potential foci for policy action. The importance of having accurate regional and local data to monitor progress and inform the England strategy is highlighted at several points in subsequent chapters.

1.1.4 Why is early conception an issue?

Whether or not early conception is regarded as a 'problem' is a matter for debate. In some countries (as in the UK going back some years), early marriage and childbearing is (and was) the norm. There are other issues to be considered, however, such as 'forced' early marriage and societal pressures to be fertile, 'shotgun' marriages, gender inequalities and other factors impacting on individual choice; these are beyond the scope of the present volume.

In a rapidly changing world, however, where extended education, growing employment for women and smaller families are becoming the norm, an increasing number of countries regard teenage parenthood as carrying significant intergenerational disadvantage, and are taking action to equip young people to avoid early conception (UNICEF, 2001; UNFPA, 2013a, 2013b; 2015). All the UK initiatives were developed with the aim of reducing social exclusion, poverty and inequalities, alongside improving young people's sexual health and wellbeing.

Meanwhile, it is worth noting variations in abortion proportions, which can be interpreted as indicating the degree of planning involved in the conceptions that do occur. Although circumstances can change between conception and birth (for example, partnership dissolution, housing and financial emergencies), most abortions arise from unplanned conceptions. In the same way that there are variations in conception rates across regions, so there are variations in abortion proportions.

Using the 1998 baseline data, and with an England overall figure of 42 per cent, across regions, the proportions of conceptions that ended in abortion ranged from 54.5 to 35.2 and, across local government areas, from 78.3 to 23.9. Lee et al. (2004) explored these variations using both qualitative and quantitative data, and found that many of the statistical associates of variation in conception rates also applied to variations in conception outcomes, and that there are many attitudinal, community and societal factors that affect the choices that young women make when faced with a pregnancy. In brief, areas with high conception rates tend to have lower abortion proportions. Over the course of the strategy, the proportion of conceptions leading to abortion increased in all England regions, including the most deprived areas. This trend may reflect an increase in the choice of outcome options offered by the wider availability of abortion services, described in Chapter 3, and/or greater awareness of the advantages of delaying early childbearing arising from the publicity surrounding the prevention strategy.

1.2 Research challenges

There are a number of methodological challenges involved in the study of teenage pregnancy. These are briefly outlined now to avoid the need for repetition as the review progresses and different studies are described.

1.2.1 Distinguishing precursors from sequelae

There is interest in how teenage parents, especially mothers, may differ, as a consequence of being parents, from others who are not parents. Some research points to downward social mobility in the form of lower income, higher unemployment, increased likelihood of poor mental health – for example postnatal depression – and other negative outcomes. Studies generally obtain their samples after the event – that is, after parenthood has occurred – and compare young parents with similarly aged non-parents.

A major challenge with this research design is that it is very difficult to disentangle any factors, attributes, conditions or qualities that may have been present *prior to* the pregnancy from those that were brought about *as a result of* the pregnancy and birth. In other words, claims that the young age of the mother leads directly to negative outcomes need to be handled with great care. Attempting to ascertain factors that pertained prior to the birth from retrospective accounts are fraught with difficulties relating to memory, post-hoc justifications and other challenges.

Examples are provided later of studies that have overcome these challenges by using longitudinal data obtained from large samples that provide relevant information before and after the transition to parenthood. Such studies, however, were not designed specifically in order to explore early childbearing, so the level of relevant detail in the topics covered is limited. Further, some were commenced prior to early pregnancy being a particular focus of policy interest, so what we would now regard as highly relevant information was not included from the outset.

Further, such studies do not necessarily capture information on young women who became pregnant but chose to have an abortion. Although this question may be asked, the stigma associated with abortion may lead to inaccurate responses. So, by just comparing young mothers with non-mothers, any potential differences between those who become pregnant and those who (perhaps) do not are hidden. A similar point can be made regarding young women who suffer miscarriages.

Even for studies that do have available data from before and after the event, confident attribution can be highly challenging. If, for example, an association is observed between a young woman's family structure at age 13 and the probability of childbearing before age 18, this does not indicate a causal relationship. It may provide clues as to where to search for explanatory links, but does no more than this.

The so-called 'gold standard' approach to research involves randomly allocating people to different controlled conditions and then comparing outcomes subsequently. Such an approach is clearly inappropriate when considering teenage conception as an outcome, although some studies have adopted this method when looking at specific issues that may be relevant, such as different approaches to sex and relationships education. Some examples are considered later.

1.2.2 Variations in levels of sexual activity and/or levels of contraceptive use

It was mentioned earlier that teenage conception data are presented as rates per thousand women within specified age ranges. What this overlooks, of course, is that not all of these women will be sexually active. There is a strong case for presenting conception data as rates *per 1000 sexually active women*, but the level of detail of local data that would enable this is not available and would take an extremely large and prohibitively expensive representative sample survey to obtain.

Consider an example: Area A has an under-18 conception rate of 50 per thousand while Area B's rate is 48 per thousand. If half of the young women in Area A have experienced penetrative heterosexual sexual activity, then the 'true' rate of conception among those at risk of conception is 50 per 500, which is 100 per thousand. In Area B, if three-quarters have had penetrative heterosexual activity then the rate is 48 per 750, which is 64 per thousand. So, apparently similar conception rates (50 and 48) can arise from different areas' behavioural characteristics. Further, it is important to note that the category of 'sexually active' in this context simply means having experienced penetrative heterosexual activity but does not measure the *frequency* of such activity, an index that will clearly also affect the likelihood of conception.

Additionally, levels of correct and consistent contraceptive use will also affect outcomes. So, for example, in the two hypothetical areas outlined above, the seeming similarity in the traditionally expressed (per thousand women) rates conceals differences in levels of sexual activity (or status), but also reveals variations in effective contraceptive use. In the two examples above, it would appear that young women (or couples) in Area B are more effective users of contraception than those in Area A, since the conception rate among sexually active women is considerably lower (64 as compared with 100).

So, in accounting for variations in rates, as well as in devising suitable policy responses, it is important to gather more detail than the official published rates provide. As mentioned earlier, good data on area-level variations in sexual activity are not available, and nor are similar detailed data on contraceptive usage (the national survey –NATSAL – does involve a large sample across the country, but this is unsuitable for detailed age-related analysis once broken down into local levels). In England, local data on attendance at community contraceptive services are recorded by age and residence, but data are not available by age on other sources of contraception, nor on actual usage. Some studies do ask about *general* usage, or general properties or attributes, such as attitudes to risk, or sensation seeking, as opposed to specific contextual factors that may account for risks occurring.

1.3 Who is more likely to get pregnant?

Bearing in mind the caveats outlined above regarding research in this complex area, this section provides an overview of key findings that have helped to identify some of the important factors associated with teenage conceptions. Consideration is given to variations at international, regional and individual levels. Finally, brief consideration is given to the issue of intentionality.

1.3.1 International variations

As mentioned earlier, because abortion is illegal or strongly proscribed and stigmatised in some countries, comparative data on conceptions from a wide range of countries are hard to access. Accordingly, emphasis is on birth rates, and reference was made earlier to the initial (dated but still relevant) Guttmacher comparative studies and to the fact that the general societal characteristics that they reported were associated with variations in national rates (Jones *et al.*, 1985, 1986). Similar general conclusions were reported by the UNICEF team based on a slightly different sample of countries. This also introduced the interesting notion of 'motive and means' as significant factors in accounting for variations in teenage birth rates between and within countries (UNICEF, 2001).

The UNICEF report draws attention to the reduced birth rates alongside higher abortion proportions in the Nordic countries, and argues that these data represent a relative failure in sex and relationships education and/or service provision (on the grounds that abortion is unlikely to be a preferred choice). In identifying the Netherlands as a country with low birth *and* low abortion rates, the report calls this a 'remarkable achievement', the underlying reason for which is 'the combination of a relatively inclusive society with more open attitudes to sex and sexuality education, including contraception' (UNICEF, 2001, p. 23).

As well as interesting lessons that can be learned from comparative national birth rate data of this kind, focus can also be directed towards possible variations in levels of sexual activity and abortion proportions in different countries.

In other words, are the birth rates higher in the USA and the UK just because more young people are engaging in sexual activity, and/or because more young people are making a positive choice of early parenthood, and are these affected by the cultural variations identified by the Guttmacher researchers and the UNICEF study?

Combining data on changes in levels of sexual activity across time in Europe, reported by Bozon and Kontula (1998), and those reported by Singh and Darroch (2000), Ingham (2007) demonstrated that the large variations in birth rates across European countries were not accounted for by the proportions of women who reported heterosexual intercourse by the age of 20 years. What was also demonstrated was wide variation in the abortion proportions across countries. So, for example, across the ten European countries compared, Germany had a teenage abortion proportion of 29 per cent, compared with Sweden's 69 per cent. These variations suggest differing attitudes to abortion in the different countries, as well as, perhaps, different availability and efficient use of reliable contraception.

Relatively little is known about reported reasons for sexual activity among young people in comparative terms; such data would be immensely helpful in the attempts to account for national variation in rates of conceptions and outcomes. One such study was reported by Ingham and van Zessen (1997, 1998), albeit based on small samples in the Netherlands and the UK but derived from detailed interview data. They report that, whereas women provided broadly similar reasons in the two countries, men in the Netherlands were much more likely to report 'love', 'commitment' and similarly intimate reasons for first sex (around 60 per cent) than were men in the UK (around 15 per cent). Among the latter, 'opportunity', 'physical attraction' and 'peer pressure' were more frequently reported reasons. More intimate reasons (as seen in the Netherlands) are associated with longer length of relationship prior to first sex, higher levels of partner communication and more effective contraceptive use.

1.3.2 Regional variations

Close links between rates of teenage pregnancy and levels of social deprivation have been identified in a number of studies. One of the earliest in the UK was carried out in Scotland, with Smith (1993) demonstrating that young women living in the most deprived areas who became pregnant were considerably more likely to give birth while a teenager and to be less likely to have an abortion.

Using multi-level modelling (to account for shared characteristics at different levels of analysis), Diamond et al. (1999) found that specially developed (and directly relevant) indices of social deprivation predicted rates of teenage conception in local authority areas across the South West of England. These indices included (for urban areas) the proportion of children under 5 years old, the proportion of households without access to a car, the percentage of 17-year-old children not in full-time education and a measure of population mobility. In rural areas, significant predictors were 'non-car ownership, the proportion of children under 5 years old, overcrowding and lack of basic amenities' (Diamond *et al.*, 1999, p. 283).

A more recent study (Office for National Statistics, 2014) reported that child poverty and unemployment are the two area-deprivation indicators with the strongest association with under-18 conception rates.

It needs to be borne in mind that this approach to the study of variations in conception rates runs the risk of falling into the 'ecological fallacy'; in other words, it should not be assumed that the characteristics of an area that relate to specific outcomes apply to all the individual people living in that area (although the chances are increased, of course).

An illustration of this distinction comes from work by Smith and Elander (2006), who demonstrated that, in terms of early sexual activity and life expectations, levels of both family and area deprivation interacted. Although early sexual activity was associated with living in deprived areas, the effect was stronger among those in deprived families. Similarly, life expectations were higher in less deprived areas, but only among those in non-deprived families.

1.3.3 Individual characteristics

Although national and regional variations, and their associated correlates, are of great interest in narrowing down the search for explanatory factors and developing policy interventions, they do not enable a level of understanding to identify individual-level risk of, and/or vulnerability to, early pregnancy. As mentioned earlier, asking women after the event of conception is not necessarily a reliable approach to the area.

A few studies in the UK have enabled a more thorough exploration of this issue. The first of these was carried out by Kiernan (1997) using data from the British Cohort Study that commenced in 1958 (BCS58). The study involved sending regular survey instruments to the parents of all children born within a specific week in 1958 and then later on to the children themselves as they became old enough to complete their own surveys. The clear advantage of this approach is that data are collected prior to key events occurring, and so issues such as (potentially misleading) retrospective accounting are not pertinent.

However, as well as studies not being designed specifically to explore teenage conception (as mentioned above), there is also the issue of attrition to consider. In other words, a certain number of the initial sample will drop out, through losing interest, moving house and becoming untraceable, or other significant life events. If these participants are more likely to be (or to have been) in one or other of the groups of interest, then bias will enter the analysis. Nevertheless, a considerable sample size remains, among which there was a sufficient number of teenage births to enable statistical comparisons to be made.

Kiernan identified a number of risk factors that predicted a teenage birth; these included reported emotional problems at ages 7 or 16, the teenager's own mother being a teenage mother, the family experiencing financial adversity when they were 7 or 16, a preference towards being a teenage mother, and low educational attainment at age 16. Women with all five of these characteristics had a 56 per cent chance of becoming a teenage mother, compared with 3 per cent for those with none of them.

Berrington *et al.* (2005a) carried out a similarly detailed analysis of data from the BCS70 survey (similar to BCS58 but using a cohort born in 1970). Key predictors of early parenthood were 'own mother was a teenage mother', 'no father figure at birth', 'father's social class 4 and 5 at birth', 'conduct disorder at age 10' and 'living in social housing at age 10'. The more of these risk factors that were present, the higher were the odds of teenage childbearing.

More recently a study in an English region explored the impact of Adverse Childhood Experiences (ACEs), defined as physical, sexual or emotional childhood abuse, family breakdown, exposure to domestic violence, and living in a household affected by substance misuse, mental illness or where someone is incarcerated. Experiencing four or more ACEs was associated with a fourfold higher risk of having or causing an intended teenage pregnancy (Ford *et al.*, 2016).

Berrington *et al.* (2005b) also considered the characteristics of fathers – these were included if their age at reported fatherhood was under 23 years (since most fathers of children born to young mothers are slightly older than the mother). Despite the risk that there is an element of under-reporting in these data, the characteristics that distinguished young fathers from others are remarkably similar to those obtained for young mothers. Again, the more risk factors that were present, the higher the odds were of being a young father.

The reliance on parenthood as the outcome in these longitudinal cohort studies does not enable the factors associated with conception (including abortion), as such, to be explored. Young women who conceive but then choose abortion will almost certainly differ from those who choose to give birth. A creative way of looking at this was devised by Ermisch and Pevalin (2003), who included in their analysis cases of teenage women who suffered a miscarriage as an additional comparison group for young mothers, the argument being that these had not opted for abortion. The analysis showed that, by age 30, the impact of early childrearing was strongest in terms of non-home ownership and, if partnered, the partner being unemployed.

A yet more recent study, using the large Millennium Cohort data set (Hawkes, 2010), reports that there are substantial differences in reported life circumstances, prior to the birth, between women who do and do not become young mothers; these include being 'more likely to have experienced the unemployment of a father at age 14, to have left school at the minimum school leaving age, to have experienced parental separation and to have lived away from home than all the other mothers' (p. 81). However, the study demonstrates that there are gradations of negative circumstances at the time of the birth itself, such that those associated with becoming a mother during the teenage years are not substantially different from those who become parents in their early twenties, in terms of partner presence, being an owner occupier, having a vehicle available and living in a disadvantaged area.

A recent study design that became feasible due to advances in data linkage cast further light on susceptibility to early conception. One of the key questions in the broader research area is why some young women avoid early pregnancy despite sharing demographic and location data with some who do. By combining individual-level data from conception and educational records, researchers from the Institute of Fiscal Studies were able to identify that educational progress between ages 11 to 14 and persistent school absence by the age of 14 were additional predictors of risk over and above all other known demographic aspects. However, it was notable that the individual data analysis found that the majority of young women conceiving before the age of 18 did not have specific risk factors. The study concluded that to achieve a significant reduction in conception rates, a strategy cannot concentrate on high-risk groups alone (Crawford et al., 2013).

In England, teenage births by ethnicity are not routinely published, so estimates need to be drawn from Census data, collected every ten years. In the 2001 Census, motherhood under 19 was significantly higher among White British, Mixed White and Black Caribbean, other Black and Black Caribbean women while all Asian groups were under-represented (Department for Education and Skills, 2006a).

During the early days of the strategy, it was observed that areas in London with higher proportions of Black African and Caribbean young people tended to have higher rates of conceptions *and* higher abortion proportions, a different association from that found in most areas. Marked changes occurred, however, in the rates observed in these localities during the life of the strategy.

Aspinall and Hashem (2010) pointed out that, despite targeted work being a priority in the Public Service Agreement targets linked to the strategy, good-quality, locally coded ethnicity data on births and abortions were lacking, making specific targeted work very challenging.

Higher birth and/or abortion rates among some ethnic groups are likely to be influenced by the disproportionate impact of disadvantage on ethnic minorities – with young people in some groups over-represented in the care system or in school exclusions – as well as marked cultural variations in norms and behaviours. The consultation to develop the England strategy also highlighted that contraceptive services were frequently not designed in a way that would reach ethnic minority young people, an issue that was addressed in the strategy action plan.

1.3.4 Degrees of intentionality

One of the key challenges in the field of early pregnancy is to disentangle the various factors that have been associated with occurrence and outcomes and assess their relative importance. As mentioned already, designing studies to collect data that would enable clear distinctions to be made poses very real challenges.

Explanations for early pregnancy and childbearing raised in the studies cited above fall, to put it simply, into one of two (or both) categories. The first is historical; factors or contexts that occurred in the past are used to explain current risk behaviour and/or vulnerability. So, for example, living in a single parent family, having a mother who was herself an early childbearer, receiving a poor level of sex education, lacking knowledge and understanding of fertility and contraception, acquiring gender-normative behaviours that have restricted communication options, and so on. Wellings *et al.* (2013), on the basis of NATSAL-3 data, reported that pregnancies among 16- to 19-year-olds were most commonly unplanned, and were associated with lack of sexual competence at first sexual intercourse (see section 2.1.6), reporting higher frequency of sex in the previous four weeks, receiving sex education mainly from a non-school-based source, and current depression (Wellings *et al.*, 2013, p. 1807).

The second group of factors relate to future orientations. So, the desire to have a baby to demonstrate capability in a non-academic or non-employment domain, or to have an object for one's affection, to cement a relationship (or attempt to maintain one), to demonstrate fertility, and so on. In practice, of course, the 'future-oriented' factors may well be a direct or indirect result of prior experiences and contexts.

Nevertheless, these different perspectives may affect the extent to which an early pregnancy is planned or unplanned. Pregnancies that are primarily driven by factors in the second category (future orientation) may well be planned, or not actively prevented, whereas those in the former category are more likely to be unplanned (which is not to say that they will not be wanted once a pregnancy is confirmed). Policy responses to these two groups of factors will vary – correcting or remediating past 'deficits' to enable more fully informed choices, and/or focusing on future orientations. A not uncommon expression in the field is that 'ambition is the best form of contraception'; although it is of course the effective use of contraception that actually prevents pregnancy! In practice, all avenues should be covered, although the practical reality is that resources do not permit this, so priorities need to be selected. Achieving a suitable balance between targeted and universal interventions is one of the real challenges in this area of work and was central to the ambition of the England strategy.

1.4 Impact of early conceptions

1.4.1 Impact on mothers

As mentioned earlier, distinguishing the impacts of early motherhood from factors that predispose young women to early pregnancy is a major challenge.

Some of the earlier studies that reported on negative outcomes for teenage parents were based on cross-sectional comparisons and so are rather restricted in what they can claim regarding the impact of parenthood. As mentioned above, all the UK-based longitudinal cohort studies have pointed to teenage mothers having greater disadvantaged circumstances prior to the birth than those who did not become teenage mothers, but additional disadvantage appears to arise from early childbearing.

In presenting data in this – and other – areas it is crucial to note that the studies identify general statistical trends and not issues that are claimed to affect each and every young mother. Nor should any of the results presented be interpreted as casting any aspersions on young women's abilities to cope with early childbearing; obviously, as in any other walk of life, some will cope better than others. Indeed, it is an important aspect of work in the area that efforts are made to identify factors that assist young parents, and to enable improved support and provision for the families involved. This was an integral part of the England strategy and is discussed in Chapter 6.

The Berrington *et al.* (2005a) research (using the BCS1970 data set) compared outcomes for mothers who had their first children at different ages. What this demonstrated was that the impact of age was incremental; in other words, the overall negative impact on parents who were teenagers at the time of the birth was somewhat more pronounced than the impact on women who were in their early twenties at the time of their first birth, but was not qualitatively different. This result is similar to that found, using a different cohort and different data-collection methods, by Hawkes (2010).

However, the analysis by Berrington *et al.* revealed that it was not age *per se* that had an impact, but factors that are often associated with early childbearing but are not inevitable. Thus, a major negative outcome – depression – was associated with other independent factors at all ages, but these are more likely to arise in the case of early childbearing. They include relative poverty, lack of partnered support and poor housing environment. The younger the mother at first birth, the more chance there is of her being un-partnered some years later.

1.4.2 Impact on fathers

Few studies have looked at the impact of early fathering on the young men involved. Again, Berrington *et al.* were able to do this (assuming that reports of being a father were fairly accurate). Key results were that, at age 30 years, men who fathered babies before the age of 22 years were more likely than matched non-fathers to be unemployed, to have separated from the mother, and to have re-partnered (Berrington *et al.*, 2005b).

Contact with the mother and their child(ren) varied but was much lower, perhaps not surprisingly, when the primary relationship with the mother had broken down and the men had re-partnered. Although this might seem to be obvious, it is not an inevitable consequence and needs to be considered where continued contact between father and child is felt to be appropriate, as close involvement has shown to benefit young fathers and their children, even if the parental relationship ends (Fatherhood Institute, 2013). The experience of young fathers has been explored in more recent qualitative studies, which are discussed in Chapter 6.

1.4.3 Impact on children

Data on the impact on the children of teenage parents do show poorer outcomes compared with children born to older mothers. Again, however, few of these outcomes are a direct result of the age of the mother, but are influenced by pre-existing factors, circumstances and behaviours. For example, the higher risk of low birth weight, stillbirth and infant mortality for babies born to younger women is likely to be affected by poor nutrition and higher rates of smoking during pregnancy – the main modifiable risk factor for a range of child health outcomes (Chan and Sullivan, 2008).

Late booking of young parents with maternity services, alongside lack of accessible and trusted services, diminishes the protective benefits of antenatal care. Accessibility of antenatal classes may be restricted due to travel costs, as well as psychological barriers experienced by some young women due to feeling stigmatised when other members of such classes tend to be older. There are excellent examples of antenatal care specifically for teenage women, as illustrated in Chapter 6, but the ability to provide special antenatal classes may be constrained by funding limits and/or because there are insufficient numbers to justify this expenditure.

So, some negative effects on children born to teenage mothers may reflect these differences. Lower birth weight may make babies more prone to infection and other forms of ill-health, and, if young parents have less money available, then visits to their doctors' surgeries may be more difficult and any required diagnosis and treatment may be delayed. Further, if young parents and their children are housed in poor and possibly overcrowded accommodation, then the probability of accidents may be higher, as well as the conditions impacting on their mental health and wellbeing.

Support for this interpretation arises from the analyses by Berrington and colleagues, using the ALSPAC data set, a longitudinal data set on all children born within a certain time in the Avon and Somerset areas (Golding et al., 2001). Analyses were carried out on children in over 9000 families aged up to 42 months old, with comparisons being made between children born to women at different ages at the time of birth. On many measures (including vocabulary, gross and fine motor development), children of teenage parents were found to be no different from others. There were, however, adverse outcomes for the children in terms of behavioural adjustment, including conduct, emotional behaviour and hyperactivity. These need to be considered as a whole, since they include factors that relate to family backgrounds of the mothers themselves, the adverse social circumstances or relationship breakdown experienced after the birth, and factors that might relate more directly to care provided by teenage mothers. Parental depression, for example, to which young mothers are particularly vulnerable, has been identified as the most prevalent risk factor overall for negative impact on child development outcomes (Sabates and Dex, 2012).

Hawkes (2010) reports on outcomes for children born to parents of different ages and, again, illustrates that some negative cognitive developmental indices are linked to age of the mother at birth in an incremental manner; these include vocabulary subscale and school readiness scores at age 3, and some other cognitive measures at age 5. Some behavioural outcomes show similar patterns, including hyperactivity, emotional difficulties, conduct problems and peer problems. Morinis *et al.* (2013), based on the UK Millennium Cohort study, found that, at age 5, children born to mothers aged 18 years or under, when compared with children born to mothers aged between 25 and 34 years, were four months behind on spatial ability, seven months behind on non-verbal ability and eleven months behind on verbal ability; however, controlling for sociodemographic circumstances and perinatal risk removed these differences, with the exception of verbal ability.

While the challenge in distinguishing the impacts of early motherhood from factors that predispose young women to early pregnancy remains, it is clear that many young women, and young men, enter parenthood with a disproportionate burden of disadvantage, which can affect outcomes for them and their children. The England strategy's approach to providing bespoke support for young parents is described in Chapter 6. Meanwhile, the next chapter describes some of what is known about means to reduce levels of unintended early conceptions.

Note

1   In other countries in the UK, Northern Ireland focuses on under-20s and under-17s, Wales monitors under-18s but has a specific focus on under-16s, while Scotland focuses prevention on under-18s and support for parents up to age 26.

Chapter 2

Reducing rates of teenage conceptions

2.1 Considerations regarding reducing rates of teenage conception

2.1.1 Overview

Much attention has been paid, especially in the USA and the UK, to whether and how levels of teenage pregnancies can be reduced. There is also major concern in many low-and middle-income countries. Although the detailed contextual features of these countries vary widely, the transferable success factors associated with the England strategy are explored in Chapter 7.

In a nutshell, relatively high rates of teenage childbearing prior to the 1960s were accepted since most of them occurred within marriage. The degree of individual choice for early parenthood at that time is not possible to ascertain, but is likely to have been compromised by the illegality of abortion and the social pressures on some to arrange a marriage if pregnancy occurred. According to the UNICEF (2001) analysis, when age of marriage and the availability of contraception started to change in the 1960s, some countries adapted well to these changes and some did not. Those that did so experienced reductions in early childbearing; some primarily through increases in abortion proportions (the Nordic pattern) and some through reducing conception rates (the Netherlands being the prime example). Factors which are generally regarded as contributing to, or enabling, these reductions include macro-level social attributes such as greater gender equality and lower levels of income inequality, societal normative positions, such as assuming the need for, and delivering, sex and relationships education and accessible contraceptive and support services for young people, and acceptance of young people's sexual development and interests (not necessarily condoning, but being realistic and responding accordingly) which are linked to more open approaches to the whole area.

In the USA and the UK, however, these wider societal changes did not occur. There are various reasons for this that are beyond the scope of the current chapter, but it did mean that teenage conception and birth rates remained relatively high compared with many other developed countries. So, when policy makers eventually turned their attention to these figures, a variety of approaches were adopted with the aim of reducing the levels (for one early overview of historic policy initiatives, see Wellings and Kane, 1999).

Basically, to reduce rates of teenage pregnancy, the levels of sexual activity need to be reduced, and/or the efficient usage of contraception by sexually active teenagers needs to be increased. Although this may sound relatively straightforward, in reality, of course, both areas are highly complex. Across the board, different approaches to these challenges rest on quite different ideological positions with regard to intentions for intervening in this area. A major approach in the USA, and in some other countries, has been driven by the view that young people should not be engaging in sexual activity until they are married, or at least very close to it with a fully committed partner. So the emphasis is on encouraging abstinence by various means, of which abstinence-only sex education is a preferred option. An alternative view is that young people cannot be prevented from having sex, so resources are better directed towards equipping them to make safe and informed choices through comprehensive sex and relationships education and improved availability and use of contraception. Some selected issues involved in these endeavours are briefly reviewed.

2.1.2 School-based sex and relationships education

Since all young people in richer countries attend school up to the age of at least 16 years (or at least should do), great emphasis has been placed on the delivery of school-based sex education, albeit called by different names in different places. As mentioned above, successive US governments encouraged states to adopt abstinence-only approaches, and for many years offered generous financial incentives to state legislatures to do so; few states declined the offer.

There were eight criteria that needed to be met to qualify for federal funding, including telling pupils that pre-marital sexual activity 'is likely to have harmful psychological and physical effects', and that 'bearing children out-of-wedlock is likely to have harmful consequences for the child, the child's parents and society', etc. (Advocates for Youth, 2007). Given that the average age of marriage is approaching 30 years in the USA, these teachings clearly place great demands on young people.

Part of the strict abstinence-only approach involves either the omission of any mention of contraception or the inclusion of negative (and often false) information about its harmful effects. It is felt that, by mentioning that contraception is available and reasonably safe, many young people will find a ready alternative to the waiting that was required of them. This is despite clear evidence that teaching about contraception is not associated with increased risk of sexual activity or sexually transmitted infections in the teenage years (Kohler et al., 2008).

Alternative approaches in the USA include the so-called Abstinence Plus programmes, which are based on the desirability of abstinence until marriage, but do include (albeit seemingly reluctantly) some information on contraception – just in case some young people simply could not wait. The third approach is called Comprehensive Sexuality Education, with programmes being designed to provide full details, to improve communication skills, gender-related concerns and other relevant topics. The aim is to equip young people with the knowledge, skills and confidence to make positive choices about relationships and sexual health (see, for example, Haberland and Rogow, 2015).

It is notoriously difficult to assess the impact of single programmes on teenage conception rates, for a number of reasons. Factors affecting conception are complex and it is most unlikely that the impact of one single programme can be identified, quite apart from the very large numbers that would be required to demonstrate statistically significant results. Nevertheless, efforts have been made to evaluate programmes, with outcome measures ranging from the (very challenging) numbers of conceptions, or the more commonly reported self-reports of specific risk behaviours that increase the likelihood of a conception occurring, to measures of knowledge of sexual issues and/or attitudes to risk.

Quite apart from issues of effectiveness, there have been serious questions raised about the medical accuracy of many of the abstinence-based programmes implemented (Santelli, 2008) and the consequent breach of human rights by imparting false information (Santelli et al., 2006), as well as much broader issues regarding their impact on, for example, gender issues and self-esteem (Fine and McClelland, 2006). So, in addition to the empirical assessments of the impact of sex and relationships education, there are powerful rights-based arguments for ensuring adequate provision to enable young people to make informed choices to protect their own and others' health; these stem, in part, from the International Convention on the Rights of the Child (UNICEF, undated). From this perspective, provision of SRE is not about *whether* it should or should not happen, but *how* best to deliver it to enable the rights of all young people to be respected and protected. This indeed was the challenge made by the UN Special Rapporteur response to the UK periodic review (UN, 2014).

Kirby was a leading researcher for many years, collecting data from large numbers of studies and reviewing published and unpublished material, some of which involved randomised allocations to conditions in different schools. In a series of reports and articles stretching over twenty years, he became more confident in asserting the lack of success of abstinence-only-based programmes, and started to identify the features of what the evidence pointed to as being essential for successful approaches to the area (Kirby, 2007, 2008). Many international agencies have drawn on his – and others' – work to develop their own guidelines (UNESCO, 2016, 2017, Advocates for Youth, SEICUS, etc.). Although specific details of these claimed key success factors vary across agencies, the UK's Sex Education Forum's identified reported characteristics of successful programmes derived from the work of Kirby, as well as Trivedi et al.'s NICE review update (2007), to produce the following list (Sex Education Forum, 2015, p. 5):

- a comprehensive range of topics is addressed, including contraception;
- trained educators are used;
- programmes begin before a young person first has sex;
- psychosocial factors which affect behaviour, including values, norms and self-efficacy, are addressed;
- participatory learning methods are used;
- children and young people are taught using small group work; and
- both school and home contribute to SRE.

In the UK, two large random control trials on SRE were funded in the 1990s. One (the SHARE programme) involved school-based delivery in Scotland, with over 7,000 pupils being involved in twenty-five schools, randomly allocated to receive a specially designed (and theoretically based) twenty-session programme delivered by specially trained teachers; the control group received their normal provision. Various measures were taken before and after the delivery (aged 13 and 14 years) as well as a longer-term follow-up to assess conception and abortion rates by age 20 years. Little impact of the intervention was found, although pupils reported higher enjoyment in the new programme (see Wight, 2011).

The other large UK programme (RIPPLE) involved the delivery of three sessions of peer education in 29 schools in London and southern England, involving over 9,000 13- and 14-year-old pupils, with the schools being randomly allocated to receive the sessions or their normal provision. Minimal short-term or longer-term impact on the large number of outcome variables was observed (Stephenson et al., 2004, 2008; Parkes et al., 2011).

The lack of positive results from these two well-funded UK studies led some critics to question the value of school-based SRE; indeed, one such example was provided when Baroness O'Loan cited the SHARE study in the House of Lords debate on whether SRE should be made statutory in UK schools (Hansard, 2010). This was, however, a quite inappropriate and unjustified reaction. All these studies show is that those specific programmes with that specific content and delivered to those specific school years did not show measurable impact on the selected outcome measure. The results certainly do not indicate that SRE is not worth delivering, or that efforts to increase its relevance and value should be reduced, or that longer-term and more sustained programmes starting much earlier in age would not be worthwhile developing.

A similar general critique can be made regarding the recent Cochrane Review on the effectiveness of school-based SRE on biological outcomes (pregnancy and HIV rates). Combining results from a large number of studies – including eight large random controlled trials (RCTs) involving over 55,000 students – the authors report that there is 'little evidence that educational programmes alone are effective' in reducing these selected biological outcomes (Mason-Jones et al., 2016, p. 3). Quite apart from the immense challenges of carrying out RCTs, combining simple outcome data from these studies (from across three continents) can be argued to detract from the content of the programmes themselves and risks reducing SRE to little more than an injection! In any event, the conclusion refers to educational programmes alone, a policy that few would propose given the complexity of the issues involved.

There are some indications that the quality of SRE in the UK is increasing, despite the failure to get it established as a statutory subject (apart from the small very biological component in the Science National Curriculum subject) until the decision finally taken by government in March 2017 (Department for Education, 2017). The most recent data from NATSAL (National Survey of Sexual Attitudes and Lifestyles) show that the reported importance of SRE received in school has increased over the past twenty years, although it should be noted that the increase in schools being cited as the 'most important source' could imply either an improvement in the actual quality of provision or a reduction in the quality of other potential sources, or some of each. However, the young men and women who cited school as their main source were more likely to experience first sex at a later age and were less likely to report unsafe sex or to have a diagnosis of an STI; young women were less likely to be pregnant by 18 and less likely to have experienced sex against their will (Tanton et al., 2015; Macdowall et al., 2015). This positive association with consensual sex was also found in Lindberg and Maddow-Zimet (2012), where girls receiving comprehensive sexuality education were less likely to have a partner with a big age difference (associated with coercion and intimate partner violence) and were more likely to describe their first sex as wanted.

2.1.3 Provision of contraception

Alongside improved sex and relationships education in school, increased availability and usage of contraception has been strongly encouraged in the UK and in parts of the USA. In recent years, there has been much greater uptake of long-acting reversible contraception (LARCs) among young people in the UK (Connolly et al., 2014) and in the USA (Lindberg et al., 2016), although discontinuation for various reasons (mainly unwanted side-effects) remains a concern (Hoggart et al., 2013; Madden et al., 2014). However, although increased use of LARCs appears to have made a major contribution towards reductions in conception rates among young people, there are steady increases in new cases of sexually transmitted infections. Some of the increase is presumably due to an increase in screening leading to more detection, but it may also imply that regularity of condom use has declined. It does appear that increased usage of LARCs is associated with considerably lower rates of condom use among US high school students (Steiner et al., 2016). The England strategy tried to promote both effective contraception to prevent pregnancy and consistent condom use to avoid STIs, but achieving equal impact from both messages remains a challenge.

2.1.4 Reducing teenage conceptions rates in the USA

There has been a decline in teenage pregnancy rates in the USA in recent years, although the reasons behind this change are disputed. The abstinence-only movement has claimed the success of their educational approach in reducing levels of sexual activity, while others have attributed success to wider availability of contraception through school-based clinics and other opportunities for access. To help resolve this dispute, Santelli and colleagues analysed data from a number of large surveys between 1995 and 2002, developing measures termed *contraceptive risk index* and *overall pregnancy risk index*, which were calculated using the former index alongside the percentage of individuals reporting sexual activity.

Among 15- to 17-year-olds, rates of sexual activity declined by about 10 per cent, but there was no decline among the 18- to 19-year-olds. In relation to the reduction in pregnancy risk among this younger age group, 77 per cent was attributable to improved contraceptive use, while this figure rose to 88 per cent across the whole age range. The authors conclude that: 'The current emphasis of US domestic and global policies, which stress abstinence-only sex education to the exclusion of accurate information on contraception, is misguided. Similar approaches should not be adopted by other nations' (Santelli *et al.*, 2007, p. 156). A more recent analysis using similar methods (Lindberg *et al.*, 2016) reports that the decline over recent years in adolescent fertility is 'entirely attributable to improvements in contraceptive use' (p. 577).

In any event, reductions in levels of sexual activity would not, in themselves, indicate any success for the abstinence-only approaches. Instead, they may arise due to increased awareness of risk among young people due to improved sex education in schools that have adopted comprehensive sex education programmes (which are associated with delayed age of first sex), from the media and within families. Greater sexual 'competence', discussed below, can include reduced gender power differentials (leading to reduced levels of coercive sexual activity), better knowledge of prevention, and other factors.

2.1.5 Other sources of sexual information

Apart from school and clinical services, young people learn a great deal about sex and relationships from other sources; these include families or carers, various media (including pornography) and friends or peers. Some of what is learned is specific (albeit correct or not), while other aspects are implicit and covert. So, for example, parents may answer specific questions about bodies, babies and related issues in various ways and with different levels of accuracy (cf. Stone *et al.*, 2012; McGinn *et al.*, 2016) but at the same time be modelling certain behaviours (for example, displays of affection or not, gender power, gender roles, reactions to scenes on television, supposedly light-hearted 'throw-away' comments) that may well seriously affect the attitudes that their children develop as they get older, in a negative or positive way.

Other examples of less direct sources of information include the likely impact of media images of sexualised bodies, images and behaviours contained in pornographic material (although there is evidence that some young people actually learn a lot about bodies from such sources in the continued absence of any more reliable sources; cf. McKee, 2007), what has become known as 'everyday sexism' (Bates, 2015, 2016), and many others.

It is interesting to note (NATSAL-3) that young people's preferred main source of information on sex and relationships is school, followed by parents and health professionals, suggesting a desire for support from trusted, authoritative sources. This contrasts with their current main sources which, after school, are friends and the media, with parents, particularly fathers, and health professionals playing an insignificant role. The importance of health professionals in providing young people with accurate information was highlighted by the American Academy of Pediatrics, who called on their members to counter the gaps and misinformation from US abstinence programmes (Breuner et al., 2016).

2.1.6 Sexual competence

What all this points towards is that calls for *simple* solutions to the challenges posed by early unplanned pregnancy – through increased services for young people and/or improved sex and relationships education, essential though they are – miss the point of the sheer complexity of the factors that affect early sex and contraceptive usage. Some years ago, Ingham and Van Zessen (1997), building on the earlier work of Rademakers (1991), pointed to the notion of 'sexual competence' as a way of accounting for the large differences between the UK and the Netherlands in aspects of sexual activity; for example reasons, protection and mutuality, and outcomes, notably early conception rates. They regarded this as being a cultural phenomenon, with various taken-for-granted assumptions (or discursive frameworks) guiding individual and policy-related decisions. Areas that are accompanied by division and debate within the UK (and USA, for that matter) – such as whether sex and relationships education should be offered in schools, whether contraception and sexual health services should be more widely available and less stigmatised – are not generally issues of dispute in the Netherlands. A fine illustration of how this general set of assumptions permeates societies is provided by Schalet's work comparing parental attitudes to their teenagers' sexual activity in the USA and the Netherlands (Schalet, 2000, 2011). A further example is provided by this summary of the underlying principles of sex education in schools in the Netherlands:

Dutch sexuality education emerges from an understanding that young people are curious about sex and sexuality and that they need, want, and have a right to accurate and comprehensive information about sexual health . . . it encourages young people to think critically about their sexual health, including their desires and wishes . . . attention is paid on discussing values, establishing personal boundaries, communicating wishes and desires, and developing assertiveness.

(Ferguson *et al.*, 2008, p. 102–03)

Similar openness is observed in Nordic countries. This is how one leading commentator described the situation in Sweden regarding sex education in schools, a stark contrast with the typical US and UK approaches and resistances:

The guiding stars are knowledge instead of ignorance, openness with regards to facts instead of mystifying and an acceptance of young people's sexuality (or sexual emotions), relationships and love, with or without a partner. The idea is that the sex education should support and prepare young people for a responsible present and/or future sexual life . . . Sexual enjoyment is also regarded as a value in itself . . . There is no opposition to sex education in Sweden.

(Sex Ed in Sweden (Katerina Lindahl, RFSU, personal communication))

These illustrations of 'competence' and how it can be instilled/enabled/encouraged make it easier to understand some of the likely reasons for the wide variations in levels of teenage conceptions between countries (alongside the economic and structural features). Note that for a broad-based sex education to be widely accepted requires the active cooperation of parents, teachers, school governors, the mainstream media, politicians and other policy makers and, of course, young people themselves. This is precisely why the notion of 'competence' can be regarded as a cultural phenomenon and not just an individual property (see also Hirst, 2012).

That said, however, some very useful work has been carried out in the UK by Wellings and colleagues using the NATSAL data. Operationally defining 'competence' at first ever sexual intercourse as comprising four elements – using a reliable form of contraception, the timing felt right, their reason for sex was an autonomous one and both partners were equally willing – they demonstrated that higher levels of 'competence' were associated with higher age at first intercourse and lower risk of conception. This individual competence measure provides a potentially helpful set of 'assets' which SRE and targeted prevention programmes should aim to develop in young people (Wellings *et al.*, 2013).

2.2 Is there a case for intervening?

2.2.1 Overview

There has been a steady series of critiques of the need for policy interventions in the area of teenage pregnancy, as well as in their implementation. Some argue that the negative health and social outcomes for young mothers and their children are exaggerated, or based on old data, or do not take sufficient account of the (often impoverished) living conditions after the birth. Others question what right the state has to intervene in personal decisions about family creation and development, whether setting targets to reduce rates simply serves to further stigmatise those already in vulnerable situations, or how the strategy is a modern-day form of eugenics since conception rates are higher in more deprived parts of the country so reductions will likely have unequal impact (see, for example, Arai, 2009 and various chapters in Duncan *et al.*, 2010).

These are important questions (albeit some are more challenging than others), and are extremely useful reminders for issues to be constantly borne in mind. But they are not reasons for governments not to develop strategies to address high rates. In England, for example, the fact that the target set in 1999 involved a 50 per cent reduction in under-18 conception rates is an indication that there was never any intention to try to prevent *all* teenage conceptions. Further, since around half of all under-18 and over 60 per cent of under-16 conceptions end in abortion, the majority of which were presumably not planned, efforts to reduce these can be justified on many grounds. It also needs to be fully recognised that beneath the headline rate data, a whole array of complex and dynamic processes are occurring that impact on early sexual activity and contraceptive use and pregnancy choices, some of which clearly indicate coercion, gender imbalances, and other features of sexually unhealthy societies.

Indeed, sometimes pregnancy choices and aspiration are shaped not by young people themselves, but by senior decision makers. As described in subsequent chapters, slow progress in reducing rates in some areas was influenced by those who believed early parenthood was an inevitable part of deprived communities and neglected to offer young people the knowledge, skills and opportunities to make different choices.

Even though targets for conceptions may have been the trigger, the introduction of the strategy encouraged a wide array of activities – based on learning from elsewhere and research evidence, as well as ideological positions based on gender equality, human rights and the importance of the centrality of choice in determining futures. It was the opportunity to address these issues that contributed to the widespread support for the strategy from many NGOs and professional organisations, including those working with young parents.

Some of the critiques pointed out that negative outcomes are more likely to be linked to poor housing conditions, poverty and lack of education and employment opportunity after the birth, than age *per se*, so efforts need to be directed towards respecting and supporting choices that young people make rather than trying to control their behaviours. The England strategy was intended to do both. Alongside the prevention target, there was a complementary target and programme of material and emotional support for young parents; these are described in Chapter 6.

2.2.2 Multi-pronged approaches

What becomes very apparent from consideration of the research in the area of early pregnancy is that there are no easy solutions. Although improving the extent and quality of sex and relationships education clearly seems to be of the utmost importance, on its own it will not achieve much in the absence of other enabling environments. To take a simple and obvious example: if young people in schools are educated about and advised to use condoms, but are then unable to access them, or if a young woman expresses a wish to use one but her male partner refuses, then the outcomes will not be positive. A whole systems approach is needed, with different agencies and concerned parties contributing what they can, with the interests of young people at the centre. This seems to be what encapsulates the situation in those countries that have adapted well to the changing circumstances of young people and society in general (UNICEF, 2001).

Within the UK, some support for this broad approach was received from research carried out when there was a national target (set by a previous government in 1990) to reduce rates of under-16 conceptions – one of the targets set in *The Health of the Nation* initiative established in 1992. Data were collected on the extent of change in under-16 conceptions rates during the 1990s. Those areas showing the twenty highest increases were compared with those showing the twenty highest reductions in relation to the extent of the provision of various initiatives. Data were collected through interviews with key agencies, close analysis of annual public health reports and other sources.

What emerged was that local government areas that showed the highest reductions (when compared with the 'increasing' sites) were characterised by a number of important features, including better youth service provision, more targeted sexual health services for young people, improved sex education in schools, listening to young people's views and other initiatives (Ingham *et al.*, 2001).

For these changes to be introduced in individual areas, a cultural change needed to have occurred in relation to young people and sexual health, along the lines of those changes that had occurred at national levels some years earlier in some countries. Further, what these early results demonstrated was that, while resources are genuinely required for change to occur, it is the cultural and attitudinal shifts that drive change; the finance facilitates and enables it. It was this comprehensive, whole systems approach to teenage pregnancy that underpinned the England strategy, the importance of which was confirmed during its implementation. The detail of how this was done is described in the following chapters.

2.3.3 Finally . . .

This chapter has provided an overview of some of the alternative ways of approaching the issue of early pregnancy, and why it is a worthwhile endeavour to attempt. It should be clear that, in introducing a public health approach to the many issues involved, the intention of the England strategy was not at all to moralise, or stigmatise, or direct, but to create contexts that would empower and support young people in managing the rapidly changing world around them so that whatever informed choices they make are respected and supported. Obviously, under the broad umbrella of the initiative, there will have been people who had their own agendas and reasons for feeling that action was needed, and various sections of the media and the political world (and academia) raised regular questions and challenges along the way. But throughout, the strategy and its various amendments were informed by the latest research as opposed to ideologies or rhetoric. Anchoring the strategy in evidence secured the support of professional organisations and NGOs and, as described in the next chapters, gave government the confidence to pursue implementation even when early progress was slow. The detailed analysis by Wellings *et al.* (2016) indicates that this approach was well justified; in brief, areas that received higher strategy-related funding showed larger reductions in conception rates after controlling for deprivation levels, and the odds of young mothers being in education, work or training doubled between 2000 and 2010.

Chapter 3

England's teenage pregnancy strategy

Rationale, development and first phase implementation

3.1 Where it began

3.1.1 The window of opportunity

The window of opportunity for England's Teenage Pregnancy Strategy was the incoming Labour government in 1997, which had an explicit ambition to reduce intergenerational inequalities. Teenage pregnancy was seen as both a cause and consequence of poor health, education and economic outcomes affecting young parents and their children. Notably, UK teenage birth rates were the highest in Western Europe and had shown no sustained downward trend. Although all countries, including the UK, had reduced rates during the 1970s, as the decline continued in other countries over the next two decades UK rates remained static. It was clear from comparative data that high rates were not inevitable and that young people in the UK were experiencing very different choices from their European peers (Figure 3.1).

The issue had not been entirely ignored by previous governments. In 1992, the Conservative government's Health of the Nation strategy had included, with other health targets, a ten-year target to halve the rate of under-16 conceptions. The initiative saw an 83 per cent increase in the number of dedicated young people's contraceptive service sessions (London School of Hygiene and Tropical Medicine, UCL and BMRB International, 2005) but lacked a clear action plan and failed to make a significant impact on the rates. It also omitted attention to 16- and 17-year-olds who experienced 80 per cent of conceptions to the under-18 age group. Notably, an assessment of the overall policy found it was largely regarded as focusing only on the health sector, omitting other services involved with children, young people and their families. It also lacked the necessary horizontal and vertical structures for effective partnership working and failed to set out the tasks and responsibilities of different agencies (Universities of Leeds and Glamorgan and the London School of Hygiene and Tropical Medicine, 1998).

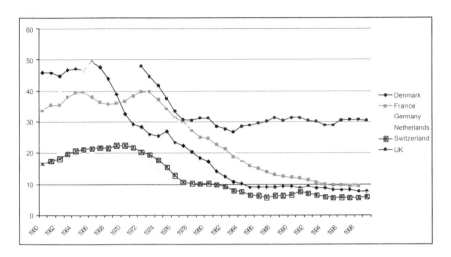

Figure 3.1 Showing comparative under-20 birth data.

Source: *Teenage Pregnancy Strategy Evaluation. Final Report Synthesis.* 2005.

3.1.2 The development of the strategy

Recognising the need for a new approach, and responding to strong advocacy from non-governmental organisations (NGOs) and professional organisations, the Labour government commissioned the newly formed Social Exclusion Unit (SEU) to do a thorough review of the evidence for the causes and potential solutions to the high rates, and develop a comprehensive ten-year strategy with a detailed implementation plan. The decision to commission the Social Exclusion Unit, rather than a government department, reflected the under-standing that teenage pregnancy was a complex, cross-cutting issue. The SEU, established in 1997, was set up specifically to 'help government action to reduce social exclusion by producing joined up solutions to joined up problems'.

One of the first tasks of the SEU was to explore the data and pattern of teenage pregnancy in the UK, look at the experience of other countries and identify the reasons for the high rates. As discussed in Chapter 1, the drivers of teenage pregnancy are complex, but following literature reviews, stakeholder consultations and interviews with young people, three factors stood out (Social Exclusion Unit, 1999):

Ignorance. The SEU found young people lacked accurate knowledge about contraception and STIs, what to expect in relationships and the challenges of being a young parent. Existing research confirmed the benefits of comprehensive SRE in both delaying early sex and increasing contraceptive use. However, despite many examples of good practice, SRE was found to be under-resourced, not supported by training and not linked to wider initiatives addressing teenage pregnancy and sexual health. Young people and parents looked to schools as the preferred route for SRE but friends were as influential a source about sex as school. The universal message the SEU received from young people was that SRE fell far short of what they would like and what they need to equip themselves for developing healthy relationships, delaying pregnancy and looking after their sexual health. Friends, the media and magazine 'problem pages' were filling the gap.

Mixed messages. Young people's reporting of mixed messages appeared to be rooted in an unhelpful combination of exposure to widespread sexual imagery, but embarrassment in discussing personal issues and asking for advice. Young people consistently over-estimated the levels of teenage sexual activity and described peer pressure to fit in with the perceived, albeit inaccurate, social norm. On the other hand, they were missing accurate information and opportunities for discussion from inadequate SRE, finding it difficult to talk to their parents, and were apprehensive about accessing contraceptive advice. Fears about confidentiality, particularly for under-16s, and judgemental attitudes of staff were the major barriers. As one young person put it, 'it sometimes seems as if sex is compulsory but contraception is illegal'. There also seemed to be more embarrassment discussing or using contraception than about sex itself. In a comparative study, Dutch boys were 2.5 times more likely than their English peers to discuss contraception with their partners before first sex and, compared with many other countries, UK teenagers were less likely to use contraception at first sex. The SEU review concluded that one of the results of mixed messages appeared to be that young people were not having less sex, but more unprotected sex.

Low expectations. Although data showed that teenage pregnancy affects all communities, young people with a history of disadvantage were at a significantly greater risk of becoming parents in their teens. Poverty and unemployment, low educational attainment, living in care, sexual abuse, mental health problems and crime were all found to be strongly associated with teenage parenthood. The effect of multiple risk factors (quantified in the 1958 birth cohort study) was particularly striking. Women with all the following characteristics had a 56 per cent chance of becoming a teenage mother, compared with a 3 per cent chance for those with none: emotional problems at ages 7 and 16; having a mother who had been a teenage mother; families who experienced financial adversity when they were 7 or 16; a preference for being a young mother; and low educational attainment at 16. Complex factors always influence individual decisions. For some, becoming a parent appeared to be motivated by a strong desire to provide a better experience for their child than they had had themselves. For others, with no expectation of employment or motivation to continue in education, early parenthood might seem to be the logical passport for making the transition from adolescence into adulthood.

3.1.3 Setting the goal and strategy themes

After eighteen months of analysing the issue, reviewing the international evidence, identifying existing good practice in England and consulting with a wide range of NGO and professional stakeholders, the Strategy was published in 1999 (Social Exclusion Unit, 1999). It had two clear goals: a headline target of halving the under-18 conception rate in England by 2010, with 1998 as the baseline year; and a complementary target to increase the proportion of 16–19-year-old mothers in education, training or employment, to reduce the risk of intergenerational poverty and social exclusion.

The Strategy set out a 30-point action plan, framed around four themes:

Joined-up action with new mechanisms to coordinate action at both national and local levels and ensure the strategy is kept on track.

Better prevention of teenage pregnancy: improving sex and relationships education in and out of school, and access to contraception for all young people, with targeted prevention for at-risk groups and a new focus on reaching young men. Boys and young men were identified as half the solution to reducing early pregnancy, but with contraception messages historically focused on girls and young women, they had lacked advice and support to enable them to take responsibility.

A national campaign involving government, media, NGOs and others to improve understanding and change behaviour.

Better support for pregnant teenagers and young parents, with a new focus on returning to education, with free childcare to enable participation; working to a position where no under-18 lone parent is put in a housing tenancy without support; and pilots around the country providing intensive support for young parents and their children. This chapter focuses on the prevention side of the strategy. Chapter 6 describes implementation of the support programme.

The action plan also included a commissioned research programme to explore issues identified in the SEU report as requiring more understanding (Teenage Pregnancy Unit, 2004–07).

Three features marked the difference in the Strategy from previous approaches. First, the recognition that the solution to teenage pregnancy was not in the gift of any one national government department or local agency. A multidimensional issue would require collective action, through successful collaboration across agencies at different levels. Second, that implementation of a complex programme needed to be anchored in robust structures and reliable resourcing. Third, that providing good support for young people who chose to become parents was an important contribution to the prevention strategy: in the short term, by helping them prevent further unplanned pregnancies; in the long term, by breaking intergenerational cycles of poverty and disadvantage and reducing the risk factors for teenage pregnancy among the next generation of young people. Notably, the new approach of the Strategy reflected the nine key characteristics of modern policy making, identified by the National Audit Office (2001).

3.2 The first phase of implementation: 1999–2005

Following a high-profile launch by the prime minister in June 1999, which helped signify its priority, the first phase of implementation began (Department of Health, 2001a; Teenage Pregnancy Unit, 2002a).

3.2.1 The structures, local targets and funding

A dedicated Teenage Pregnancy Unit (TPU) was set up in the Department of Health to lead the strategy, with cross-department funding. This was the engine room of the strategy and essential for leading such a large programme of work. The team of staff combined external experts and civil servants. Blending the unique skills of civil servants with specialist policy expertise was a new approach taken by the Labour government and helped increase the credibility of the strategy with stakeholders. An inter-departmental Teenage Pregnancy Board was established to reflect the cross-cutting nature of the policy challenge and the shared responsibility for implementation. A Teenage Pregnancy Independent Advisory Group (Advisory Group) was appointed, bringing together experts on all aspects of the strategy. The Group met every three months, with sub-groups formed to focus on specific aspects of the strategy, and had a remit to monitor implementation, advise and make recommendations to ministers and hold government to account for the strategy's progress. Regional Teenage Pregnancy Coordinators (regional coordinators) were appointed by the TPU for each of the nine government office regions. Locally, every local government area and their health partner was asked to appoint a Teenage Pregnancy Coordinator (local coordinator) and a Teenage Pregnancy Partnership Board (partnership board) with representation from health, education, social services, youth services, housing and relevant voluntary sector organisations. A national NGO Forum was established to harness additional expertise and involvement in the Strategy from organisations working closely with young people. An Inter-Faith Forum was set up to discuss and inform implementation of the Strategy in different faith contexts.

Local under-18 conception rate reduction targets for 2010 were agreed with each area: ranging from a 60 per cent target in high-rate areas to 40 per cent in lower-rate areas. The local targets were calculated on the progress needed to reach the national goal. If all areas achieved their local reductions, the 50 per cent goal for England would be met.

A Local Implementation Grant was provided to each area. The grant allocation was determined by the size of the local population of 15–17-year-old young women, and the baseline under-18 conception rate, which indicated the degree of challenge the local area would have in meeting the reduction target. Annual allocations ranged from £150K to £600K, with most areas receiving around £300–400K. The grant was ring fenced, with conditions on how it was spent. This included appointing a coordinator, establishing a partnership board and providing the TPU with annual progress reports. In addition, the grant could be used for pump-priming new initiatives or extending existing work, but was not intended to replace mainstream funding from other agencies. The total annual grant was around £25M. A further £7M was held centrally by TPU to support the national campaign and other strategy activity most efficiently commissioned at a national level.

Progress towards the strategy's goal was monitored through the quarterly and annual conception data. Independent academic researchers were commissioned to evaluate the first four years of the strategy's implementation and report in 2005 (London School of Hygiene and Tropical Medicine, UCL and BMRB International, 2005).

> I was appointed as the first Head of the Teenage Pregnancy Unit based on my experience as a former Chief Executive in successfully implementing health strategies in a number of local areas. In the early days I was encouraged by the then Permanent Secretary[1] to break all the normal rules to ensure a truly effective cross-government approach. The Unit as a mixture of civil servants and experts from the field was focused on ensuring that the strategy's detailed relevant policy was jointly developed across government departments, as well as having a significant outward face to ensure the right action was taken across every part of England. This outward focus continued when I set up some years later the Teenage Pregnancy National Support Team, referred to in the next chapter. It was an exciting time to develop from scratch the detailed implementation of the Social Exclusion Unit strategy and start to see the impact across the country.
>
> (Cathy Hamlyn, first head of the Teenage Pregnancy Unit and former senior civil servant in Department of Health)

3.2.2 National guidance and support for local strategies

Every local partnership board was asked to develop a local teenage pregnancy strategy, led by the coordinator. Guidance was provided by TPU with a template to complete. Each strategy was expected to (a) reach all young people in the area, with additional focus in high-rate areas or with groups of young people most at risk, (b) be informed by the pattern of teenage pregnancy in the area and an audit of service provision to identify gaps, (c) involve young people and local communities, and (d) make links to other relevant local plans and initiatives. The regional coordinator and TPU assessed each strategy and provided feedback to the coordinator and partnership board.

3.2.3 National action to support local delivery

To assist local implementation, the action plan tasked the TPU with providing additional guidance and support across the different strands of the Strategy.

To improve the provision of sex and relationships education (SRE): the education department published new SRE statutory guidance for schools (Department for Education and Employment, 2000). To help dissemination and take-up of the guidance TPU funded the Sex Education Forum to run regional seminars for local coordinators and their school and education colleagues. The Sex Education Forum is the leading NGO on SRE, with a diverse membership including faith and parenting organisations, and is well respected by stakeholders. A video and training pack was provided for school governors to increase their understanding of SRE and strengthen school leadership. A new national Continuing Professional Development (CPD) programme was established for teachers and school nurses on SRE and Personal Social and Health Education (PSHE), to increase the capacity of a skilled and confident workforce – identified as a key factor for delivering effective SRE. To help ensure SRE reached neglected or at-risk groups, TPU funded the development by NGOs of targeted SRE; for example, resources to reach boys and young men (Davidson, 2003) and an accredited social and life skills module on SRE for young offenders.

To embed SRE within wider school programmes, there were strong links with the National Healthy Schools Programme (NHSP). Introduced in 1999, the NHSP aimed to support children and young people in developing healthy behaviours, and help raise pupil achievement, reduce health inequalities and promote social inclusion. Schools achieved National Healthy Schools Status (NHSS) if they met forty-one criteria across four themes: PSHE, healthy eating, physical activity and emotional health and wellbeing (Department of Health and Department for Education, 2001). All areas were asked to have NHSP representation on their partnership board, and schools in the most deprived areas with high teenage pregnancy rates were encouraged to join the programme.

To help increase the provision of youth-friendly contraception and sexual health services: the Department of Health published best practice guidance on youth-friendly contraception services (Department of Health, 2000). The guidance drew on previous research with young people describing the ingredients of a service they would trust and find easy to use; in particular from a report by Brook, the leading young people's sexual health NGO, titled, with advice from a young person, '*Someone with a smile would be your best bet*' (Brook, 1998). The guidance was disseminated to local areas through a series of regional seminars for coordinators, sexual health leads and commissioners. To see how well current services were meeting the criteria in the guidance, areas were asked to audit their community contraceptive services and general practices and use the results to improve their provision. To address young people's concerns about confidentiality, identified as a key barrier to accessing early advice, the Department of Health provided best practice guidance to health professionals on providing contraceptive and sexual health advice to under-16s (Department of Health, 2000, updated 2004).

TPU provided separate guidance to increase uptake of services by boys and young men and young people from black and minority ethnic (BME) communities, which were also disseminated through regional and local networks (Teenage Pregnancy Unit, 2000a, 2000b). To ensure young people were well informed about local services, each local strategy was required to produce credit-card-size publicity booklets and have a plan for effective dissemination.

To encourage young people to visit their general practice for contraceptive advice, TPU worked with the Royal College of General Practitioners (RCGP) to develop practical tips and a checklist for making general practice more young people friendly (RCGP and Royal College of Nursing, 2002). *Getting it right for young people in your practice* was sent to all general practices in England. As young people had particular concerns about the confidentiality of their 'family doctor', TPU funded regional events to promote training of practice staff using a *Confidentiality Toolkit*, developed by the RCGP, British Medical Association, General Practitioners Committee, Royal College of Nursing and the Medical Defence Union (RCGP *et al.*, 2001, revised 2016). Accompanying confidentiality posters and leaflets for general practice were made available free to local areas.

Measures were taken through the Department of Health's Sexual Health and HIV Strategy to reduce later abortions among young people; in 2000, 16 per cent of under-20s had abortions at thirteen weeks or later, compared with 10 per cent of women over 20. The Sexual Health and HIV Strategy, published in 2001 and implemented alongside the teenage pregnancy strategy, included a requirement that all women meeting the legal requirement for abortion should have access to an NHS-funded abortion within three weeks of their first appointment. Partnership boards were asked to develop plans to increase early access for pregnant young women under 18 and to monitor numbers accessing abortion over 12 weeks' gestation. The Sexual Health Strategy also helped to hugely expand access to free emergency hormonal contraception through pharmacies, a health setting which is very local, open long hours and trusted by young women (Department of Health, 2001b).

To help build the capacity of a trained nursing workforce TPU funded the Royal College of Nursing, the UK's professional nursing organisation, to develop a distance learning course to help meet the staff needs of an increasing number of nurse-led contraceptive and sexual health services and outreach work.

To strengthen links between SRE and services: TPU funded the Sex Education Forum to publish a guide for local areas, *Secondary Schools and Sexual Health Services: Forging the links* (Sex Education Forum, 2003) and to run an e-mail network to support schools with, or considering setting up, an on-site service. Government also published guidance on establishing on-site sexual health services as part of the Extended Schools programme (Department of Children, Schools and Families, 2006). Extended Schools, prioritised in poorer areas, provided a range of support services on one site, including access to health advice. Teenage pregnancy, sexual health and young parenthood were all identified as health priorities for school nursing, and a practice development resource pack highlighted the importance of school nurses providing confidential support to pupils. Resources to integrate school SRE and contraceptive services for young men were commissioned from Working with Men, a respected NGO. To help schools discuss abortion and ensure young people had accurate information, the NGO Education for Choice was funded to publish a cross-curricula resource exploring the issue of abortion in a number of different subjects (Education for Choice, 2004).

> National evidence-based guidance from the TPU made a huge difference, particularly on innovations that were seen as challenging. For example, guidance on the value of locating sexual health services in schools was enormously helpful as schools could see that this approach was being nationally endorsed and it certainly helped them to accept this as a new way of working. It opened doors for us, which might otherwise have been closed.
>
> (Anne Colquhoun, Teenage Pregnancy Coordinator, Bristol)

To engage the non-health wider workforce: TPU published guidance for youth support workers (Department of Health (Teenage Pregnancy Unit) and Connexions, 2001, updated by Department for Education and Skills, 2005) and social care practitioners (Department of Health (Teenage Pregnancy Unit), 2001, updated by Department for Education and Skills, 2004b) on supporting young people to access contraception and sexual health advice. Specific resources were also commissioned to help local areas address the additional needs of young people in or leaving the care system (National Children's Bureau and tpa, 2003). The Connexions service, established in 2000, to provide information, advice and guidance for young people aged 13–19, included advice in their diploma training on linking young people into services. TPU also commissioned a diverse communities project to explore the faith and cultural influences on teenage pregnancy and sexual health issues and provide resources for local areas. This included a resource for practitioners, examples of multi-faith schools working with parents to develop a values framework for SRE, and a video and training materials for SRE in Catholic schools (Teenage Pregnancy Unit, 2002c).

To involve young people: TPU published guidance for local areas on how to engage young people (young men and women), including teenage parents, in the development and monitoring of their strategies (Teenage Pregnancy Unit, 2002d) and later commissioned a practical guide with examples of effective practice (National Children's Bureau, 2006). A guide was also published on developing sex and relationships peer education projects (Teenage Pregnancy Unit, 2002b). Young men and young women were recruited onto the Advisory Group to contribute views from their constituency groups on the strategy implementation, and to inform annual recommendations to government. Recruited through NGOs and serving two-year terms, they were paired with an Advisory Group member and supported in preparing for, and contributing to, meetings.

The first young members of the Teenage Pregnancy Independent
Advisory Group

> I've been working on a major project to find out the main barriers young mums face in getting back to work or training. I bring real experience and have already provided feedback to ministers.
>
> (Rhoda Thomas, a young parent and advice
> worker for Connexions)

> One of my driving concerns is that there are good accessible clinics and services so that teenagers can easily get the information and contraception they need. As a peer educator I was involved in mystery shopping of sexual health services, as well as delivering sexual health workshops in schools and informal settings. This frontline experience was invaluable for informing my contributions to the Advisory Group and enabled me to gather other young people's views on a range of issues and experiences.
>
> (Rhiannon Holder MBE, a sexual health peer
> worker and volunteer)

3.2.4 The national media campaign

The media campaign aimed to improve knowledge, address mixed messages and encourage communication. The design was informed by international desk research commissioned to identify which messages and advertising campaigns had worked best with young people (Eborall and Garmeson, 2000). The findings shaped the aims of the campaign: to inform and support young people to take control; not feel pressured into having sex before they felt ready; and be confident in asking for contraception and sexual health advice. Importantly, the messages needed to be delivered in a tone that neither scared nor lectured young people. Parents were identified as children and young people's preferred source of information, but caution and embarrassment appeared to block

Figure 3.2 Example of *ruthinking* campaign message. 2001.

communication. Informed by the research, two campaigns were developed: one for young people, one for parents.

Sex. Are you thinking about it enough – 'ruthinking' – was launched in 2000, aimed at reaching all 13–17-year-old girls and boys. Running on radio and in teenage magazines, the campaign focused on resisting peer pressure, reassurance about the confidentiality of accessing advice and contraception, and using condoms to prevent pregnancy and STIs (Figure 3.2).

Secondary messages about the full range of effective contraception were communicated through articles in magazines and websites.

To help maximise the impact of the campaign locally, regional road shows were organised to help local areas amplify the messages. Materials such as posters, leaflets, key rings and bus pass wallets were free for local areas to distribute in schools, colleges and other settings used by young people, as part of the media and communications plans required as part of their strategy. For efficiency, some distribution of materials was organised nationally – for example, to general practices. Partnerships were developed with youth brands to place the campaign messages alongside popular products in retail outlets, including Superdrug, a leading high-street pharmacist which ran an in-store campaign with radio and window displays.

To ensure the campaign had a targeted as well as universal reach, the messages and visuals were developed and adapted after testing with young people from ethnic minorities and vulnerable groups, such as looked-after children and care leavers. Posters were distributed to shopping-centre wash-rooms in high-rate areas, partnerships were formed with relevant NGOs and local areas were encouraged to disseminate the materials through practitioners such as social workers, leaving care teams and youth offending teams. Popular BME radio stations, including the BBC Asian network, ran campaigns, supported with phone-ins providing advice from experts from NGOs and the Advisory Group.

The campaign was supported by the *ruthinking* website and a free telephone helpline, Sexwise, which was open from 7 a.m. to midnight, seven days a week.

Figure 3.3 Example of a *Time to Talk* poster. 2002.

The Sexwise helpline had been funded by the Department of Health since 1995, but calls increased by 58 per cent after the campaign was launched, with half the calls from boys and young men. Young people needing further advice or an urgent clinical service – such as emergency contraception – were referred on to their nearest local service from the helpline's database, which was regularly updated with information provided by local coordinators.

The campaign for parents – *Time to Talk* – encouraged parents to talk to their children about sex and relationships. To avoid being construed as 'nannying by government', and to use the expertise of parenting specialists, the campaign was delivered through Parentline Plus, the leading and well-trusted national NGO which provided support and a free helpline for parents on a wide range of issues. Posters, leaflets and booklets were again free for local areas to distribute through schools and other community settings and by practitioners trusted by parents (Figure 3.3). A set of *Time to Talk* materials was sent nationally to every general practice for display in waiting rooms. The campaign was also integrated with government's wider parents communications strategy, enabling the *Time to Talk* leaflets to be widely distributed in community settings, including supermarkets. Parentline Plus helpline advisors received training on how to answer parents' specific questions on sex and relationships but also how to raise the topic opportunistically when parents called with concerns about potentially related issues; for example, queries about alcohol, peer pressure or staying out with friends.

3.3 Supporting the strategy through joint working

3.3.1 Establishing collaborative partnerships

By 2005, the strategy was regarded as a model for joint working, forging strong vertical links between national and local and strong horizontal links with relevant partners. There had not previously been a strong tradition of successful collaboration between health, education, youth and social services, and the strategy was seen as succeeding in implementing joint working where others had not (London School of Hygiene and Tropical Medicine, UCL and BMRB International, 2005). Key success ingredients were the near-universal support for the strategy's aims and actions and the dynamism of the support structures.

Local partnership boards met regularly, often forming sub-groups to give detailed attention to specific aspects of the strategy. Partner agencies were keen to be involved, as one coordinator discovered when establishing their local board:

> In the first few weeks I visited all the agencies that could possibly be involved in teenage pregnancy and invited them along to the group – my fault it got so big – because they all came – they were interested.
> (London School of Hygiene and Tropical Medicine, UCL and BMRB International, 2005)

Regional coordinators facilitated regular network meetings for local coordinators to communicate policy information and share problems and solutions. TPU met regional coordinators bi-monthly to review progress and identify and address any barriers to implementation, and there was active engagement from the TPU with local areas. Annual conferences and policy events for coordinators were organised by TPU. Members of the Advisory Group visited local areas to inform their annual report and recommendations to government, as well as adding weight to local strategies by meeting local senior leaders. TPU hosted regular meetings with the NGOs and inter-faith forums to maintain a two-way exchange of information and discussion on strategy-related issues.

> As a teenage pregnancy coordinator I never felt lonely. The local partner-ship board was always well attended with multi-agency commitment and interesting debate about the direction of our local strategy. There was a spirit of mutual support to spend the grant in the best way possible to get the best outcomes. The local meetings were supported by a fantastic regional and national network.
>
> (Anne Colquhoun, Teenage Pregnancy Coordinator,
> Bristol)

> The support provided nationally and regionally was invaluable to me as a local coordinator. It helped to be able to learn from other areas, especially statistical neighbours[2], and developed a peer support network for local coordinators. The information shared by the TPU and regional coord-inators helped the local strategy progress quicker, as if we hit a problem locally we could get advice from others tackling the same issues and find solutions quicker. It saved time and energy and was more efficient than each area developing policies and interventions in isolation.
>
> (Gail Teasdale, Teenage Pregnancy Coordinator,
> Kingston-upon-Hull)

> One of the key strengths of the strategy was the continuous feedback loop from local areas, via the regional coordinator to the TPU, with bi-monthly two-day meetings giving sufficient time to discuss and address barriers. Having national government so close to the reality of local implementation, and being able to nimbly adapt the support provided, was crucial to success and totally unheard of before, or since.
>
> (Kate Quail, Regional Teenage Pregnancy Coordinator
> and later Head of the Teenage Pregnancy National
> Support Team)

3.3.2 . . . and integration into wider government programmes

During the first five years, much effort was put into maintaining the priority and embedding the strategy actions into relevant government policy and programmes. The teenage pregnancy target was included in the government's renewed national Public Service Agreement and as a performance indicator for local government and their health partners (Department for Education and Skills, 2004b). A Government Green Paper on Children – *Every Child Matters* (Department for Education and Skills, 2004a) – set out a new joined-up and holistic vision for children and young people, against five outcomes: being healthy, staying safe, enjoying and achieving, making a positive contribution and enjoying economic wellbeing. The under-18 and under-16 conception rates were included in the Be Healthy Outcome, alongside rates of STIs in under-20s to indicate the importance of addressing teenage pregnancy together with young people's sexual health. Joint working was strengthened by the Change for Children programme being enshrined in the Children Act (2004), which placed a duty on local authorities and their partners to cooperate towards meeting the five outcomes.

To reflect the more integrated approach, in 2003 the TPU was moved from the Department of Health to a new Children, Young People and Families Directorate in the Department for Education and Skills, with a new role of Children and Families Minister taking lead responsibility for the Strategy implementation. However, strong joint working continued with ministers and officials in the Department of Health and through the Teenage Pregnancy inter-departmental board.

Integrating SRE with the National Healthy Schools Standard programme helped to support improvements in SRE. In 2004, achievement of the NHSS required schools to deliver a planned SRE programme, informed by consultation with young people and parents. To help ensure good SRE reached more vulnerable young people excluded from or not able to be in mainstream school, a new definition of NHSS for pupil referral units included a requirement to provide a good-quality PSHE programme. The increased priority of SRE and PSHE was reflected by 80 per cent of Local Authorities having a PSHE coordinator in place by 2004 (London School of Hygiene and Tropical Medicine, UCL and BMRB International, 2005).

Efforts to increase provision of young-people-friendly contraceptive, sexual health and abortion services were bolstered by linking teenage pregnancy to the Sexual Health and HIV Strategy; a new public health programme, *Choosing Health* (Department of Health, 2004a), which confirmed the importance of easily accessible contraception and sexual health services linked to improved SRE; and a new National Service Framework (NSF) for improving services for children, young people and maternity (Department of Health, 2004b). Following a recommendation from the Advisory Group for a universally recognised symbol to denote young-people-friendly services, the principles of the strategy best practice guidance on contraceptive services and the NSF standards were translated into the Department of Health's *You're Welcome* criteria, later endorsed by the World Health Organization (Department of Health, 2005, updated 2007 and 2011).

Underpinning the first phase of implementation was government leadership, with explicit endorsement by ministers and an active and responsive national unit. Locally, senior leaders brought agencies together to collaborate on joint action and maximise funding opportunities. The local implementation grant signalled the importance of the strategy, provided a reliable source of funding for the coordinator and helped attract matched funding from other agencies.

The role and seniority of the local coordinator was critical. The small number of areas where setting up the strategy was slower were characterised by periods when there was no coordinator in post, the post was not full time or the role was not sufficiently senior to provide the necessary leadership.

> Local coordinators were described as the lynchpin of implementation. Their status in the community, their professional experience and the support they have received have been key to the success of their role.
>
> (Teenage Pregnancy Strategy Evaluation, 2005)

> In the first four years, the strategy has been implemented with energy and enthusiasm, in an atmosphere of cooperation and consensus of those involved.
>
> (Teenage Pregnancy Strategy Evaluation 2005)

> In 2000, during the early days of the Strategy, I was working in a local Teenage Pregnancy Team coordinating an SRE programme. It was an exciting time as it felt like an army was being mobilised all over the country. We were part of a network of individuals with a shared set of values and a deep commitment to see the Strategy succeed.
>
> (Anna Martinez, later national coordinator of the
> Sex Education Forum)

Notes

1   Permanent Secretaries are the most senior civil servants of British government ministries. They generally hold their position at a ministry for a number of years, as distinct from the changing political Secretaries of State to whom they report and provide advice.
2   Local government areas identified as having similar demographic characteristics.

Chapter 4

The second phase of implementation

Reviewing, redoubling effort and reaching the target

4.1 The mid-course review

4.1.1 Taking stock of progress

In 2005, the independent evaluation of the first phase of the strategy (London School of Hygiene and Tropical Medicine, UCL and BRMB International, 2005) and monitoring of the data prompted a mid-course review (Department for Education and Skills, 2006b). Although there had been a fairly steady decline in the national under-18 conception rate of 11 per cent, the reduction lagged significantly behind the trajectory needed to meet the target. It also masked a very wide variation in progress between local areas (Figure 4.1). The majority of areas had achieved declines but at one end of the spectrum rates had fallen by 42 per cent and, at the other end, increased by 43 per cent. If all local areas had achieved the reductions of the top quarter, the fall in the national rate would have more than doubled.

4.1.2 Comparing areas with varying performance

This variation in performance prompted two 'deep dive' in-depth reviews, the first led by the TPU and the second carried out in partnership with the Prime Minister's Delivery Unit (PMDU). The PMDU was a high-profile unit established in 2001 to strengthen government's capacity to deliver its key priorities, and to monitor performance of indicators in the Public Service Agreements.

The reviews compared three local areas with declining rates and three areas – with similar populations and levels of deprivation – where rates were static or increasing. The review team, including members of the Unit, the Advisory Group and the regional coordinators, visited each area for two days. Interviews were conducted with all partner agencies, from senior managers through to frontline practitioners and young people. Questions focused on how the area had implemented the strategy actions, including the establishment of joint working, leadership and accountability. Detailed interview notes were compiled and the results compared.

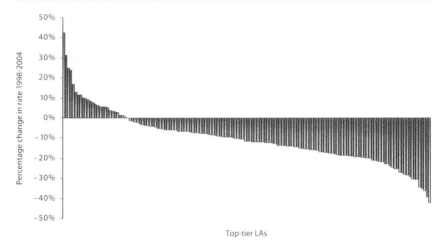

Figure 4.1 Illustrating variation in progress between 1998–2004.

The findings clearly identified that the high-performing areas were implementing all aspects of the strategy effectively, supported by senior leadership with a strong coordinating function. Areas with slower progress had certainly not been idle, but they had implemented only some actions, or had focused on small geographical areas and at-risk groups, rather than combining a universal and targeted approach. Notably, they lacked senior leadership.

The key factors evident in the areas showing progress were:

- a strong senior champion who was accountable for and took the lead in driving the local strategy and coordinating the contribution of partner agencies;
- active engagement in joint working of all of the key mainstream delivery partners who have a role in reducing teenage pregnancies – health, education, social services and youth support services and the voluntary sector;
- the availability of well-publicised young-people-centred contraceptive and sexual health advice services, with a strong remit to undertake preventive work, as well as delivering reactive services;
- a high priority given to SRE and PSHE in schools, with support from the local authority to develop comprehensive programmes of sex and relationships education (SRE) in all schools;
- a strong focus on targeted interventions with young people at greatest risk of teenage pregnancy, in particular with looked-after children;[1] the availability (and consistent take-up) of SRE training for professionals in partner organisations working with the most vulnerable young people (such as Connexions Personal Advisers, youth workers and social workers); and

- a well-resourced youth service, providing things to do and places to go for young people, with a clear focus on addressing key social issues affecting young people, such as sexual health and substance misuse.

4.2 Actions following the mid-course review

4.2.1 The critical importance of a 'whole systems' approach

The mid-course review was an important milestone for the strategy. First, the contrasting progress of very similar areas made it clear that continuing high rates were not inevitable. With leadership and the right actions, rates could be reduced, even in the most deprived areas. This was an important message for areas where some senior leaders believed the high rates of teenage parenthood were an intractable part of the local culture and impermeable to prevention. Second, it confirmed the underlining principle of the strategy that the complex issue of teenage pregnancy had to be addressed through a collaborative 'whole systems' approach. The benefits of youth-friendly contraceptive services would only be realised if other agencies and practitioners in touch with young people were part of the prevention pathway and linked them into services; and specific teenage pregnancy actions needed to be integrated into wider programmes addressing underlying risk factors of low aspirations and poor educational attainment. In essence, teenage pregnancy needed to be everybody's business, and, if the right actions were taken, everybody benefited.

4.2.2 New and more prescriptive guidance and self-assessment toolkit for local areas

To provide a more detailed road map for local areas, ministers published new and more prescriptive guidance setting out more clearly the practical actions for all relevant partner organisations (Department for Education and Skills, 2006b).

Figures 4.2 and 4.3 were used to illustrate how to translate the complex issue of teenage pregnancy into a whole systems approach, with every agency understanding their contribution. Senior leadership was at the centre to signal the critical importance of commitment and accountability. How the ten key factors were implemented locally is described in Chapter 5.

To strengthen local performance management, TPU developed a self-assessment toolkit to enable areas to review their strategy against the ten key factors and to identify and address gaps. To underline the importance of joint working and strategic leadership, the toolkit was jointly published by DfES and DH (Teenage Pregnancy Unit, 2006).

Local self-assessments were led by the coordinator working with the partnership board, and moderated by the regional coordinator. Results were

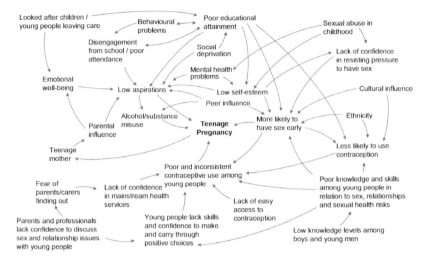

Figure 4.2 Translating the complex issue of teenage pregnancy with a range of risk factors . . .

Acknowledgement Dilwyn Sheers *et al.* Teenage Pregnancy Unit.

. . . into a collaborative 'whole systems' approach with clear actions for each agency

Figure 4.3 The ten key factors for effective local strategies.

shared with local senior strategic leaders to provide summaries of local performance and informed commissioning decisions to address any gaps and weaknesses. TPU and regional coordinators used the self-assessments to gain a better understanding of the problems in under-performing areas, identify common themes and provide additional support.

TPU also provided detailed data analysis sheets for each local area showing their conception trend, broken down by conceptions leading to maternity and conceptions leading to abortions. The analysis also included other relevant data on education attainment and data from local areas, identified by a recognised set of criteria as 'statistical neighbours', to allow like-with-like comparisons (Department for Education and Skills, 2006b).

4.2.3 Direct ministerial contact with local areas

Recognising that improving progress in the poor-performing areas was essential for accelerating the national downward trend, DfES and DH ministers decided to establish direct communication with the 21 local areas with high and increasing rates. Senior leaders of local government and their health partners were requested to submit progress reports three times a year, setting out the actions they were taking, which received joint ministerial feedback. They were also invited, with an elected councillor, the Director of Public Health and the local coordinator, to attend an annual ministerial meeting to discuss and share effective practice.

> There was tension between the desire to support local areas but at the same time to push the poorest performers closer to the achievements of the best. The key to progress, I was convinced, was having a dedicated senior person at local level who was committed to driving the necessary change across key agencies. This was supported by having ministerial meetings with the key local players to examine with them their progress, or lack of it, and agreeing what needed to happen next. We expected very senior people, including Chief Executives, to attend these meetings. The sharing of good practice from successful areas was important encouragement that change was possible.
>
> (Baroness Hughes of Stretford, Beverley Hughes, former Minister of State for Children and Young People)

The areas were provided with additional support from the regional coordinators, supplemented by more intensive in-depth reviews and recommendations from a newly appointed Teenage Pregnancy National Support Team (TPNST). The National Support Teams were established by the Department of Health in 2006 to work directly with health and local government to support them to deliver their public health priorities (including teenage conceptions, sexual health, obesity, mental health and infant mortality). The TPNST was made up of highly respected experts from across the country and headed up by a previous regional coordinator with extensive experience of implementation. Visits involved members of the Advisory Group, the Unit and the regional coordinator and took a similar approach to the mid-course deep dives, interviewing key informants, analysing local data and exploring how the ten key factors were being implemented. Feedback was rapid, with constructive recommendations and the offer of further support if needed (Department of Health, 2011).

4.2.4 Strengthening targeted prevention to reach young people most at risk

In response to the findings of the mid-course review and recommendations from the first phase evaluation, TPU carried out further evidence reviews and data analysis to help all areas strengthen their targeted prevention work (Department for Education and Skills, 2007).

Investigation into the very small area data found that 50 per cent of the under-18 conceptions occurred in 20 per cent of wards, with almost all local government areas having at least one very high-rate ward (Figure 4.4). This was a particularly important message for senior leaders in areas where, because rates were at or below the national average, teenage pregnancy was not necessarily identified as a priority.

Local areas were also given updated evidence briefings on the characteristics of young people most at risk of early pregnancy, to help them identify the practitioners, services and relevant programmes that needed to be part of the prevention pathway. Divided into different categories, the following risk factors had the strongest association:

- *Risky behaviour*: early onset of sexual activity; poor contraceptive use; poor mental health, conduct disorder or involvement in crime; and alcohol and substance misuse.
- *Education-related factors*: low educational attainment; disengagement from, and dislike of, school; and leaving school at 16 with no qualifications.
- *Family and background factors*: low parental aspirations; living in care; being the daughter of a teenage mother; and
- *Ethnicity*: having a Mixed White and Black Caribbean, Black Caribbean or Other Black ethnicity.

Data also showed that teenagers with a previous pregnancy were at greater risk. An estimated 20 per cent of births to under-18s were to young women who were already teenage mothers. Of abortions among under-19-year-olds, 11 per cent were to young women who had had one or more previous abortions, but the percentage varied significantly between local areas, ranging from 5 to 39 per cent.

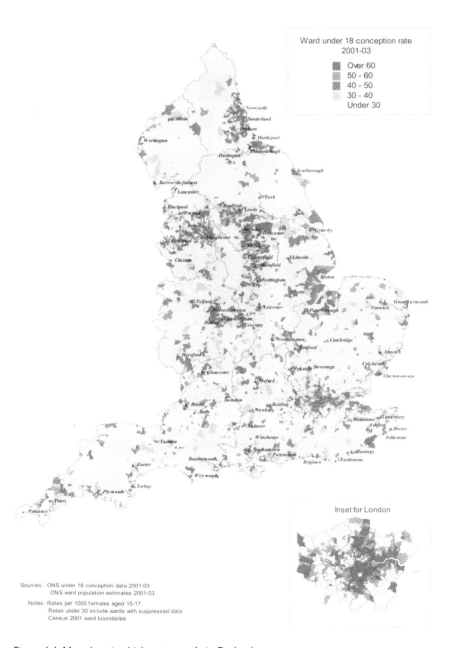

Sources: ONS under 18 conception data 2001-03
          ONS ward population estimates 2001-03

Notes: Rates per 1000 females aged 15-17
        Rates under 30 include wards with suppressed data
        Census 2001 ward boundaries

Figure 4.4 Map showing high-rate wards in England.

4.2.5 Reviewing and revising the national campaign

To support the next phase of the strategy and include a more targeted approach, TPU also reviewed and revised the national campaign, A new-look *ruthinking* continued to provide universal messages for younger teenagers on delaying sex until they felt ready, challenging myths about the proportion of young people having sex under 16, and encouraging early uptake of confidential contraception and sexual health advice from local services. Partnerships with popular youth brands continued. Collaboration with the commercial sector not only helped to carry the campaign messages into retail outlets, but also secured additional advertising exposure at no cost. Materials were free for local areas to use in relevant settings and to support targeted work. They were also made available to schools in areas with high and increasing rates and in schools serving high-rate wards.

To complement *ruthinking*, messages targeting slightly older sexually active teenagers were delivered through a new campaign. *Want Respect: Use a Condom* was based on the principle of gaining peer respect from practising safer sex, and shifting the social norms around carrying and using condoms (Figure 4.5). The campaign adverts included a focus on condom negotiation and empowering women as well as men to carry condoms with confidence. *Want Respect* was communicated through media channels popular with the target audience and in conjunction with youth brands that lent credibility to the message, particularly with young men. Partnerships with condom manufacturers and retailers helped to improve easy access to condoms, which was identified as key to increasing use (Department for Children, Schools and Families, 2008a). The Sexwise helpline answered calls from around 1.4 million young people per year – 50 per cent of whom continued to be boys and young men.

The *Time to Talk* campaign for parents continued, with advice provided through the Parentline Plus helpline and website, with materials free for local areas. To amplify local dissemination, there was national distribution of the *Time to Talk* materials through both the National Healthy Schools and Extended Schools Programmes. National funding was provided for the Family Planning Association *Speakeasy* programme, which had been commissioned by many areas to support parents and carers in discussing sex and relationships with their children. Speakeasy is an eight-week course, run one evening a week in small groups, which aims to equip parents and carers with an understanding of the physical and emotional changes taking place at puberty, awareness of what sex and relationships education means in the context of family life, confidence and skills in identifying and responding to the needs of their own children, awareness of societal and cultural attitudes towards sex and sexuality as it relates to children, knowledge of the different kinds of contraception that are available, information on sex and relationships education in schools, and information and knowledge on child protection strategies. The funding enabled local areas to sustain the programme by training their own practitioners to become Speakeasy facilitators.

Figure 4.5 Example of a *Want Respect* ad. 2006.

TPU led regional seminars for coordinators and sexual health leads, to ensure they understood the new campaign approach and were supported to extend it effectively at a local level. The self-assessment toolkit included a media and communications strategy checklist and TPU provided an additional Communications Guide for local areas.

4.2.6 Maintaining the priority, joint working and integration into wider government programmes

Government's sustained priority and leadership were signalled by continuing to include the teenage pregnancy target in the new joint DfES[2] and DH Public Service Agreement to 2008, and as an indicator in the performance frameworks for health and local government (Department for Children, Schools and Families, 2008a). Increasing recognition of the importance of teenage pregnancy was reflected in the high numbers of local government areas choosing teenage pregnancy as a priority in their local plans. To help ensure all areas maintained a focus, TPU provided guidance showing how progress on teenage pregnancy helps support achievement of other local priorities, such as reducing child poverty and increasing the proportion of young people in education and training.

Implementation of the new guidance and actions following the mid-strategy review was supported by wider government initiatives to promote a more joined-up and holistic approach to improving outcomes for children and young people; notably, the further embedding of *Every Child Matters*, the expectation of local areas to integrate their teenage pregnancy strategies into the new requirement to develop a Children and Young People's Plan to meet the five *Every Child Matters* outcomes, and a new Targeted Youth Support (TYS) programme aimed at addressing the underlying risk factors that can result in a range of poor outcomes (Department for Education and Skills, 2007). To have the maximum impact on reducing teenage pregnancy, TYS practitioners were given guidance on providing young people with the knowledge and skills they need to develop positive relationships and good sexual health and to promote access to contraception when they need it (Department for Children, Schools and Families, 2008b). A strengthened National Healthy Schools Standard programme continued to reinforce the links between SRE and sexual health services, and through the Extended Schools programme, schools were encouraged to offer on-site contraception and sexual health advice as part of a range of services. New guidance was published on establishing on-site services in further education colleges to provide easy access to contraceptive advice for large numbers of 16–17-year-olds (Department for Education and Skills and Department of Health, 2006a).

The joint departmental guidance highlighted the mutual benefits of collaboration. Reductions in pregnancy would contribute to local health targets but also helped improve student retention rates, one of the FE college inspection criteria, by reducing numbers of young women dropping out of courses due to pregnancy. The drive to increase the provision of young-people-friendly services was strengthened by national funding to help areas implement the *You're Welcome* quality criteria. This included recruiting and training young people to 'mystery shop' local services to assess whether or not they met the quality criteria, with a feedback report and constructive recommendations provided to services to help shape improvements.

The local implementation grant funding continued at the same level, but in 2006 the ring fence was removed to encourage joint planning and collaborative funding. The location of the Unit in the newly named Department for Children, Schools and Families (DCSF) continued to foster integration of the strategy actions into relevant programmes aimed at reducing underlying risk factors, building aspiration and increasing education attainment. However, strong joint working with the Department of Health ensured improvements in access to contraception, STI screening and pregnancy options were complemented and strengthened by the National Strategy for Sexual Health and HIV. Integrated working was supported and reinforced by the very strong and visible joint ministerial team from the two departments.

> Strong ministerial engagement was crucial to the effective implementa-tion of the strategy, as well as the knowledge that the Teenage Pregnancy Strategy was but one strand of a much wider government commitment to ending child poverty.
> It also helped that my position as Minister of State for Children and Young people was deliberately a cross-departmental brief. However, the personal commitment of another female Minister of Health was equally important, especially in forging the collaboration needed both between government departments and at local level.
> > (Baroness Hughes of Stretford, Beverley Hughes, former Minister of State for Children and Young People)

4.3 2008–2010: a further review of progress

4.3.1 A strengthened focus on SRE and effective contraception

Over the next two years, there was close monitoring of local progress, with an updated self-assessment toolkit for all areas to complete (Department for Children, Schools and Families and Department of Health, 2009). Local areas under ministerial focus were taken off the list when data showed evidence of improvement, and new high-rate areas added if the pace of change was slow. The regional coordinators, complemented by the National Support Team, provided expert support. By 2010, an NST in-depth review and bespoke recommendations for further actions had been received by 68 areas, with local areas strongly welcoming the specialist advice and constructive support model.

> The National Support Team visit played a vital part in embedding local work and ensuring the strategy left a legacy in the quality of the services for young people. The thorough review of our strategy by a highly regarded national team helped to validate the investment of commitment and resources by celebrating our good practice, but also highlighted gaps and the need for multi-agency collaboration. The NST engagement with senior officials opened doors and led to strengthened partnership working.
> > (Claire Whiteley, Teenage Pregnancy Coordinator, Bradford)

> We gained a better understanding of the scale of the issue in our area . . . For us 'a light came on'!
> > (Local Authority Chief Executive, NorthWest)

In addition to supporting improved local performance, further thought was given to what national action would help accelerate progress. An updated international research review, commissioned by TPU, confirmed the original evidence base for the Strategy: that the provision of high-quality comprehensive sex and relationships education, and improved use of contraception, were the componenets with the strongest empirical evidence for reducing teenage pregnancy rates. Furthermore, within the overall reduction in the conception rate, the data showed that conceptions leading to birth were declining faster than those leading to abortion. In other words, fewer young people were getting pregnant but, of those who did, an increasing proportion was deciding against teenage parenthood and choosing abortion instead. These were clearly unwanted pregnancies, underlining the need to strengthen the prevention programme. Some step changes were needed to further improve SRE and access to effective contraception.

4.3.2 A concerted push for statutory sex and relationships education

From the start of the Strategy there had been a sustained call to government from the Advisory Group, the Sex Education Forum and other NGOs and stakeholders to make SRE within Personal Social, Health and Economic (PSHE) education a statutory part of the curriculum; a recommendation reiterated in the independent evaluation of the strategy's first phase. This was considered essential to increase the priority in schools and address the unacceptable variability between young people in relation to the amount and quality of SRE they received (Ofsted, 2007). While statutory status alone would not guarantee quality, it would secure a place for SRE/PSHE in the curriculum, require training of specialist teachers and continuing professional development, and ensure inspection of school provision. Following a survey of 20,000 young people from the UK Youth Parliament (UK Youth Parliament, 2007), which showed that 40 per cent rated their SRE poor or inadequate, and a campaign – *Beyond Biology* – from the Sex Education Forum (Sex Education Forum, 2006), government accepted the need for change and commissioned an external review of SRE and PSHE (Department for Children, Schools and Families, 2008c). In 2008, at a national Sex Education Forum conference, Jim Knight, the schools minister, announced that government intended to make PSHE, including SRE, statutory (Department for Children, Schools and Families, 2008d), receiving a standing ovation from delighted stakeholders!

To determine the most effective ways of achieving this, government commissioned an independent review. Led by Sir Alastair Macdonald, a prominent education leader, the review confirmed that statutory SRE and PSHE, at both primary and secondary levels, was key to raising status and improving provision, and made recommendations for government to take forward into legislation (Department for Children, Schools and Families, 2009). However, to widespread dismay and strong criticism by the Advisory Group and stakeholders, the Bill failed to get passed in the final legislative session before the general election in May 2010.

Nevertheless, during the preparation for the Bill important progress was made in improving the understanding of SRE and building consensus for universal provision. Once myths about the sexual content of SRE at primary level were dispelled, and parents understood that good SRE delayed rather than lowered age of first sex, opinion polls and focus groups demonstrated strong support for provision in all schools. 'We are not talking about five-year-old kids being taught sex. What we're talking about for key stage 1 is children knowing about themselves, their differences, their friendships and how to manage their feelings' (Jim Knight, Schools Minister, *Guardian* 23 October 2008).

Similarly, discussions with faith communities and organisations also elicited support for statutory status. The Advisory Group and NGOs played a critical role in calmly making the case for the benefits of SRE, and supporting ministers to explicitly support the move to statutory status. The expectation of statutory status also prompted some local areas to raise the priority of SRE and develop programmes and training to prepare schools.

> It was hugely disappointing that the legislation fell at the final hurdle. However, the review which led to the decision for statutory status demonstrated that when evidence and testimonies are presented from those affected by poor provision, and the content of SRE is explained, fears and misconceptions fall away and a consensus emerges that SRE is essential to protect and promote the health and wellbeing of children and young people.
> (Jane Lees, Chair of Sex Education Forum 2008–2017)

4.3.3 Improving young people's knowledge and access to effective contraception

The importance of improving young people's access to and use of contraception was highlighted by new research attributing 86 per cent of the recent decline in US teenage pregnancy rates to better contraceptive use (Santelli *et al.*, 2007). To support local areas in improving access to effective contraception, the Department of Health secured £33M additional funding from the Government Spending Review settlement for 2008–11 (Department for Children, Schools and Families, 2009). The primary aim was to increase access for all women, including young people under 18, to all types of contraception and particularly to ensure that the choice of long-acting reversible contraceptive (LARC) methods was easily available in all areas. Expanding availability of LARC methods had also been a recommendation of the first phase evaluation.

Funds were distributed through the regional network of Strategic Health Authorities,[3] which were asked to ensure investment was made in activities that would be sustainable beyond the three-year lifetime of the funding.

A proportion of funding was earmarked to support local areas expand the collaboration with Further Education colleges to set up on-site services. To continue the important promotion of condoms to protect against STIs, Brook was funded to develop guidance for local areas on condom distribution schemes (Brook, 2008a). TPU also funded Brook to develop guidance on sexual health outreach to help local areas take services to young people who might be wary of accessing other settings (Brook, 2008b), and to provide updated guidance and best practice examples of engaging with boys and young men (Brook, 2010).

4.3.4 A new national campaign to normalise discussion about contraception

As part of the drive to improve awareness and uptake of contraception, there was a rethink of the national campaign and the Department of Health commissioned an evidence review to identify the most effective role of communications (Department of Health and Department for Children, Schools and Families, 2009). The review found that while there were multiple influences on behaviour, the strongest predictors of young people practising safer sex was not their attitudes or stated behavioural intention, but their 'preparatory' behaviours – accessing condoms, carrying condoms and discussion about condom use. Discussion about condom use prior to sex had the strongest overall influence. The biggest impact of a communications campaign would be through normalising everyday discussion about contraception and sexual health to reduce the stigma and embarrassment, which young people reported as deterrents to seeking early advice.

Developed in close consultation with stakeholders and NGOs, a new campaign was launched in November 2009, aimed at young people up to the age of 25. *Sex. Worth Talking About* – a notable shift of emphasis from the earlier teenage pregnancy strategy campaign, 'Sex. Are you *thinking* about it enough?' – ran on TV, radio, cinema and online ads showing conversations about contraception and chlamydia between young people, with parents and with health professionals in a range of everyday scenarios (Figure 4.6). For the first time, government ads about the range of contraceptive choices and the importance of STI testing were brought into the living room, before the 9 p.m. 'watershed'. The notable absence of complaints from the public was a further reflection of the growing consensus that providing young people with good information was important in helping them prevent early pregnancy and to look after their sexual health.

Young people seeking further information were directed to a new *Sex. Worth Talking About* website and the Sexwise helpline was rebranded 'Worth Talking About'. To help extend the messages into local settings, a separate campaign website was developed for coordinators and sexual health professionals, with a campaign toolkit, free posters and resources to disseminate to young people and health professionals. A new guide for parents – *Talking to*

Figure 4.6 Sex. Worth Talking About campaign logo. 2009.

your teenager about sex and relationships, co-branded with the NHS logo and Parentline Plus – was also distributed to all independent pharmacies in England. Pharmacies were chosen as a frequently visited and trusted source of health advice with a presence in all local communities, including the most deprived.

Owing to the election and change of government in May 2010, and although materials continued to be available for local areas, the national campaign activity ran for only four months, significantly limiting its impact. Nevertheless, there were some encouraging signs. Despite the short duration, follow-up evaluation found there was very high recognition of both the contraception and chlamydia adverts, and increased awareness of long-acting reversible contraception, particularly the implant. Interestingly, the chlamydia messages particularly appeared to increase parents' intention to talk to their teenagers about sexual health. Service data also suggested some positive impact, with a 10 per cent increase in chlamydia screening between 2009 and 2010 and a rise in the proportion of young people choosing a LARC method from 24 per cent in 2008/09 to 26 per cent in 2009/10 and 28 per cent in 2010/11. Although it is not possible to attribute it directly to the campaign, the under-18 conception rate showed the largest single-year decline of 8 per cent between 2009 and 2010.

4.3.5 Maintaining the priority, joint working and integration into wider government programmes

As well as these specific actions and the close monitoring of local progress, government signalled the continuing priority of teenage pregnancy in the new Public Service Agreements. To further integrate the strategy into wider programmes, teenage pregnancy was included as one of five leading indicators in a new Youth PSA – increasing the number of young people on the path to success. Each PSA was underpinned by a cross-department delivery agreement. Although DCSF led on the Youth PSA, all departments, including DH, shared responsibility for the PSA and progress on the under-18 conception rate. The indicator also continued to be included as a priority in the NHS

Operating Framework. Locally, the under-18 conception rate was now chosen by 106 out of 150 areas as a priority indicator, second only to the proportion of young people not in education, employment or training (Department for Children, Schools and Families, 2009). To support local areas strengthen the monitoring of progress and accountability, TPU provided a revised self-assessment toolkit and a local monitoring data set, with suggested indicators to measure the delivery and impact of the different strategy actions. To help ensure the self-assessment was part of the overall commissioning cycle, the toolkit included a one-page summary of progress and further required actions for sign off by senior leaders (Department for Children, Schools and Families and Department of Health, 2009).

The importance of joining up teenage pregnancy work was reinforced by a strong ministerial presence. The Children's and Health ministers spoke together at regional conferences for coordinators and senior leaders; ministers responsible for healthy schools, extended schools and further education spoke publicly about the benefits of on-site contraception and sexual health services; and ministerial promotion of a new Child Health Strategy reinforced the benefits of SRE, easy access to confidential services, early targeted help and support for parents (Department for Children, Schools and Families, 2009).

Improvements in SRE were supported by a new statutory duty on schools to improve pupil wellbeing, and continuing inclusion in the National Healthy Schools Programme and in a new Enhanced Healthy Schools Programme. In addition to the contraceptive investment, the drive for increased youth-friendly services was strengthened by a new Healthy Child Programme for 5- to 19-year-olds and continued funding for the *You're Welcome* accreditation programme. Early help for young people most at risk was extended through the Targeted Youth Support programme.

By 2010, the strategy was regarded by many as being the vanguard of joint working between government departments, local partners and professionals and, in particular, a catalyst for partnership working between health and education.

> The Teenage Pregnancy Strategy wasn't just successful in reducing teenage conceptions and supporting young parents, it also rewrote the book on how to effectively deliver complex, often believed impossible, changes within society. The model of integrating national policy with local implementation created strong vertical links through national, regional and local coordinators, but also wove together diverse services across local areas. One of the lasting impacts of the strategy has been to engender a new way of joint working.
>
> (Jo Nichols, Local and Regional Teenage Pregnancy
> Coordinator, and Associate National Delivery Manager
> Teenage Pregnancy National Support Team)

The strategy forged the way for improved joint working on addressing other young people's risk taking, such as alcohol. Partner agencies saw the benefits of collaboration between services and practitioners.

(Gail Teasdale, Teenage Pregnancy Coordinator,
Kingston-upon-Hull)

4.4 2010 and beyond

4.4.1 Keeping the focus beyond the end of the strategy

In 2010, government published new guidance for local areas for two key reasons (Department for Children, Schools and Families and Department of Health, 2010). First, this was the final year in which local areas could take action to influence the original target. Second, the guidance made an important statement that the strategy was not ending. The original reasons for the strategy remained, and although the downward trend was starting to accelerate, there was much more to do. It was clear that, with the right actions, rates could be reduced, but the priority needed to continue. *Teenage Pregnancy Strategy: Beyond 2010* was informed by an updated evidence review, summarised the progress and learning so far, illustrated by a range of local case studies, and set out proposals for further national actions.

In May 2010, a new coalition government was elected, marking the end of thirteen years of continuous Labour administration. Ministers from the renamed Department for Education and the Department of Health decided against publishing a further stand-alone strategy or setting new national and local targets. Instead they made clear they wanted teenage pregnancy to remain a priority but for the actions to be integrated into wider programmes to narrow inequalities and address child poverty. Local areas were asked to continue to prioritise reducing teenage pregnancy rates, using the international evidence and lessons from the areas where rates have fallen fastest to accelerate progress. The Advisory Group published its final report and recommendations to new ministers in December 2010. *Past successes – future challenges* stressed the importance of a continued focus from the new administration and the economic, as well as human, costs of disinvestment (Teenage Pregnancy Independent Advisory Group, 2010).

The reduction in the teenage pregnancy rate over the last decade – to the point where it is at the lowest level for over twenty years – is very welcome and reflects the hard work of people working at a local level to help young people make safe and healthy choices about sex and relationships. But we still have very high rates compared to many other countries and clearly there is still much more to be done. I want local areas to maintain their efforts to reduce teenage pregnancy rates further, making a vital contribution to their strategies to reduce child poverty and health inequalities.

(Sarah Teather, Minister for Children and Families, 2010)

To signal an ongoing national focus on teenage pregnancy, reducing the under-18 conception rate was one of eight ambitions in the Department of Health's new policy guidance on improving sexual health (Department of Health, 2013a), and the under-18 conception rate was included as one of three sexual health indicators in a new Public Health Outcomes Framework, designed to monitor national and local progress (Department of Health, 2013b). The benefits of SRE were highlighted in a new Schools White Paper (Department for Education, 2010), and the importance of youth-friendly services underlined by revised *You're Welcome* quality criteria (Department of Health, 2011). A cross-government youth policy, *Positive for Youth* (HM Government, 2011), emphasised the importance of building young people's knowledge and confidence to delay early pregnancy and look after their sexual health. Notably, the policy included a case study of Brook's Sex Positive Campaign, a marker of progress in government's ease in discussing sexual health.

The Sex Positive Campaign was developed by Brook young volunteers, as part of 'V talent year', a national full-time volunteering programme for young people. The campaign was prompted by their personal experiences of poor sex and relationships education, overwhelmingly negative attitudes to young people's sexuality and a lack of information about sexual health services. Recognising that many young people had the same experiences, the young volunteers were inspired to start a campaign to encourage societal attitudes to be sex positive, making it easier for young people to talk about and make well-informed and positive choices about sex, and remove the stigma about asking for advice on sexual health. The campaign evolved into a Sex Positive movement, as subsequent cohorts of young volunteers took ownership, leading their own social action projects at national and local level, meeting with MPs and ministers and promoting awareness and discussion online.

However, national funding for the strategy, including the media campaign, stopped, visible government leadership ceased and the structures for strategy implementation began to be dismantled. The regional coordinator posts, government offices and National Support Teams ended in 2011 and the Teenage Pregnancy Unit closed in 2012. So too did the national and regional structures for supporting local implementation of the *National Healthy Schools Programme* and the *You're Welcome* standards. Decisions about coordinators, partnership boards and accountability arrangements were left to local government, which, following the Health and Social Care Act, now had responsibility for public health, including the commissioning of clinical sexual and reproductive health services. However, a study in 2011 found one-third of the dedicated coordinator posts had been cut (Nichols, 2011). In 2013, the previous head of TPU established a new independent Teenage Pregnancy Knowledge Exchange at the University of Bedfordshire, to ensure a national source of expertise continued, and shortly after became teenage pregnancy adviser to Public Health England to develop further national guidance and provide support to local areas.

A teenage pregnancy briefing was published for elected councillors highlighting the need for continued attention and further development, and illustrating effective local practice (Local Government Association and Public Health England, 2016, updated 2017). Guidance was published for local areas, which restated the principles for implementing the ten key factors and provided a checklist for reviewing progress (Public Health England and Local Government Association, 2017). A framework for supporting teenage mothers and young fathers set out the evidence and multi-agency contribution for improving outcomes (Public Health England and Local Government Association, 2016). These, and other new policy and guidance documents which include teenage pregnancy strategy actions, are referenced in Chapter 5 and also in Chapter 7's discussion on sustaining momentum beyond the end of the strategy.

4.4.2 Reaching the target

The original reduction target of the strategy was finally achieved in 2014. The under-18 conception rate of 22.8 per 1000 15–17-year-olds marked a 51 per cent reduction from 1998, with the number of conceptions dropping from 41,089 to 21,282. The under-16 conception rate also fell by over 50 per cent. Both had reached the lowest levels since 1969 when conception data collection began. All areas had seen reductions, including those with previously slow progress (Figure 4.7), and abortions and maternity rates were declining in parallel (Figure 4.8). The impact of the strategy was also explored in an independent observational study. Routinely collected area-level conception data, deprivation and local implementation grant expenditures were combined with individual-level risk factor information from the three waves of the National Surveys of Sexual Attitudes and Lifestyle (NATSAL) to describe changes in conceptions, abortions and maternities to under-18s in England. The study reported a marked decline in conceptions, which was greater in areas of higher deprivation and also in areas of higher teenage pregnancy strategy investment (Wellings et al., 2016)

National data on monitoring indices of the strategy implementation are limited. However, there was a doubling in the number of youth-specific community contraceptive clinic sessions between 1997/98 and 2009/10, a large increase in the use of LARCs by under-18s accessing contraceptive clinics (Health and Social Care Information Centre, 2008/09, 2009/10), a significant expansion in the number of school and college-based clinics providing reproductive and sexual health advice (Sex Education Forum, 2008a, 2008b) and an upward trend in the proportion of young people reporting school as

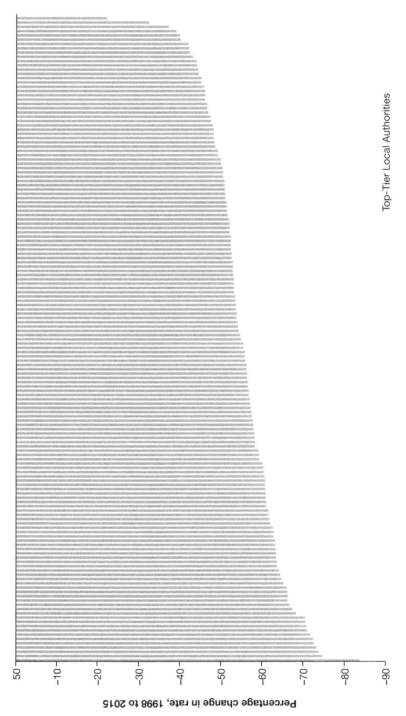

Figure 4.7 Under-18 conception rates: change in conception rate per 1000 girls aged 15–17: 1998–2015.

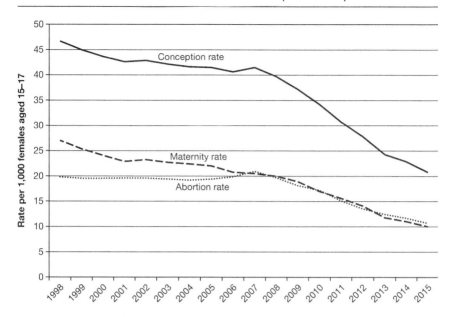

Figure 4.8 The national trend in under-18 conceptions, maternities and abortions: 1998–2015.

their main source of SRE, which is associated with lower under-18 conception rates and STI diagnoses (Tanton *et al.*, 2015).

As Figure 4.8 illustrates, the decline accelerated after 2008, with a 39 per cent reduction between 2010 and 2015. As teenage pregnancy is a complex issue requiring a multifaceted approach, it is unlikely that one factor drove the steeper decline in the later stages of the strategy. More probable is a combination of factors, including the increasing priority given to teenage pregnancy by local areas after the mid-strategy review in 2006, with increased ministerial focus and additional support, the cumulative impact of a long-term programme of prevention work through service improvements, workforce training and wider government initiatives to strengthen partnership working and improve wider outcomes for children and young people, an increase in under-18s choosing one of the LARC methods and the benefits of time in changing the culture of strategic leaders and service providers that, when young people are given choices, high rates are not inevitable.

> I have been a Teenage Pregnancy Coordinator since the beginning of the strategy and now have a lead commissioning role for young people's health in Public Health.
>
> I have never since experienced the enormous benefits of the strong vertical communications between national, regional and local. The strengths in collaborative working and true partnerships were evident for

local young people – teenage pregnancy wasn't inevitable and it was part
of everyone's responsibility to support young people.

(Kerry Clarke, Teenage Pregnancy Coordinator,
Brighton and Hove)

This last point is particularly important given that the downward trend
continued despite the impact of the recession. During the UK recession in the
early 1980s, there had been a marked increase in the under-20s conception
rate, mainly accounted for by a rise in conceptions leading to maternity
(Brook, 2014). Based on the trend in the 1980s, and the strong association
between teenage pregnancy and deprivation, government scenario planning
for the 2008 recession anticipated a potential reversal of the downward trend
and a disproportionate increase in maternities. However, the data did not follow
the anticipated pattern, despite the increase in young people not in education,
employment or training between 2008 and 2012. The conception rate
continued to fall, with both abortion and maternity rates declining.

As pointed out in Chapter 1, it is important to avoid a reductionist approach
to explaining the very significant reduction in rates, although the association
between local reductions and strategy funding is an important sign of impact.
It appears to be the multifaceted and multi-level approach, implemented with
sufficient time, facilitated by a government committed to change, and an
enthusiastic, dedicated workforce that was instrumental in achieving the goal.

The UK Teenage Pregnancy Strategy is an impressive example of how a
sustained, multilevel, and multicomponent intervention, such as that
advocated by the recent Lancet Commission on adolescent health, can
impact a complex health and social issue, with high cost effectiveness.

(Skinner and Marina, 2016)

4.4.3 What were the success factors and what might have been done differently?

Understanding the success factors is important for maintaining the downward
trend in the UK and for other countries seeking to address high rates. So too
is reflecting on what might have been done differently to strengthen the
strategy. The points summarised below are explored in more detail in
Chapter 7, described under the WHO criteria for effective national adolescent
sexual and reproductive health programmes.

Features of success

• Creating and maximising the opportunity for collaborative action
• Developing a credible, evidence-based strategy with national and local
  targets

- Establishing the structures and support for effective strategy implementation
- Regularly reviewing the strategy and tailoring actions to address the findings
- Embedding the strategy in wider government programmes aimed at improving health, education and economic outcomes
- Maintaining leadership and accountability throughout the strategy, with sufficient time to bring about change.

What might have been done differently to strengthen the strategy?

- Making SRE statutory as an action of the strategy
- Issuing more prescriptive guidance from the start, with stronger performance management of strategy inputs
- A stronger campaign focus on effective contraception, with condom use as a secondary rather than primary message
- An annual national survey of young people to monitor impact of strategy actions, which could be used by local areas
- More proactive work with the media from the start of the strategy to highlight consensus and counter misleading media reports.

Note

1 A child or young person is looked after if they are in the care of the local authority for more than 24 hours.
2 In 2001 the Department for Education and Employment became the Department for Education and Skills, following the move of employment functions to a new Department for Work and Pensions. In 2007, DfES split into a new Department for Children Schools and Families, and a Department for Innovation, Universities and Skills. In 2010 DCSF was renamed the Department for Education.
3 Strategic health authorities (SHA) were part of the NHS structure in England between 2002 and 2013. Each SHA was responsible for implementing policies of the Department of Health at a regional level.

Chapter 5

Translating evidence into action

The ten key factors for an effective strategy

5.1 Local implementation

5.1.1 Overview

The previous chapter described the journey of implementing the prevention programme of the strategy, mainly from a national perspective. This chapter focuses in more detail on local implementation and how the ten key factors for an effective strategy, confirmed in the mid-course review, were translated into action to create the essential whole system approach. The contribution of the ten factors is described with reference to the supporting national actions. Each is illustrated by local case studies, written in collaboration with the local teenage pregnancy lead. These are chosen from a mix of urban and rural areas which had achieved significant reductions in their under-18 conception rates[1], although, by focusing on one aspect, they do not reflect the totality of the local strategies. They also only represent a very small sample of effective implementation across the country. The vast majority of the case studies, although originally supported through the teenage pregnancy grant, secured funding from mainstream resources. This reflects the strategy's intention that work on teenage pregnancy should not 'stand alone', but be integrated into commissioning of wider programmes. Inevitably, in time, some of the case studies will become historical, but they are nevertheless valuable as a reminder of 'what good looks like'.

Each section concludes with the key principles for successful implementation. These are drawn from the mid-course review, subsequent learning over the ten years of the programme, and consultation with experienced teenage pregnancy coordinators who led local implementation. The principles deliberately do not refer to England-specific policies or structures, so that they can be applied in a range of policy and commissioning landscapes to meet the needs of different local populations.

Figure 5.1 The ten key factors for effective local strategies.

5.2 Senior leadership and accountability

5.2.1 National and local actions

The mid-course review (Department for Education and Skills, 2006b) and the first phase evaluation (London School of Hygiene and Tropical Medicine, UCL and BMRB International, 2005) both identified committed senior leadership as central to the success in high-performing areas. Conversely, lack of commitment partly explained poor progress in areas struggling to reduce rates. This was commonly manifested either by a passive acceptance of teenage pregnancy as the norm and impossible to influence, or by a failure to recognise the link between early pregnancy and the inequality of young people's life chances. Both resulted in the issue not being given sufficient local priority. This was sometimes compounded by a long-held assumption that teenage pregnancy was solely a health issue and not also the concern and responsibility of other agencies, an assumption that can require continued challenge.

Strong and visible leadership needs to be accompanied by senior engagement from partner agencies to act as agents of change for the necessary whole systems approach. All partners need to understand why reducing teenage pregnancy is important, the relevance to their own priorities, and how their agency can contribute, and agree funding and responsibility for monitoring measures of progress. Making teenage pregnancy everybody's business is essential for effective implementation but, without clear accountability, it can quickly become nobody's responsibility!

During the course of the strategy, government action at the national level was crucial in supporting local leadership and prioritisation. This included having a ten-year goal and agreed local reduction targets; embedding the target in local government and health performance frameworks; providing briefings for locally elected councillors on how progress on teenage pregnancy and improved outcomes for young parents contributed to other outcomes; requiring annual reports from all areas and senior sign-off for self-assessment reviews; and more frequent reporting and ministerial engagement for areas showing slow progress. The engagement of senior leaders markedly strengthened after the mid-course review, direct ministerial involvement and the additional support from the regional coordinators and the National Support Team (Department for Children, Schools and Families and Department of Health, 2010).

In England, the under-18 conception rate is now included in the Public Health Outcomes Framework along with several indicators to which progress on teenage pregnancy directly contributes; for example, young people not in education, training or employment, infant mortality and children in poverty. Public Health England and the Local Government Association published a new briefing for local councillors, highlighting the continuing importance of teenage pregnancy and need for further progress (Local Government Association and Public Health England, 2016, 2017). PHE and LGA also issued revised guidance restating the principles for implementing the ten key factors and provided a checklist for reviewing progress (Public Health England and Local Government Association, 2017).

5.2.2 Senior leadership and accountability – in practice

CASE STUDY 5.1:

Establishing a joined-up strategic vision and governance arrangements

Brighton and Hove, a coastal city in South East England, has a population of 273,000. From the start of the strategy the council had a joint teenage pregnancy and substance misuse commissioner, a representative partnership board and a local strategy, in line with national guidance. However, early progress was slow, with only a 13 per cent reduction in the under-18 conception rate between 1998 and 2007.

In 2008, following the mid-course review, assistant directors in the Council's Children and Young People Team led a comprehensive challenge to test a hypothesis that the high conception rates were widely accepted by local staff. An attitudinal survey was completed by 80 staff across all partner agencies and at all levels, from senior leaders to frontline practitioners. While a high proportion considered themselves or their organisation to be addressing teenage pregnancy, the results showed over half believed early parenthood was inevitable and part of Brighton culture.

This led to a new action plan for 2009, with two key messages: 'teenage pregnancy is everybody's business' and 'early conception is not inevitable'. The action plan had a high-profile launch to signal its importance, presented at a senior leaders' conference by the Lead Elected Member for Children and Director of Public Health, and at a staff conference by the Chief Executive of the Primary Care Trust and the Director of Children's Services. SMART[2] objectives were set under six key themes: leadership, culture and behaviour, integrated planning and review, workforce development, service provision and effective monitoring.

The visible senior leadership and new action plan had a clear impact. Partnership work was strengthened, with specific targets and outcomes included in service contracts. Frontline staff welcomed the accompanying policies and procedures that supported a more directive approach. There was increased investment brought together in the form of a 'pooled budget' (Section 75 agreement), with specific work funded through mainstream budgets. Improved quantitative and qualitative data from provider services enabled the dedicated performance analyst to monitor and understand better the profile of young people accessing services.

A comprehensive performance management system was developed for tracking progress and holding partner agencies and services to account for their contribution to the strategy. An Operation Delivery Group with frontline champions from all contract holders met quarterly. Performance boards attended by senior heads of partner agencies also held quarterly meetings to review progress of agreed actions. Recommendations for additional action were put forward for ratification to the Teenage Pregnancy and Substance Misuse Partnership Board attended by senior heads of all partner agencies. Overall progress against the action plan was regularly reported to, and scrutinised by, the Board of the Children and Young People's Trust, the Primary Care Trust, the Local Strategic Partnership and the Joint Strategic Management Group for the Section 75 pooled budget arrangements.

In the years following the launch and implementation of the action plan, there was an accelerated decline in Brighton and Hove's under-18 conception rate. By 2015, the rate had reduced by 48 per cent.

CASE STUDY 5.2:
Maintaining strategic leadership beyond the strategy

Cornwall, a county in South West England, has a population of 532,000. Following the Health and Social Care Act (2012) and the move of public health to local councils, Cornwall Council's new Sexual Health Commissioning Board and Sexual Health Partnership Group took the lead on teenage pregnancy, reporting to the Health and Wellbeing Board through the Director of Public Health. The role of the coordinator and the key principles of multi-agency working were maintained, with a continued priority to reduce under-18 conceptions embedded in the council's sexual health strategy. The partnership group includes the elected member for children's services, public health, sexual health commissioner, education, youth services, maternity, early years and social care and family support services, sitting alongside clinical providers; data and performance are included in the Public Health Service plan and Director of Public Health's annual report. By 2015 Cornwall's under-18 conception rate had declined by 56 per cent.

5.2.3 Key principles for senior leadership and accountability

- Agree the governance arrangements and senior accountable board for monitoring implementation and impact of the strategy.
- Identify a senior official or elected member of the local government structure, to be a 'teenage pregnancy champion', providing visible leadership on the ambition and implementation of the local strategy, including liaising with the local media.
- Appoint a teenage pregnancy coordinator or nominated lead, with sufficient seniority to engage partner agencies, and who reports directly to the senior accountable board.
- Provide briefings for elected officials and all key partners on the importance of teenage pregnancy, the relevance to their own priorities and the required contribution of their agency.
- Agree named senior teenage pregnancy champions and accountable leads in each partner agency for commissioning and monitoring their agreed contribution.
- Integrate teenage pregnancy actions with commissioning of relevant programmes for maternity, early years, children and young people and sexual health services.
- Agree arrangements with partner agencies for a regular review of data and performance, with overall progress regularly reported to the senior accountable board.
- Establish regional and national networks to maintain the priority, support multi-agency collaboration and share practice.

5.3 Strong use of data for commissioning and monitoring of progress

5.3.1 National and local actions

Detailed, accurate data are essential for assessing need, planning, commissioning and monitoring progress. The strategy had the benefit of very accurate data on under-18 conceptions at a national, regional and local government level (Public Health England, 2014). These are collected from the statutory notifications of all births and abortions. By estimating gestation of the pregnancy, the data are adjusted to the age at which the young woman conceived. The data are supplied quarterly with a full annual data set including district data. Three-year aggregated data for smaller geographical areas are also supplied annually. The robustness of the data was crucial for national and local monitoring of progress towards the targets, and for the comparisons between areas which facilitated the mid-course review. The drawback on the nationally supplied data is the time taken for the data to be processed, checked and published, which results in a fourteen-month time lag. This poses a difficulty for local areas in closely monitoring real-time trends and the impact of their strategy actions.

To help areas better monitor the implementation of their strategy, the self-assessment toolkit included a data monitoring set with suggested local indicators (Teenage Pregnancy Unit, 2006, updated 2009). This included the quarterly collection of numbers from maternity and abortion services to provide more current conception trend data, and indicators to monitor the 'inputs' of strategy actions. For example, the proportion of schools with a teacher completing the PSHE/SRE certification; the number (and proportion of sexually active teenagers in the local population, estimated from national survey data[3]) attending local contraceptive and sexual health services; the proportion of youth and social care practitioners receiving training on relationships and sexual health; and the proportion of 16–19-year-old women not in education, employment or training who are young mothers.

Combining data with local intelligence provides additional detail for planning. For example, mapping schools and colleges onto a map of small geography ward-level conception rates, illustrated in Figure 5.2, will show which education settings are in high-rate areas. But only locally sourced data on individual school catchment areas will confirm which schools are attended by young people living in the high-rate areas and which should therefore be prioritised for SRE improvements. Similarly, consultation with young people is essential to find out where they spend their time out of education settings so that support and services can be designed around their lives.

Under-18 conception data continue to be published by the Office for National Statistics and made available alongside other related indicators and those relating to the wider determinants by PHE. Local areas can view trends,

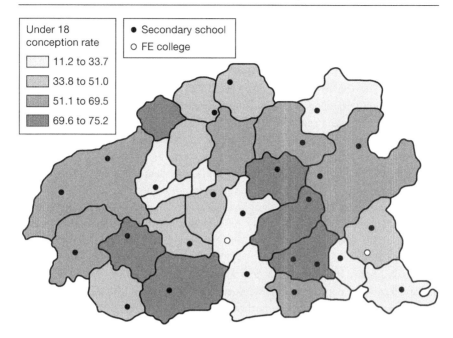

Figure 5.2 Local government ward map showing schools and colleges: an illustrative example.

explore the data and benchmark themselves against a range of comparators. Indicators available include the under-18 and under-16 conception rates and other related outcomes such as children in poverty, the proportion of young people not in education, employment or training, and uptake of long-acting reversible contraception.

5.3.2 Strong use of data for commissioning and monitoring – in practice

CASE STUDY 5.3:

Developing a local data dashboard to monitor the strategy's impact

Salford City Council is a metropolitan borough of Greater Manchester in North West England, with a population of 246,000. Salford started the strategy with an under-18 conception rate 25 per cent higher than the overall England rate. Senior leaders in the council, Primary Care Trust and public health recognised the impact of early pregnancy on the life chances of young people and future generations, and there was strong shared commitment to reducing rates.

Effective use of local data was seen as essential both to inform commissioning decisions and to closely monitor progress. A data dashboard was developed with a set of indicators to help track implementation of the strategy actions, and the trend in the under-18 conception rate. Getting more timely conception data was a priority. The fourteen-month delay in the official statistics was a significant barrier to understanding local trends and monitoring the impact of the actions put in place, and was a real concern to senior leaders who were accountable for progress. To address the time lag, the raw abortion and maternity data were collected at source from the relevant providers, as part of contract agreements. Using the same methodology as ONS, the data were calculated to the age at conception. The data were then pseudo-anonymised to allow for further analysis, for example by smaller geographical area. The data set was programmed to run automatically on a monthly basis providing conception numbers and rates, and a breakdown of conceptions into live births, abortions and repeat abortions.

The dashboard included indicators for five other areas – visits by young people under 18 to local contraception and sexual health services; the number of long-acting reversible contraception methods fitted in under-18s in both community services and primary care; a benchmarking indicator for individual schools' provision of SRE, informed by assessment against a set of engagement and quality criteria; the percentage of young parents attending children's centres; and the percentage of schools implementing the local targeted support service, the number of young people identified and the proportion of those identified receiving support. This was considered a particularly useful indicator of schools' support for young people at risk.

The dashboard indicators were tracked monthly, with performance against each of the eight areas RAG (Red Amber Green) rated to indicate the direction of travel. Amber or red ratings becoming green provided evidence of improved performance; for example, increasing attendance at contraceptive services in geographical areas with very high rates. Conversely, a green report becoming amber or red alerted managers to investigate and potentially target resources to address an unmet need.

Having reliable early warning signs of the trend in both conception data and implementation of the agreed actions enabled the strategy to have a more proactive and targeted approach to local need. It also provided reassurance to senior leaders and elected councillors that Salford was taking a strategic, rather than knee-jerk approach, and that the contribution of each agency was being coordinated and carefully monitored. Salford's under-18 conception rate dropped by 48 per cent between 1998 and 2015.

5.3.3 Key principles for effective use of data and local intelligence

- Identify a named lead with responsibility for collation and analysis of teenage pregnancy data and local service uptake statistics.
- Agree with senior officials in partner agencies a set of lead indicators for monitoring the implementation and impact of strategy actions, and invest time to establish consistent data sets.
- Establish data-sharing agreements between partner agencies and service providers.
- Agree arrangements for regular review of the agreed data set, with a RAG or other rating system to identify trends and identify early warning signs, with reporting up to the senior accountable board.

5.4 Improving sex and relationships education (SRE) in schools and colleges

5.4.1 National and local actions

Improving SRE for all children and young people, as part of Personal, Social and Health Education (PSHE), was a foundation stone of the strategy, and identified as a key success factor in the mid-course review. National actions to support local areas included new government guidance for schools, including SRE as one of the criteria for schools to achieve the National Healthy Schools Programme accreditation, and funding to increase the skills of teachers and school nurses through participation in the PSHE/SRE Continuing Professional Development (CPD) programme. A range of additional resources were also commissioned from the Sex Education Forum and other NGOs, including a toolkit for primary and secondary schools to audit pupils' views of SRE and identify and address gaps (Sex Education Forum, 2008a), a web-based inter-active drama involving young people in developing and filming scenarios around relationships (Department for Education and Skills, 2006b), resources to provide high-quality SRE for young people with learning disabilities, and help them access services (Image in Action, 2010), and a guide on developing sex and relationships peer education projects (Teenage Pregnancy Unit, 2002b).

Over the course of the strategy, increasing numbers of young people cited school as their main source of SRE and reported improvements in the SRE they received. However, the progress needed to ensure all young people's entitlement to high-quality SRE was significantly hampered by the continued non-statutory status. Nevertheless, through good local leadership some areas developed effective approaches which reflected the international evidence for effective SRE delivery. These include senior strategic commitment by the local authority; systematic delivery of comprehensive SRE/PSHE in primary and secondary schools, linked to other relevant programmes and embedded in a whole school approach; an LA dedicated advisory team to support school improvement with training for staff and governors; a curriculum and lesson plans reflecting the government SRE guidance; clear links between SRE and access to one-to-one confidential advice through school nurses and local services; consultation with, and involvement of, students; and engagement with parents. Many areas also provided targeted support for schools with the highest number of students at risk and commissioned additional small group or one-to-one SRE for most vulnerable young people.

From 2010 to 2017, the Coalition and then Conservative government maintained the non-statutory status, but continued to state the importance of SRE and the expectation that all schools should provide it. It also supported new supplementary advice for schools developed by three leading NGOs. *Sex and relationships education for the 21st century* explains high-quality SRE and its contribution to the health, emotional wellbeing and safeguarding of children and young people, and provides advice to teachers on addressing challenges posed by new technology; for example, sexting, cyberbullying and easy access to pornography (Brook, PSHE Association and Sex Education Forum, 2014). Revised statutory guidance for schools and colleges, *Keeping children safe in education*, refers to the contribution of SRE to safeguarding, and a new judgement in the school inspection framework on personal development, behaviour and welfare provides a potential lever for increasing the priority of SRE (Department for Education, 2016).

In March 2017, after persistent lobbying from NGOs and recommendations for statutory status from five parliamentary select committees, the government announced its intention to introduce legislation for compulsory relationships education in all schools for children aged 4–11 and compulsory relationships and sex education for children aged 11–16 (Department for Education, 2017). The decision was celebrated by stakeholders and received minimal criticism from the media. However, ensuring the legislation (Children and Social Work Act, 2017) translates into high-quality provision for all children and young people will depend on the new guidance for schools, the level of investment government puts into the training of educators and the arrangements for quality assurance.

5.4.2 Improving sex and relationships education – in practice

CASE STUDY 5.4:
Local leadership in improving SRE

Shropshire is a rural county with a population of 306,000. It has 19 state secondary schools and 127 primaries. Shropshire Council's strategic approach to improvement stemmed from three main drivers: the council's belief that they had a moral and ethical duty to provide all young people with good-quality relationships and sex education (RSE),* whichever school they attended; evidence from review meetings that schools wanted to provide high-quality RSE but felt isolated, with untrained and unconfident teachers, and inadequate schemes of work; and Shropshire young people voting for improved RSE as a council priority.

In 2009, a curriculum development adviser was appointed to lead and implement a cross-county programme. The programme provides primary and secondary schools with an award-winning and PSHE Association quality assured comprehensive package of training, lesson plans and resources to deliver RSE through a spiral and cross-phase curriculum, starting in year 1 (age 5) through to year 11 (age 16). It is coordinated with other school and community-based services such as pastoral care, school nurses, Targeted Youth Support, contraception and sexual health services and the Condom Distribution Scheme. In order to receive the support, schools must meet the conditions of allocating specified curriculum time (a minimum of five one-hour lessons for each year group), updating their policy, consulting and involving pupils, parents and governors and releasing teachers for training to help ensure delivery of quality RSE is embedded and sustained. Young people's views influenced the strategic decisions throughout the development and current implementation of the programme. Formally, members of the Youth Parliament (MYPs), and now Health Champions and Shropshire Safeguarding Board young people's group, report and feed into strategic decision making. A Shropshire young people pledge for RSE was produced and endorsed by councillors.

Originally resourced from the teenage pregnancy grant, the programme is now fully funded through a joint commissioning approach. This reflects the senior recognition that high-quality RSE makes a significant contribution to other council objectives, particularly early help, health and wellbeing and safeguarding. Questions on RSE are now included in the annual schools safeguarding quality assurance audit and included in training for Safeguarding link governors. The adviser reports to Children's Trust, Safeguarding and Child Sexual Exploitation and is based in Public Health as part of the Children and Young People's Team, Healthy Child programme.

Over 92 per cent of the primary schools and 17 out of 19 secondary schools (including the 12 academics and two private schools) now deliver the RSE programme. The programme is highly valued by head teachers who value the support in integrating RSE into a whole school approach and the adviser's input at governor and parent meetings; by teachers who welcome the training and externally verified schemes of work; and by pupils who report increased knowledge, confidence and support. The programme has also led to systemic changes in schools: additional time and budget allocations to RSE, specialist RSE/PSHE school teams, monitoring of RSE in governor and senior management meetings and better identification and support for vulnerable pupils.

The strategic approach to improving SRE across all schools is associated with an accelerated downward trend in Shropshire's under-18 conception rate, which declined by 25 per cent between 2010 and 2015.

* Shropshire amended SRE to RSE to emphasise the central importance of relationships, an approach taken by some other areas. RSE is the term used in the Government's very recent legislation for statutory status.

CASE STUDY 5.5:
SRE in faith and diverse community schools

Nottingham, a city in the East Midlands region of England with a population of 311,000, began its strategy with the sixth highest under-18 conception rate in England. By 2012, the rate had halved but still remained significantly higher than the overall England rate. To continue the downward trend, Nottingham City Council developed a city-wide 'Sex and Relationships (SRE) Charter' calling on schools to commit to good-quality SRE.

The Council funded a package of specialist support, which includes help to run consultation sessions with pupils, identifying school-level data about gaps in knowledge, support to facilitate meetings with parents, and training for school staff. The Charter was launched with support from the Director of Public Health, the Corporate Director for Children and Adults and the Directors of Education. The Lead Elected Member for Education, Employment and Skills also sent a letter to schools in support of the charter.

Middleton Primary and Nursery School is one of the schools that accepted this package of support in September 2015. A third of the pupils speak English as an additional language and about a quarter of the pupils are of Pakistani heritage. More than 100 parents completed a survey asking what topics they thought should be taught in SRE, and if they felt able to talk to their child about sex and relationships issues themselves. There was high turnout for a meeting where parents could see the new resources the school planned to use from Year One (age 5) through to Year Six (age 11).

Frequent communications with parents continue. For example, on the day that SRE is taking place a message is sent home via a mobile phone 'app' enabling parents to be prepared to pick up on questions at home that flow from the lessons.

Key to success was the open and honest approach of the school and the involvement of a parent-governor from the Pakistani community who acted as a conduit for other parents if they had questions. She said: 'I feel my knowledge in Islam helped in breaking down issues that were alien to their comfort zones, as well as raising awareness about female genital mutilation, abuse and grooming and helping them recognise that these were real problems affecting children in all communities, including our own. I wanted to dispel any misconceptions about SRE and highlight its importance in protecting our children.'

Commitment to the Charter from schools in the first eight months has reached 43 per cent. Several Elected Members of the Council are involved giving shared ownership of the initiative and effective accountability. The Lead Elected Members for safeguarding, schools, health and teenage pregnancy are all involved and readily make links across Council priorities.

CASE STUDY 5.6:
Using text messaging to link SRE to 1:1 advice

Leicestershire is a rural county with a population of 609,000, and Leicester City a unitary authority with a population of 330,000. To engage effectively with vulnerable young people and empower them to take ownership of their health, Leicestershire Partnership NHS Trust (LPT) developed the ChatHealth secure text messaging service. ChatHealth offers young people the opportunity to consult with a school nurse on a 1:1 basis. Co-designed with young people, it keeps messaging conversations safe and provides timely, confidential access to help from health professionals.

Since ChatHealth was introduced there has been a significant increase in the number of contacts with school nurses, who have been able to provide advice to many young people who would have been reluctant to access the service in a face-to-face context. Young people report that they like ChatHealth because it is a quick and easy way to get advice about their physical and emotional health and wellbeing, with many feeling more comfortable and confident talking about sexual health via text message. Queries include young people discussing whether they feel ready for sex, contraception support, what to do following unprotected sex, wanting to know where they can access sexual health services and much more.

In particular, ChatHealth has helped school nurses connect with boys and young men, who had been reluctant to engage face to face. One in five service users using ChatHealth are boys and young men, double the proportion visiting clinics.

Since 2015, the ChatHealth team in Leicestershire has supported other school nursing teams across the country to adopt this safe and secure messaging model. The platform is now used by some 25 teams nationwide and is also being introduced into health visiting and other community services. Numbers of staff trained to use the software have increased tenfold, from 50 originally in Leicester to more than 500 nationwide, responding to around a million young people using the service.

Since the start of the strategy, the under-18 conception rate has fallen by 57 per cent in Leicestershire County and 60 per cent in Leicester City.

CASE STUDY 5.7:

Supporting young people with learning disabilities

In 2009, with increasing numbers of young people attending Further Education Colleges, meeting the SRE needs of those with learning disabilities was identified as a key gap. The leading NGO, Image in Action, was commissioned by the Department of Health to develop a practical resource to support students with moderate learning disabilities or autism spectrum conditions, such as Asperger's syndrome. Designed to help students understand and navigate their increased independence and sexual awareness in a new social context, the resource focuses on public and private behaviour, personal space, consent, developing relationships and looking after their sexual health. The two resources, Going Further: Getting Started and Going Further: SRE Course, provide staff with a framework for setting up a programme, and a twelve-week detailed course including session plans with activities, methods and picture resources. Both remain free for FE colleges to download and, with adaptation, can also be used to support young people with severe learning disabilities.

5.4.3 Key principles for local improvements in SRE

- Provide briefings for senior leaders and school heads which dispel myths and address common concerns, explain the content of SRE by age, and how SRE contributes to attainment, achievement and school ethos, by equipping pupils to stay safe, develop healthy relationships and positive self-esteem, and to look after their sexual health.
- Appoint a dedicated lead for SRE in the local area and in individual schools or colleges, providing training and support for teachers to deliver SRE and support for schools in engagement with parents and faith communities.
- Provide a specific, age-appropriate SRE programme of study, for primary, secondary and post-16 settings, reflecting the internationally recognised effectiveness factors, with flexibility for local adaptation.
- Integrate SRE with a whole school approach promoting healthy and respectful relationships, with clear links to relevant policies on anti-bullying, alcohol and drugs, emotional health and safeguarding.

- Establish clear pathways between SRE and 1:1 confidential advice within school and college or local services, with the details of how to access 1:1 advice well publicised to students.
- Agree arrangements to monitor improvements in SRE delivery across the local area. For example, the proportion of schools with a policy and trained teacher, and in individual schools through assessment of learning outcomes, and a regular audit of student views, inclusive of gender, sexuality and ethnicity.

5.5 Youth-friendly contraception and sexual health services and condom schemes

5.5.1 National and local actions

In the mid-course review, young-people-focused contraceptive services, which were trusted by teenagers and well known by practitioners working with them, were the factor most commonly cited as having the biggest impact on reducing rates. Key features of effective service provision were applying the criteria of the strategy's best practice guidance: offering choice of all methods of contraception; having a strong focus on sexual health promotion, including clear links with SRE in schools and colleges; systematic and visible publicity to young people; service information for agencies and professionals to link young people into early advice, particularly practitioners working with most vulnerable young people; strong links with pharmacies offering emergency contraception, with pathways back to services offering the full range of methods; and outreach clinics in schools and colleges. All high-performing areas had also established well-publicised condom distribution schemes, with a range of accessible outlets informed by consultation with young people.

The Department of Health's *You're Welcome* quality standards, first published in 2005 and subsequently endorsed by the World Health Organization (Department of Health, 2011) include a specific section on sexual and reproductive health services. A further review of the standards is underway, with young people's views central to the process. The overarching standards contained in *You're Welcome* reflect the same principles as the original strategy best practice guidance: accessibility for all young people, including marginalised young people; publicity of the service and what it offers, in languages and formats understood by the local population; confidentiality and consent policies, publicised and explained to young people, and supported by staff training; a young-people-friendly environment, including the physical space, atmosphere and behaviour of staff; training for staff covering attitudes and values, and understanding, engaging and communicating with young people to support informed choice; joined-up working and pathways between services, with co-location of services in a one-stop shop where possible; and involvement of young people in monitoring and evaluation of the service. This often includes mystery shopping of services against the *You're Welcome* criteria, which can have a significant impact on reshaping services and changing staff behaviours.

Since 2012 and the organisational changes following the Health and Social Care Act, the strategy actions for improving young people's access to contraception have been incorporated into a number of guidance documents. *Contraceptive services for under 25s*, published by the National Institute of Clinical Excellence, makes 12 recommendations, which include applying the *You're Welcome* standards in all services (NICE, 2014). *Making it work: a guide to whole system commissioning for sexual health, reproductive health and HIV*, published by PHE, highlights the importance of young-people-friendly services and joined-up prevention pathways (Public Health England, Local Government Association, Association of Directors of Public Health and NHS England, 2014, revised 2015). *C-card distribution schemes: why, what and how*, first published in 2008, was revised and reissued (Brook, 2008b, updated 2014), and new NICE guidelines were published on a *Quality Standard on Contraception* (NICE 2016) and *STIs and Condom Distribution Schemes* (NICE, 2017).

5.5.2 Youth-friendly contraception and sexual health services – in practice

CASE STUDY 5.8:

Establishing a network of youth-friendly services to improve uptake of contraception

North Tyneside is a metropolitan borough in North East England with a population of 200,000. North Tyneside Council began its strategy with an under-18 conception rate 20 per cent higher than the overall England rate. Forty-three per cent of the conceptions ended in abortion, significantly higher than the regional proportion of 35 per cent. Alongside the other actions, improving young people's access to effective contraception was a key priority in the local action plan.

The service model was based on a hub and spoke approach, complemented by other access points across the area. The Hub Clinic, based in a central area close to public transport, is *You're Welcome* accredited, and provides the full range of contraceptive choices, sexual health screening, condoms, pregnancy testing and pregnancy options advice. Five spoke clinics are located in areas identified as optimum access points for the local population: two clinics in geographical wards with high levels of deprivation and under-18 conception rates, one within easy walking distance of two large secondary schools, one in a high-population area with a heavy 'footfall', and one in a more remote area without easy access to public transport. The spoke locations and opening times are regularly reviewed to check they are meeting local need.

The hub and spoke model is complemented by a wider service network. A sexual health outreach nurse, based in the Hub Clinic, provides peripatetic support and can be contacted directly by young people or by partner agencies and practitioners needing specialist advice for a young person in their care. Every secondary school has a health drop-in run by school nurses who can provide swift referral to the hub or spoke clinics for any pupil needing clinical advice, and the large FE college provides twice weekly chlamydia screening and condom sessions. Forty-nine pharmacies offer the local Plan B scheme for free emergency hormonal contraception and chlamydia and gonorrhoea screening, and link young people into the full service as required. An area-wide c-card condom distribution scheme helps reach boys and young men and increases contact points for advice and pathways into other services.

An unusual feature of the North Tyneside service network model was having the teenage pregnancy coordinator, who was also the adolescent sexual health coordinator, based in the Hub Clinic, alongside the sexual health promotion specialist who led the *You're Welcome* accreditation and coordinated the c-card scheme and the young parent midwife. This team approach helped to strengthen the coordination and publicity of the service network as well as balancing both the prevention and support work. Having a visible presence in a service setting also provided an easy point of contact for other practitioners and agencies supporting young people on contraception and sexual health advice, or any other aspects of the teenage pregnancy strategy. Another helpful feature was the local branding of the Hub Clinic as the 'one-to-one' service, which was widely recognised by young people, parents and practitioners. Although known to be a sexual health service, the shorthand 'dropping into one-to-one' or a 'referral to one-to-one' appeared to normalise discussion about the service and remove some of the stigma and embarrassment of accessing advice.

From 2007, the improvements in SRE and other prevention work of the strategy, combined with offering easy access to trusted youth-friendly services, was associated with a significant increase in the number of young people using the services and a big jump in the proportion choosing to use a long-acting reversible contraceptive method. Between 2007 and 2015, North Tyneside's under-18 conception rate dropped by 53 per cent.

CASE STUDY 5.9:
Developing an area-wide condom distribution scheme

While London is England's most populous region, it contains 33 Local Authority districts, which are small relative to those found elsewhere. Consequently, young Londoners are more likely to move between districts for school, college, work and recreational opportunities.

Condom-supply (or C-Card) schemes operated in a minority of districts, the delivery models varied, the scale was usually limited and activity data were problematic. In areas where young people were formally registered onto the scheme, paper cards were issued with boxes to initial every time condoms were supplied. However, many young people mislaid their cards and had to go through repeated registration processes, staff didn't routinely record or report data, and a young person had to register on multiple schemes if they moved between districts. Furthermore, research with college students found that some young people could only access condoms for free if they were repeatedly tested for chlamydia.

When the Department of Health provided additional funding in 2008 to improve access to contraception, London's stakeholders proposed the development of an integrated London-wide C-Card scheme for young people. Four local areas, at different stages of development for condom distribution, volunteered with developing and testing new approaches. A range of solutions to recording data were tested with young people, including biometrics, bar codes and RFID or 'contactless' technology. A new brand was developed with young people, comprising an easy-to-identify logo and the name 'Come Correct' to help distinguish it from existing C-Card schemes. 'Come Correct' has highly moral connotations for the target group, being concerned with preparedness and righteousness – emphasising respect for women. The scheme expanded to include all but six of London's thirty-three districts, registering over 100,000 young people with a condom demonstration session and distributing over 1.5 million condoms, and is included in the NICE guidance as an example of how collaborative commissioning can increase young people's easy access to condoms.

CASE STUDY 5.10:
Throwing the net wide for accessible c-card venues

Lincolnshire is the fourth-largest county in England, situated in the East Midlands region, with a population of 737,000 people. One of the key challenges of the Teenage Pregnancy Programme was to develop services that young people could access which addressed the issues of rurality and a limited transport infrastructure. The focus therefore was ensuring that services, including condom distribution, were provided where young people were already meeting for social activities in the evening or for educational purposes, and delivered by people with whom they already had a trusted relationship. An example of this is the C-card provision in a teaching centre for young people who have been permanently excluded from school. The centre is in the middle of a wood, providing a range of outdoor skills including forestry, wood turning and machine operating. Young people who attend the centre discuss relationships and sexual health with their C-Card-trained trusted instructors, and are able to easily access advice, information and condoms in a place they value as being informal and calm. Since 1998, the under-18 conception rate in Lincolnshire has reduced by 63 per cent.

5.5.3 Confidentiality and safeguarding

A fear that services won't be confidential has always been, and continues to be, young people's primary concern about asking for contraception or sexual health advice, particularly for teenagers under the age of consent. There has been considerable effort by medical and nursing professional organisations to move out of the shadow cast by the legal case in the 1980s, and clarify the position that contraception can be provided to under-16s without parental consent, provided the guidelines issued by Lord Fraser are followed (fpa, 2016).

As confidentiality worries were identified by the Social Exclusion Unit as a key barrier to contraceptive uptake, the strategy included a specific action for the Department of Health to issue new guidance for health professionals (Department of Health, 2000/2004). Support was also provided to disseminate the *Confidentiality Toolkit* for general practice (RCGP *et al.*, 2001, revised 2016). The confidentiality of services was highlighted in all the national campaign materials and included in the range of guidance for non-health practitioners.

Balancing young people's right to confidentiality with keeping them safe has always been an important skill for sexual health practitioners. Reassurance about confidentiality is essential to encourage young people into services so they can get contraception and sexual health advice, establish relationships with practitioners and discuss issues affecting their lives. In the small minority of cases where young people are experiencing or at serious risk of significant harm, practitioners may have to consider involving other agencies to help to keep the young person safe. In the later stages of the strategy, reports into cases of child sexual exploitation significantly increased the focus on the role of sexual health services in safeguarding, with resources commissioned to increase awareness and skills. With funding from the Department for Education, Brook designed a *Sexual Behaviours Traffic Light Tool* to help practitioners understand better the spectrum of 'normal' and 'concerning' sexual behaviour in order to help them identify warning signs of coercion or abuse and provide early help before problems escalate (Brook, 2013). The *Spotting the Signs* resource, developed with practitioners and young people, provided questions sexual health practitioners could integrate into a consultation to explore any concerns (BASHH and Brook, 2014). Translating concerns into action requires careful protocols and staff training to ensure services hold the trust of the young person while sharing essential information. Brook has been in the forefront of developing clear policies and protocols and developing a confidentiality statement for young people, which is honest about the limit of confidentiality but doesn't frighten them away from asking for help. A supplementary leaflet and information on the Brook website give more detail about what the confidentiality policy means in practice (Brook, 2017).

Confidentiality at Brook

'Here to listen, not to tell. At Brook we offer a confidential service. This means that we do not talk about your visit to anyone outside Brook without your permission unless you or another young person is in serious danger. If you have any worries or questions about confidentiality, don't hesitate to ask us.'

5.5.4 Key principles for youth-friendly contraceptive and sexual health services

- Identify an accountable local lead for the commissioning of young people's contraception and sexual health services.
- As part of the commissioning process, undertake a needs assessment to match service capacity to the estimated number of sexually active young people in the local population, using available national survey data.
- Develop process maps with young people representative of the local population, to identify convenient points of access and potential barriers, to ensure the service network provides easy access to the full range of effective contraception, sexual health screening and condom distribution schemes.
- Commission services using the World Health Organization endorsed *You're Welcome* standards.
- Agree a set of service indicators to monitor attendance and method uptake by the local population.
- Agree arrangements for regular evaluation of services by young people representative of the local population, paying particular attention to the views of marginalised young people and those from different ethnicities.

5.6 Advice and contraception in non-clinical education and youth settings

5.6.1 National and local actions

In the mid-course review, a well-resourced youth service with a clear remit to address teenage pregnancy and young people's sexual health was one of the features in high-performing areas (Department for Education and Skills, 2006b). Some areas trained youth workers to initiate and facilitate sexual health discussions with young people, and provide free condoms within local condom distribution schemes. In others, youth service managers worked with health partners to bring sexual health practitioners into the youth setting to provide 1:1 consultations, and make it as easy as possible for young people to access specialist advice and contraception. This was particularly important for reaching young people who wanted information and advice but might be wary of clinical services.

Over the course of the strategy, an increasing number of areas recognised the benefits of blending the unique skills of youth workers with sexual health practitioners to create trusted services in a range of non-health settings, including schools, FE colleges, youth centres and homeless units. The strategy guidance for youth practitioners and establishing school and college-based clinics provided local areas with national support for breaking the mould of traditional service delivery and developing innovative approaches.

Providing school and education-based contraceptive services and free condoms is a specific recommendation in the NICE guidance(s), *Contraceptive services for under 25s* and *STIs and Condom Distribution Schemes* (NICE, 2017).

5.6.2 Advice and contraception in non-clinical education and youth settings – in practice

CASE STUDY 5.11:
School-based drop-ins as part of a network of contraception and sexual health service provision

Bristol is a city in South West England with a population of 450,000. From the start of the strategy Bristol City Council established a strong partnership between the local authority and the health sector and developed a multi-agency action plan. However, early progress was slow and there was particular concern that more vulnerable young people living in high-rate areas weren't attending contraception and sexual health services. School-based drop-in clinics were explored as a way of making access to early advice as easy as possible. After a small pilot project in one school after which the head teacher reported the benefits to pupil attendance and learning, drop-ins were extended across the city, with priority given to schools serving neighbourhoods with high conception rates.

Central to the success of the drop-ins was the staffing partnership of sexual health nurses from Brook and youth workers, many of whom worked in the locality so were known by young people and provided a reassuring friendly face to the service. The youth workers provided an informal triage system, putting young people at ease, facilitating small group discussion and condom teaching. Young people needing clinical 1:1 advice were referred to the sexual health nurse, who could offer emergency hormonal contraception, oral and injectable contraception, pregnancy testing and advice, and chlamydia screening. The skill blend helped to create an atmosphere which young people described as relaxed and cheerful, with the staff seen as friendly, helpful, trustworthy and discreet. The youth workers were also able to follow up individual young people in the community if they needed additional support.

School-based drop-ins are now in 18 schools and visited by 4,000 young people a year, 25 per cent of whom are new contacts. Notably, the drop-ins attract young people least likely to visit community contraceptive services: boys, who make up 48 per cent of those attending, and young people who have not yet started a sexual relationship, suggesting the service is meeting its intended aim of offering early help. This offers a valuable opportunity for youth workers to discuss healthy relationships, consent and safer sex to help young people delay sex until they feel ready and make better-informed choices. The popularity of the drop-ins prompted additional funding of community sexual health outreach workers to offer more time and intensive help to young people at higher risk, a role which was integrated into youth work contracts.

Key lessons include offering an assurance of confidentiality and a 'teacher-free' space for young people; having frequent meetings with schools to develop and run the service smoothly, address apprehensions and respond quickly to any problems; regular data collection to monitor the use of the services, the issues raised by young people which can be fed into the school's SRE programmes and any safeguarding concerns; and proactive work with the media to ensure accurate reporting and avoid misleading headlines. Having head teachers speak publicly about the benefits to pupils gave confidence to other schools and reassured parents. Interestingly, the overwhelming majority of parents welcomed the service; only one complaint has been received in ten years.

Through increasing the uptake of early advice and strengthening the pathway between SRE and 1:1 advice, and between services, the drop-ins have significantly increased contacts with young people. Bristol's under-18 conception rate dropped by 68 per cent from 2007 to 2015.

CASE STUDY 5.12:

Taking contraception out to other services

The 'Choose it and Use it' initiative was developed by Brook to support vulnerable young women who may be apprehensive or find accessing services difficult. The session is relevant to all young women, but is targeted at those living in supported accommodation, care leavers receiving social care support and/or young parents.

'Choose it and Use it' is a two-hour educational session, first piloted in Wirral in 2011, and designed to improve the knowledge and uptake of long-acting reversible contraception (LARC). Delivered by an education worker and a sexual health nurse, the session discusses contraception in a fun and interactive way, helping young women understand their fertility, how different methods work and any potential side effects. The trusting relationship developed with the Brook team gives the young women the confidence to ask questions and choose the method they feel is right for them. It also enables them to talk openly about their relationships, which helps identify any additional support they may need.

Following the session the nurse offers a private consultation with all the young women. On average, 70 per cent of the young women opt for a consultation, with around 80 per cent prescribed contraception or booking an appointment to have an implant or IUD fitted at a later date. The service has been delivered to over 500 young women in Liverpool and Wirral.

Each 'Choose it and Use it' session is evaluated using feedback forms and the resulting uptake of a private consultation with a nurse is monitored. The sessions always have a positive evaluation, with young women commenting on how they enjoyed the opportunity to meet with a nurse and how they feel more confident accessing a Brook service in the future.

> I didn't realise how important it was that I use contraception. I feel like I understand how my body works now and how to prevent pregnancy and STIs. I enjoyed talking to the Brook staff and was really comfortable asking questions.
>
> (Young woman, aged 17, living in supported accommodation)

5.6.3 Key principles for providing advice and contraception in non-clinical education and youth settings

- Identify education and other non-clinical settings used and trusted by young people.
- Consult with young people (inclusive of gender, sexuality and ethnicity), staff, and (in education settings) parents, to explore the benefits and challenges of providing 1:1 sexual health advice and support.
- Pilot the initiative to gauge the views of young people and staff before further development or extending to other services.
- Agree a joint confidentiality policy and protocol and inform young people and staff.
- Establish referral pathways with other relevant services, including clinical services, offering the full range of contraception and sexual health screening if required.
- Agree arrangements for monitoring young people's use of the service and evaluation of impact while respecting confidentiality.
- Ensure senior leaders and service managers are well briefed and that accurate information about the service is provided to the media before the service opens.

5.7 Targeted prevention for young people at risk

5.7.1 National and local actions

The strategy was grounded in the principle of proportionate universalism (Marmot, 2010). It aimed to ensure all young people received high-quality SRE and had easy access to services, but with additional attention given to meeting the needs of more vulnerable young people. Data analysis confirmed that most young women conceiving before 18 did not have specific risk factors (Crawford et al., 2013). However, reducing inequalities relies on reaching out to the minority of young people who, for a range of reasons, may have missed out on the knowledge and confidence from school SRE, have had no trusted adult in their lives and are wary of visiting statutory services for advice. Targeted prevention, informed by consultation with young people, has been a key success factor, particularly in high-rate and deprived areas where the prevalence of vulnerabilities is likely to be greater.

A number of national strategy actions supported local areas in their targeted work. The annual publication of conception rates by electoral ward showed the geographical areas with higher than average rates; briefings on the vulnerabilities associated with early pregnancy, drawn from research and data analysis, provided guidance on identifying young people needing extra support; a resource commissioned from an NGO offered practical strategies for SRE and sexual health outreach services; and teenage pregnancy risk factors were included in other relevant government policies and programmes; for example, those focused on looked-after children and care leavers and improving young people's education and post-16 participation.

The NICE guidance, *Contraceptive services for under 25s* recommends targeted and outreach work in tailoring services to reach socially disadvantaged young people (NICE, 2014).

5.7.2 Targeted prevention for young people at risk – in practice

CASE STUDY 5.13:
A strategic approach to targeted support

Kingston-upon-Hull is a city in the Yorkshire and Humber region of England with a population of 256,000. Hull started the teenage pregnancy strategy with the third-highest under-18 conception rate in England and the Council faced a huge challenge in meeting their reduction target. In the first few years, progress was slow and it was evident that many sexually active young people were not accessing the mainstream clinical services for contraception. This prompted the teenage pregnancy partnership board to place a much stronger emphasis on targeted work: providing support on healthy relationships and sexual health in settings which young people felt were safe and non-threatening, with links to clinical services when needed.

The approach was informed by extensive consultations with young people to identify the barriers to using sexual health services, and to make recommendations for improving access through targeted projects. A specific consultation was undertaken with young men on their service needs as very few were accessing advice from clinics. Additional consultations took place with school and community-based practitioners to explore how any gaps in provision could be best addressed.

Following successful pilots, three projects were commissioned to work with vulnerable young people and those displaying risk-taking behaviours: a peer education project which co-delivered SRE in schools and ran community-based drop-ins for young people providing one-to-one information and support; a boys' and young men's project, offering one-to-one and group work support and access to condoms; and a city centre young people's drop-in providing access to condoms, pregnancy testing, chlamydia testing and information and support, combined with street-based outreach in the communities with high rates of teenage pregnancy.

Cornerhouse, a local sexual health charity, using a youth work approach, delivered all three projects in non-clinical venues. The charity also provided training for non-health practitioners and established a condom distribution network across statutory and voluntary sector youth services. In addition, a team of three outreach contraception nurses were commissioned to deliver 'clinic in a box' services providing contraception in schools, colleges and looked-after children's residential homes, and in partnership with Cornerhouse, at their community drop-ins. They also worked with the Teenage Pregnancy Support service to provide contraception to teenage mothers within four weeks of birth to help prevent subsequent unplanned pregnancies.

The targeted programmes led to a significant increase in the numbers of young people seeking advice, with around 8,000 per year under-18s accessing the services, of whom 50 per cent were young men. This was in stark contrast to the previous 1,800 annual attendance at the clinical services, with minimal numbers of young men. The services helped young people to access advice much earlier, often before they began to have sex and before a crisis situation arose, and enabled swift referral to clinical services if additional contraception and sexual health advice was needed.

In 2014, the principles of the successful targeted services were used to inform the recommissioning of sexual health provision. Cornerhouse continues to provide the support for young people alongside clinical services. Notably, the principles have also been applied to the commissioning of a service to reach vulnerable adults who are less likely to access mainstream clinical provision.

Since the start of the strategy, Hull's under-18 conception rate has declined by 55 per cent, with a notable reduction in the proportion of conceptions to younger teenagers under 16.

CASE STUDY 5.14:
Targeted SRE outreach programme

Newcastle-upon-Tyne is a city in North East England with a population of 282,000. In 2007, Newcastle City Council established an outreach team of experienced youth workers to take high-quality SRE to young people most at risk of early pregnancy, for whom sexual health is often a very low priority in the midst of other difficulties they are facing. Delivered in small groups using participatory and youth work exercises, the Teenage Kicks six-hour programme focuses on building young people's understanding of healthy and positive relationships and consent, increasing their confidence in assertiveness and negotiation, and linking them into the city's young people's contraception and sexual services when needed. The programme is run in a range of settings. Where there is a high and ongoing need, a rolling programme is provided; in other services the team will be invited in when there is a new group of young people. In residential children's homes where the age range of young people makes group work more difficult, the team offer a drop-in for one-to-one support. The programme reaches over 900 young people each year, and is monitored through participatory evaluation during each session, in-depth focus groups with young people and evaluation questionnaires to the referral agency. Implementation of the programme was associated with an accelerated reduction in the under-18 conception rate of 48 per cent from 2008 to 2015.

Teenage Kicks is now based within the New Croft Sexual Health Service, part of Newcastle Hospital Trust, and works closely with the wider team, including the mobile outreach nurses. Its success in reaching young people at the highest risk, not only of early pregnancy but also of other poor health and education outcomes, has secured mainstream funding as part of Newcastle's early intervention programme.

5.7.3 Key principles for effective targeted prevention

- Identify a local accountable lead for early help and intervention, and identification of young people needing additional support.
- Regularly review local data and intelligence to inform targeted work.

- Consult with young people most in need of additional support, inclusive of gender, sexuality and ethnicity, to identify their needs and any barriers to service access.
- Commission targeted support services which take a youth work approach, delivered in non-clinical, young-people-friendly settings and supporting young people on a range of issues relating to sexual health and relationships.
- Publicise the targeted support services to young people and encourage practitioners working with vulnerable groups to proactively promote the services.
- Agree the indicators and process for monitoring young people's use of the service and evaluation of impact.

5.8 Workforce training on relationships and sexual health for health and non-health practitioners

5.8.1 National and local actions

Training the wider workforce on relationships and sexual health helps to join up and strengthen the prevention pathway and is often described as the glue that holds the local strategy together. A trained and confident workforce significantly increases the opportunities for young people to discuss healthy relationships, access accurate information and be linked early into contraception and sexual health services if and when they need specialist advice.

Training is important for all practitioners in contact with young people, but particularly those supporting vulnerable young people who may be wary of visiting services and feel more comfortable discussing personal issues with someone with whom they already have a trusted relationship. These may be practitioners working in statutory or NGO youth support services, and in wider programmes aimed at increasing educational attainment, building aspiration and improving emotional wellbeing.

National actions to support workforce development included specific guidance for social care practitioners, foster carers and youth practitioners and a set of sexual health competencies for youth workers, and e-learning modules for the health and non-health workforce. Training programmes were designed and implemented locally, with monitoring of uptake included as part of the self-assessment toolkit. In 2012, the Department of Health supported the Royal College of Paediatrics and Child Health to develop an e-learning module on adolescent sexual and reproductive health covering pregnancy prevention and contraception, teenage parents, sexually transmitted infections and sexual assault in young people (Royal College of Paediatrics and Child Health, 2015). Public Health England commissioned the Royal College of General Practitioners to provide an e-learning resource for non-specialist practitioners to increase their knowledge and promotion of accurate information about the full range of contraception (Royal College of General Practitioners, 2017).

5.8.2 Workforce training – in practice

CASE STUDY 5.15:
Building the knowledge and skills of non-health practitioners

Warwickshire is a county in the West Midlands region of England, with a population of 550,000. The Council's consultation with 1,000 young people identified
youth workers as a trusted source of information and support on relationships
and sexual health. This led to a county-wide relationships and sex education (RSE)
policy and workforce training programme for all professionals working with young
people. The programme sits within Warwickshire's Respect Yourself Campaign
(RYC), developed with young people with the aim of building their knowledge
and self-esteem so they can make positive informed decisions about their
relationships and sexual health. A commitment to the vision of the Respect
Yourself Campaign is a requirement for all practitioners taking the training.

The training programme has three tiers, starting with the RSE Foundation
Training. These aim to build professionals' confidence in initiating conversations
with young people about healthy relationships and sexual health; raise awareness
of their own values and attitudes and the factors influencing young people's
decisions; and increase their knowledge about local sexual health services. Once
completed, practitioners can move onto tiers 2 and 3. Supporting young people
in non-clinical settings enables non-clinical staff to be able to discuss and provide
condoms, encourage access to contraception and sexual health screening,
including, if required, accompanying vulnerable young people to access emergency
contraception, and provide pregnancy testing. Exploring issues around peer-to-
peer exploitation prepares practitioners to support young people in developing
healthy relationships, with a specific focus on issues of consent, sexting and
pornography. All courses are one day in length, have clear learning outcomes
and are free for any professional working with young people in the county.

More than 300 practitioners have attended the RYC training and over 150
are trained up to provide condoms. The universal training offer has contributed
to Warwickshire's overall conception rate reduction of 53 per cent between
1998 and 2015, with some targeted workforce training for professionals working
in a high-rate area having a particular impact.

In 2010, the Respect Yourself Campaign was strengthened by a new 'sex
positive' website, designed by young people to respond openly and honestly to
questions about relationships and sexual health. As well as including a sex
terminology glossary, a genitalia gallery, a consent quiz and answers to frequently
asked questions gathered through extensive consultation, the website also aims
to remove barriers to young people seeking early advice. 'What to expect' videos
show what the services look like, explain what will happen during a visit and

offer reassurance about confidentiality from practitioners. Request slips – such as 'I'm here to talk about emergency contraception' or 'I need a pregnancy test' – can be sent to mobile phones so nervous young people can show them to the service receptionist. The website is actively publicised through schools, colleges and social media and other channels recommended by young people.

Key to success of the Respect Yourself Campaign was the Council's leadership and support, the strong teenage pregnancy partnership and partner agency commitment to maximise numbers of professionals trained, and the meaningful involvement of young people. Originally funded through the teenage pregnancy grant, the training and the website are now supported by mainstream funding, as an important contribution to early help and safeguarding of young people.

CASE STUDY 5.16:
Helping practitioners understand healthy sexual development and support young people experiencing or at risk of sexual exploitation

In Cornwall, a comprehensive review of the Council's guidance on relationships and sexual health found practitioners lacked confidence in their ability and role in assessing young people's sexual behaviour and responding to identified concerns about abuse or exploitation. Brook's Sexual Behaviours Traffic Light Tool was chosen to develop a consistent framework for all practitioners working with young people, and integrated into the development of multi-agency relationships and sexual health best practice guidelines. Supported by the Health and Wellbeing Board, the Local Safeguarding Children's Board and the Children's Trust, the Traffic Light Tool is now the agreed protocol across health, education, social care and NGOs, with over 600 local professionals trained to use it. Ninety-eight per cent of participants rated the training as excellent (79.5 per cent) or good (18 per cent), with confidence in applying the training in practice rated 4.7/5. Evaluation of the first wave of training concluded that the training had raised the profile of young people's sexual behaviour, and provided staff in different agencies with a common language and clarity in risk assessment (King-Hill, 2016).

5.8.3 Key principles for workforce training on relationships and sexual health

- Identify agencies and practitioners in touch with young people and assess training needs on relationships and sexual health, including safeguarding.

- Provide a training programme on relationships and sexual health, prioritised for agencies and practitioners working in areas with high conception rates and those working with vulnerable young people.
- Embed the training programme in service commissioning, including induction and updating of staff, and ensure this is monitored as part of the contract management.
- Make clear the expectation of providing support for young people in relationships and sexual health by inclusion in the practitioner job description.
- Agree a senior lead in all relevant agencies to prioritise and monitor uptake of training by practitioners.
- Agree indicators and process for monitoring impact on practitioner knowledge and confidence.

5.9 Supporting parents and carers to discuss relationships and sexual health with their children

5.9.1 National and local actions

Children and young people who can talk openly and without embarrassment to their parents about relationships and sexual health are more likely to have first sex later and to use contraception when they become sexually active. Parents themselves also want to talk to their children and believe that more discussion would lead to fewer teenage pregnancies. Importantly, although school is young people's preferred source of information about sex and relationships, parents come a close second. Yet the gap between young people's preference and the reality remains significant. Forty per cent of girls would like their mother to be the main source of information, but only 14 per cent report this to be the case. Boys particularly miss out: although 23 per cent would prefer their father to be the main source and 15 per cent their mother, this is the case for only 3 and 4 per cent of boys, respectively (Macdowall *et al.*, 2015).

Supporting parents and carers to feel confident in opening conversations and responding to their children's questions without embarrassment was an important strand of the national strategy. The national *Time to Talk* campaign materials were distributed nationally to all general practices, available for areas to display in community settings most used by local parents, and provided for practitioners involved in parenting programmes such as those supporting parents in their child's transition between primary and secondary school. The booklet, *Talking to your teenager about sex and relationships*, part of the parents' strand of the *Sex. Worth Talking About* campaign, was distributed to independent pharmacies to take the messages into a trusted high-street health setting and help normalise discussion (NHS and Parentline Plus, 2010). National funding was provided for expansion of the fpa *Speakeasy* programme, to help areas train local facilitators and sustain the programme as part of mainstream parenting support, including for foster carers who are often supporting some of the most vulnerable children and young people.

5.9.2 Supporting parents to discuss relationships and sexual health – in practice

CASE STUDY 5.17:

Mandatory training for foster carers and online advice for parents

In Cornwall, the Speakeasy programme is used to train foster carers and the children in care workforce to be confident in discussing relationships and sexual health. Children and young people in care often miss out both on formal SRE, due to disrupted education, and on informal SRE from a trusted adult. Their experiences of abuse or neglect that led to them coming into care may also have left them with a distorted view of relationships and poor self-esteem. The training was co-delivered by the designated nurse for children in care to provide foster carers with the additional advice needed to understand and support the children and young people they were caring for.

To help ensure all foster carers participate, Speakeasy is included in the *Foster Carers' Training Handbook*. The teenage pregnancy coordinator also visits each foster carer support network to raise awareness of children and young people's relationship and sexual development needs, throughout the life course, and to promote the Speakeasy training. Emphasising the life course approach was vital. Many foster carers commented at the beginning of the session that they only looked after younger children, so felt the information was not going to be relevant. By the end of the session, which had a strong focus on relationships and used the Brook Sexual Behaviours Traffic Light Tool to illustrate development from childhood to adolescence, participants recognised the importance of the issues for children of all ages.

The programme was well attended from the outset, with participants reporting significantly increased knowledge and confidence in raising and responding to issues on relationships and sexual health. As a result, Speakeasy training has become mandatory for all local authority foster carers, and mainstream funding secured to extend delivery.

To extend the reach of Speakeasy, Cornwall's Health Promotion Service and Public Health team have been working to develop an online resource for parents and carers to address frequently asked questions and provide top tips on talking to children and young people in age-appropriate ways about relationships and sex. An audit of online resources found there were many sources of advice or information on the internet, but that they could be difficult to find. In addition to this, a local survey on sexual health services found 79 per cent of the 539 respondents wanted information and guidance about sexual health online. With Speakeasy providing a framework, and using video clips of Cornish parents and foster carers sharing advice, experience and answers to common questions, this resource aims to address a gap by bringing together key information, guidance and expertise to support parents and carers talking to children and young people at home.

CASE STUDY 5.18:
Dispelling myths and increasing knowledge in informal settings

Nottinghamshire is a county in the East Midlands region of England with a population of 785,000. The Council's partnership board was committed to helping parents and carers talk more confidently with their children about sex and relationships.

Attempts had been made to engage with parents and carers through invitations to school meetings, but these were often not well attended. Ways of reaching parents in settings where they already met were explored as a more effective way of integrating information and advice. Pubs were identified as a key venue, used by both parents, so a guarantee of reaching fathers as well as mothers.

The teenage pregnancy coordinator attended a Pub Watch meeting in Mansfield, the district with the second-highest rate in the country, to discuss and agree a partnership to offer their customers information on different aspects of teenage pregnancy and sexual health. In October 2004, a campaign was launched in eight pubs to include a number of teenage pregnancy and sexual health questions in the weekly pub quizzes.

The campaign had dual benefits. Providing accurate information helped dispel myths and provided parents with a sound basis to talk to their children, and discussing issues in a relaxed and informal environment helped to normalise the issue and take away embarrassment. The campaign also reached other relatives young people might choose as a trusted adult with whom to discuss issues.

In addition to the quiz questions, the pubs were supplied with a set of beer mats with campaign messages: 'Time to Talk about the birds and the bees', 'Don't bury your head in the sand' and the ParentlinePlus helpline number for anyone needing further information or advice. The beer mats were also available to order from the teenage pregnancy team so were distributed extensively across the county. Data from the Parentline Plus helpline showed a significant increase in calls following the campaign.

5.9.3 Key principles for supporting parents to discuss relationships and sexual health

- Identify a local accountable lead to coordinate and commission work supporting parents and carers.
- Ensure information and advice on talking to children at different ages about relationships and sexual health is displayed and offered to all parents and carers in universal locations, for example via schools as part of SRE, family health services, pharmacies and appropriate community settings identified by local consultation with parents.
- Commission specific programmes to provide parents and carers with more detailed information and opportunities to discuss and develop their confidence, prioritising parents in areas with high conception rates.
- Consult with faith communities to identify any specific concerns and the most appropriate settings for providing information and support.
- Agree arrangements to sustain the programme by training practitioners in agencies most in contact with parents to become facilitators.
- Include information in other programmes supporting parents and carers, particularly programmes addressing underlying risk factors for teenage pregnancy, for example improving school attendance and attainment, aspiration and emotional wellbeing.

5.10 Good communications: consistent messages to young people, parents and practitioners

5.10.1 National and local actions

Good communication is essential for effective strategy delivery and was key to maintaining the priority and keeping people connected over the ten-year period. The scope of a communications plan is necessarily wide. Senior leaders need clear messages on why teenage pregnancy matters and the evidence for what works; young people need accurate, reassuring information and to know where to go for advice; parents need encouragement to start discussions with their children; and practitioners need clarity about how they can help and be kept up-to-date with local programmes and services.

A number of national actions supported local communications. The national campaign provided messages to young people and parents, supported by free helplines, with local areas amplifying the messages through additional campaign activities and local websites. Regular communications from ministers to local areas were supplemented by briefings published by the Advisory Group aimed at elected councillors, senior leaders and parliamentarians (Teenage Pregnancy Independent Advisory Group, 2009). Good communication was greatly helped by the vertical and horizontal structures of the strategy. National information and updates were sent directly to the regional and local coordinators and swiftly disseminated to relevant partners. Negative or misleading media reporting was addressed by the TPU sending rapid responses to coordinators to help them prepare press statements, and by the proactive media work of the Advisory Group. Positive press reporting was more likely when local coordinators engaged directly with the media (London School of Hygiene and Tropical Medicine, UCL and BMRB International, 2005).

5.10.2 Good communications – in practice

CASE STUDY 5.19:
Consistent messages for young people

Enfield is an outer London borough with a population of 310,000. A proactive communications strategy was seen as key to providing young people in Enfield with the support to help them develop the knowledge, skills, motivation and confidence to make informed positive choices around relationships, contraception, sexual health and parenting.

Combining the national campaign resources with publicity promoting the local 4YP ('for young people') youth-friendly clinics, messages were prominently displayed on buses, in cinemas and in other settings used by young people, and campaign resources were systematically disseminated through partner agencies to schools, colleges and local services. Campaign activity was boosted in the months of December and January – identified by local data analysis as the peak months for under-18 conceptions – with additional targeting for high-rate areas and vulnerable groups. Young people were involved in the planning and evaluation of the campaign initiatives.

A free texting service, txtm8, was commissioned for young people to ask advice on any relationship and sexual health question, with a response from a trained adviser within 30 minutes. The service was available to all young people in Enfield, 24 hours a day, seven days a week and throughout the year.

All the information, advice and service publicity were subsequently adapted for new media channels and incorporated into the Council's Youth Enfield website. A comprehensive sex and relationships section provided information on a wide range of issues, answers to frequently asked questions and promoted the 4YP services, including the 4YP pharmacies for free emergency hormonal contraception. The names and mobile telephone numbers of three sexual health outreach nurses were also publicised for one-to-one text or phone advice. Separate pages offered support for parents in talking to their children about sex and relationships and information for professionals about local strategy policy and protocols. The website was publicised to young people through the Council's social media activity, with alerts about new clinics or changes in opening hours and a continued focus on sexual health promotion messages before and during 'risky' times of the year. To help ensure young people received consistent, clear and accurate information from all agencies, website updates were sent to partner agencies through established e-mail networks and all the information included in the Council's training programme for professionals.

To supplement the information on the website, the *Youth Enfield* magazine was published three times a year, and included sex and relationships topics in every issue, with young people contributing to the articles. Copies of the magazine were available online and were distributed in schools, colleges, libraries and other youth settings.

The benefits of embedding the communications strand of the teenage pregnancy strategy into the broader Youth Enfield programme were twofold. Including detailed information about sex and relationships on the Council's website helped to normalise the issue and take the stigma out of asking for advice, and the resources of the Council's communications team helped publicise the website widely to all young people. The communications activities were supported by mainstream funding as part of Enfield's commitment to further reduce their under-18 conception rate, which reduced by 51 per cent between 1998 and 2015.

CASE STUDY 5.20:
Keeping partner agencies and practitioners well informed

While having a strong senior partnership board is essential for leadership and accountability, maintaining the momentum and energy of the strategy relies on the daily contribution of service managers and frontline practitioners.

In Lincolnshire, a county in the East of England with a population of 737,000, getting communications right for professionals was considered key to effective engagement, particularly with services scattered across a large geographical area. The Concepts newsletter, published three times a year, provided information on national, regional and local developments, summaries of new research and offered a forum for practitioners to submit articles on good practice. The content was planned to provide timely updates, for example reporting Lincolnshire's progress after the annual data publication, with comparisons with other areas, or alerting services and practitioners to forthcoming campaigns.

The newsletter was distributed to over a thousand professionals, included in all workforce training packs and available on the Council's website. Providing a channel for coordinated and regular communications, it played a key role in establishing a collective understanding of and commitment to making the strategy a success. Lincolnshire's under-18 conception rate declined by 63 per cent between 1998 and 2015.

5.10.3 Key principles for good communications

- Identify a local accountable lead to coordinate communications on teenage pregnancy.
- Provide regular briefings or newsletter to keep elected councillors and practitioners informed and updated on strategy activities and progress.
- Develop a media strategy to promote well-informed reporting and normalise discussion about relationships and sexual health, with an agreed protocol for quick responses to negative stories.
- Ensure accurate and consistent messages about relationships and sexual health and service publicity reach all young people in the local area, inclusive of gender, sexuality and ethnicity, through a mix of digital and other communication channels.
- Publicise information, advice and sources of support to all parents.
- Establish and maintain an up-to-date database of local services to inform practitioners and strengthen partnership working.

5.11 Support for pregnant teenagers, through abortion or into parenthood, including contraception

5.11.1 National and local actions

Good support for teenagers who become pregnant is the last but critical piece of the prevention jigsaw. Advice and access to effective contraception following pregnancy helps young women prevent subsequent unplanned conceptions, and dedicated support to improve outcomes for young parents and their children reduces the intergenerational risk factors for early pregnancy.

Support begins with providing easy access to pregnancy testing. Teenagers remain at highest risk of unplanned pregnancy, with only 14 per cent of teenage mothers in the Family Nurse Partnership trial having planned their pregnancy (Robling et al., 2015). They are more likely than women aged 20–34 to have later abortions at 13+ weeks (Department of Health, 2016) and to book later for antenatal care. Early pregnancy confirmation and access to unbiased advice on pregnancy options is therefore essential for supporting young women to make informed choices and ensuring swift referral to either early abortion or maternity care. Details of the support programmes for young parents are described in the next chapter.

The importance of pregnancy testing and advice was included in the strategy best practice guidance on contraceptive services and in the *You're Welcome* standards. To help dispel myths and correct any misinformation young people may have received about abortion, a cross-curricula abortion education resource for schools was commissioned from the NGO Education for Choice (Education for Choice, 2004). Commissioning guidance was also published to ensure all women considering abortion, including teenagers, had access to unbiased decision-making support – and avoided inadvertently visiting anti-choice organisations (fpa and Brook, 2014).

Providing accurate information about post-pregnancy contraception and access to the chosen method is a key recommendation in the NICE guidance *Contraceptive services for under 25s* and the *Contraception Quality Standard* (2016) and the *Contraception after Pregnancy Guideline*, jointly published by the Faculty of Sexual and Reproductive Health Clinical Effectiveness Unit and Royal Colleges of Midwives, Nursing and General Practitioners (2017). The provision of pregnancy testing and referral for NHS-funded abortion or antenatal care is also one of the *You're Welcome* quality standards for sexual and reproductive health services (Department of Health, 2011).

5.11.2 Support for pregnant teenagers – in practice

CASE STUDY 5.21:
Reducing second and subsequent pregnancy in teenagers in Bristol

The Teenage Pregnancy Outreach Nurse service was commissioned in 2008 due to a high repeat pregnancy rate (22 per cent) for teenagers in Bristol. They work with two distinct groups of young people: those having termination of pregnancy, miscarriage or ectopic pregnancy, and those continuing with their pregnancies, both under-18s and those 18 years old with vulnerabilities.

The service sees all Bristol teenagers who come to the Pregnancy Advisory (Abortion) Service at Bristol Sexual Health Services to formulate a contraception plan and then individually support teenagers in contraceptive use for six months, or longer if needed. They also work with those who continue with their pregnancies by taking direct referrals from midwives and the Family Nurse Partnership (FNP) and contacting young women at 36/40 weeks' gestation to discuss their contraception plan. They can fit or arrange for teenagers to have their implant fitted on the postnatal ward or have a bridging method such as Depo Provera. They encourage and facilitate starting a method of contraception by day 21 post-delivery if the mother is not breastfeeding on demand and again offer support for six months or longer. All young mothers have direct access to members of staff via text or phone. Overall, uptake of LARC methods is high.

The proportion of under-19-year-old women having an abortion in Bristol, who have had one or more previously, is now down to 5.2 per cent, against England's proportion of 10 per cent. The proportion of young mothers having another pregnancy has also declined.

As well as working closely with the FNP team, the service also offers sexual health screening and outreach, and networks with a variety of agencies, including a specialist school for young mothers, supported housing projects, the Youth Offending Team and the Barnardo's Project against Sexual Exploitation.

CASE STUDY 5.22:
Young women's post-abortion support worker

As part of Brighton and Hove's ongoing commitment to reduce rates, the local abortion data were reviewed. Not only were an increasing number of pregnant under-18s choosing abortion rather than maternity – underlining the need for strengthened prevention – but the proportion of under-19s having more than one abortion was significantly higher than the national average. The review identified some key gaps in the pregnancy pathway: young women leaving the abortion service without contraception in place; no formal process for assessing and addressing other health and emotional wellbeing needs; and a missed opportunity to gather information from young women about how the SRE/PSHE programme could be further developed to help prevent unwanted pregnancies.

After a three-month pilot, the young women's support service was established with the local NGO abortion provider to ensure all under-19s received post-abortion support from a specialist youth worker. Based in the abortion service to ensure a coordinated care pathway, the youth worker sees the young woman and, if requested, her partner and family, either in the clinic or a community setting of her choice, for an average of six sessions. As well as helping her choose and maintain an effective method of contraception, the youth worker can provide support around other issues that may influence unplanned pregnancy, such as healthy relationships, protective behaviours and self-esteem. Referrals are made to additional specialist services if required. The service is also publicised to other practitioners who can make a direct referral to the youth worker. The post continues to be funded as part of the Council's prevention programme.

Since the service started, the proportion of under-19s having an abortion who have had one or more previously has dropped from 19.1 to 8.3 per cent.

5.11.3 Key principles for supporting pregnant teenagers

- Provide free and well-publicised pregnancy testing in easily accessible locations.
- Provide and publicise sources of unbiased pregnancy options advice. Young people should be clearly informed if other organisations offering pregnancy testing and supposedly objective advice are in reality opposed to abortion.
- Provide access to counselling if required, with referral pathways to maternity services or abortion care.
- Commission abortion services which are accessible to all young people, including those relying on public transport.

- Ensure information about post-pregnancy contraception is provided during the abortion care pathway or antenatal period, with the chosen method provided at time of abortion or immediately postnatally, and post-pregnancy contraception follow-up support.
- Monitor subsequent pregnancy data to measure the impact of contraception commissioning arrangements.

Notes

1   The under-18 conception reductions quoted in the case studies reflect progress to 2015, the latest annual data available at time of publication.
2   Specific, measurable, agreed upon, realistic and time based.
3   National Survey of Sexual Attitudes and Lifestyles (NATSAL).

Chapter 6

Improving the lives of teenage mothers, young fathers and their children

6.1 The strategy's support programme

6.1.1 Overview

The Teenage Pregnancy Strategy was the first government initiative to include a focus on improving support for young parents alongside the prevention programme (Social Exclusion Unit, 1999). While the primary goal was to halve the under-18 conception rate by equipping young people to delay early pregnancy, the strategy recognised that those who did choose to become young parents should have high-quality support to enable them to fulfil their ambitions, to promote independent living and to decrease the risk of longer-term social exclusion. This chapter discusses the factors that can influence poorer outcomes for some young parents and their children and describes the initiatives introduced to address the challenges they may face. Case studies written in collaboration with local areas, and quotes from teenage mothers and young fathers, are included to illustrate different aspects of the programme.

The aim of the strategy's support programme was threefold: to improve the health and wellbeing of young parents and their children; to help young parents to avoid further unplanned pregnancies – an estimated 20 per cent of births were conceived to young women under 18 who were already mothers; and to contribute to the long-term prevention of teenage pregnancy by enabling young parents to return to education, training and employment, thereby reducing inequalities and consequent risk factors for early parenthood in their own children. As a measure of progress, the strategy set a secondary ambition to increase the proportion of 16- to 19-year-old mothers participating in education, training or employment, estimated in 1996 to be only 17 per cent (Teenage Pregnancy Unit, 2002a).

Importantly, at the same time as support and advice were being improved for young parents, not only was there a 55 per cent fall in the conception rate between 1998 and 2015 but, of this diminishing number, fewer chose to continue their pregnancy (Office for National Statistics, 2017a). This confounded speculation from some critics of the strategy that improving support would incentivise teenage parenthood.

The strategy support programme was implemented through the same national, regional and local structures described in Chapter 3. The key actions were: the development and piloting of Sure Start Plus, a new programme to give coordinated support for pregnant teenagers and young parents; support to improve young parents' engagement with education and training, including dedicated childcare funding; and models of supported housing to reduce isolation and exclusion. These were complemented by the Family Nurse Partnership, introduced in England in 2007, and other initiatives and guidance, outlined in the chapter, which focused on specific aspects of the lives of young parents and their children.

6.2 Outcomes for young parents and their children

6.2.1 The influence of pre-existing disadvantage

Consultation with teenage mothers and young fathers shows no difference between them and older parents in wanting to do the best for their children, and reflects a strong desire among young parents to continue, or return to, education and gain future employment (Kane and Wellings, 2007). Many manage very well but, for some their health, education and economic outcomes remain disproportionately poor, with consequent impact on the life chances for them and their children.

Every young parent has their own individual story, but the area and individual risk factors for early pregnancy highlight the vulnerabilities with which some young people enter parenthood: family poverty, persistent school absence by age 14, slower than expected educational attainment between ages 11 and 14 (Crawford et al., 2013), and being looked after or a care leaver, where a combination of negative experiences can compound vulnerability (Fallon and Broadhurst, 2015).

These risk factors were reflected in the young parents involved in the Sure Start Plus programme and the Family Nurse Partnership trial participants. Forty-six per cent had been suspended, expelled or excluded from school and 48 per cent were not in education, employment or training at the time of joining the programme (Robling et al., 2015).

There are fewer data collected on young fathers, but studies show similar vulnerabilities. Boys who become young fathers have been found to be three times more likely than non-fathers to not complete secondary education and also tend to be far less satisfied with their educational experience. When compared with older fathers and other young men of similar age, they are more likely to have been subjected to violent forms of punishment at home and are twice as likely to have been sexually abused; to have pre-existing serious anxiety, depression and conduct disorder; to have poor health and nutrition; to drink, smoke and misuse other substances; and to have had contact with the police or been in a young offenders' institute or prison (Fatherhood Institute, 2013). Among under-25-year-old men attending drugs and alcohol services, one in six is a young father and nearly half of young offenders under 22 are, or about to become, fathers (Public Health England, 2016).

As a result of these experiences prior to pregnancy, some young parents will have missed out on the protective factors of high quality sex and relationships education, emotional wellbeing and resilience, positive parenting role models and having a trusted adult in their life. For a minority, these vulnerabilities may make parenting very challenging. Almost 60 per cent of children involved in serious case reviews were born to mothers aged under 21 years (Department for Education, 2012). Of families involved in repeat care proceedings, 50 per cent of the mothers were aged between 14 and 24 at the first care application, and one in three of those who returned to the family court had their first child as a teenager (Broadhurst et al., 2015).

As discussed in Chapter 1, it has always been difficult to quantify the extent to which poor outcomes are due specifically to teenage parenthood or to pre-existing factors of disadvantage, such as poverty and low education attainment. These factors may themselves contribute to early pregnancy choices, which is why the strategy's prevention work was, and needs to continue to be, embedded in wider programmes to improve education and reduce inequalities. That said, many young parents do carry a disproportionate burden of disadvantage, which can lead to poorer outcomes affecting their own and their children's lives.

The extent of this impact is captured in Ofsted's report on serious case reviews of babies dying in the first year of life, in which the children of young parents were over-represented. The report highlighted concerns about teenage parents who had received inadequate support, or young parents who should have been considered as 'children in need' in their own right. In most such cases, the lessons learned from the reviews were not just about the challenges for young parents of bringing up a baby, but also about the associated and cumulative risks arising from, for example, a troubled childhood, unsettled parental relationships and a lack of long-term accommodation. The report also noted that, on occasions, professionals were over-optimistic about young parents' resilience to cope with the new responsibilities and fragility of a young baby (Ofsted, 2011).

However, as also discussed in Chapter 1, very few of these outcomes are due to the biological age of the parents. The majority are affected by experiences, behaviours and circumstances that can be influenced, as the evidence described later suggests, by early, sustained and trusted support.

6.2.2 Poor health outcomes[1]

Most recent data for England show babies of teenage mothers have a 75 per cent higher risk of infant mortality, a 21 per cent higher risk of low birth weight

(Office for National Statistics, 2017b), a 13 per cent higher risk of preterm birth (Office for National Statistics, 2017c) and are three times more likely to experience a sudden unexpected death in infancy (Office for National Statistics, 2016). The risk of preterm birth increases significantly for second pregnancies (Khashan *et al.*, 2010). These outcomes are strongly influenced by late booking for antenatal care; high rates of smoking during pregnancy; lower breastfeeding rates; and poor maternal nutrition.

Booking with maternity services before the 12th week of pregnancy and regular antenatal care protect against poor outcomes (NICE, 2008). However, young mothers, on average, book later than older mothers (Cresswell *et al.*, 2013), with a higher percentage booking very late (Smith, 2015), and are less likely to keep appointments and attend antenatal education. Late confirmation of pregnancy, fear of disclosing the pregnancy, apprehension about attending antenatal classes, prioritising crisis issues – such as housing and financial problems – and difficulty travelling to services all contribute to poor uptake of antenatal care (Royal College of Obstetricians and Gynaecologists and Royal College of Midwives, 2010). As a result, teenage mothers and young fathers are more likely to miss out on the support that can help address the factors contributing to the poor outcomes.

For women of all ages, smoking during pregnancy is one of the most important modifiable risk factors for improving infant health (Royal College of Paediatrics and Child Health, 2017), accounting for one in five cases of low birth weight in babies carried to full term, and one in three Sudden Unexpected Deaths in Infancy. Teenage mothers are three times more likely to smoke throughout pregnancy, with high numbers smoking prior to pregnancy. The challenge of stopping smoking is compounded by many young parents-to-be living in crisis situations and experiencing poor emotional health.

Breastfeeding in the first year of a baby's life makes a significant contribution to improving child health outcomes, with exclusive breastfeeding for four to six months reducing the risk of sudden unexpected deaths in infancy by 36 per cent (Horta *et al.*, 2007). Teenage mothers are a third less likely to initiate breastfeeding and half as likely to be breastfeeding at six to eight weeks (Health and Social Care Information Centre, 2012). Low awareness about the health benefits, lack of confidence in their ability to breastfeed, apprehensions about public attitudes to breastfeeding and negative views of breastfeeding from the young father or wider family all appear to contribute to the lower rates. Without good support, maintaining breastfeeding while re-engaging in education and training presents a further challenge, as the later case study (p. 126) illustrates. However, it is notable that young black mothers are much more likely to breastfeed, suggesting that family and community views may have an overriding positive influence.

Good nutrition during pregnancy is critically important because the foetus competes with the mother for nutrients. This is particularly the case for teenage mothers who may not have stopped growing themselves and are likely to have additional need for nutrients (Burchett and Seeley, 2003). Many young women may already be eating a poor diet, due in part to poverty, but also to the well-documented irregular and unbalanced eating pattern of many teenagers (Food Standards Agency, 2000). For some, this means starting their pregnancies in a compromised nutritional state.

As well as pregnancy-related outcomes, children of teenage parents have a higher rate of accidents. This appears to be due to the fact that young mothers are more likely to suffer from depression and anxiety, which in turn are associated with poor housing and not having the support of a co-residential partner (Berrington *et al.*, 2005a).

Young parents' higher levels of deprivation will also exacerbate the risks. Unintentional injuries to children are more common in families on a low income and living in rented and/or overcrowded accommodation. Deprivation and poor housing are also strongly associated with accidents and accident and emergency attendance and hospital admission (Public Health England, Royal Society for the Prevention of Accidents and Child Accident Prevention Trust, 2014).

6.2.3 Poor emotional health and wellbeing

Poor emotional health and wellbeing affects the lives of parents and, because of the critical importance of attachment and positive parenting in the first two years of child's life, also has a significant impact on their children (Martins and Gaffen, 2002). Poor maternal mental health has been identified as the most prevalent risk factor overall for negative impact on child development outcomes (Sabates and Dex, 2012). Existing vulnerabilities, unstable family background, relationship breakdown, domestic abuse and poor housing all contribute to poor maternal mental health and emotional wellbeing.

Teenage mothers and young fathers are more likely to experience the risk factors for poor emotional health, so are particularly vulnerable. Mothers under 20 suffer from poorer mental health in the three years after birth compared with older mothers – with a 30 per cent higher level two years after the birth, after which they converge to the population average (Teenage Pregnancy Unit and Department of Health, 2004). Young fathers are more likely than older fathers, or other young men, to have pre-existing serious anxiety and depression and to display conduct disorder (Fatherhood Institute, 2013).

Some pregnant teenagers and young fathers may therefore already be experiencing poor emotional health as they become young parents. This is particularly the case for young people in care who may have been exposed to disruptive, neglectful or abusive family relationships. Prior experience of intimate partner violence and unstable partner relationship also contribute to the risk of domestic abuse, and consequent poor emotional health, during and after pregnancy. Only a third of young mothers experience a stable relationship throughout pregnancy and for three years after the birth, compared with 88 per cent of older mothers (Department of Children, Schools and Families and Department of Health, 2007). Of the Family Nurse Partnership trial participants, 40 per cent had experienced violence in the twelve months preceding their child's second birthday (Robling *et al.*, 2015).

6.2.4 Poor economic wellbeing

Poor educational attainment and lack of qualifications are strongly associated with low-paid work or unemployment, which, in turn, drives family and intergenerational poverty. Children of young parents have a 63 per cent higher risk of experiencing child poverty and a higher risk of unemployment and low income in adult life (HM Government, 2014).

Although reliable data on young parents' participation are not available, it is estimated that a significant proportion of young parents are not in education, training or employment (Department for Work and Pensions, 2006). This will include those who have recently given birth and some young mothers who make a positive choice to delay returning to education until their child is older. However, lack of participation often follows prior disengagement from school and low attainment at 16. It is also strongly influenced by barriers such as lack of foundation level programmes,[2] inflexible course entry points sometimes causing long delays before the young parent can re-engage, and difficulties with childcare and transport (Reddington, 2007). There are no comparable data collected on the fatherhood status of young men who are not in education or training. However, young men with a negative educational experience are likely to be most affected and, as a result, have double the risk of being unemployed at age 30 – even after taking account of deprivation (Berrington *et al.*, 2005b). Some young fathers may also choose to stop further education or training in order to bring income into the family, and get trapped in low-paid employment. That said, as described below, there is clear evidence that, for both teenage mothers and young fathers, parenthood is often a catalyst for continuing education and reshaping their own ambitions (Florsheim and Ngu, 2003).

6.3 What helps?

6.3.1 The evidence for improving outcomes

Although the inequality in outcomes experienced by some young parents is stark, this is not inevitable if they are given positive support that is early, sustained, multi-agency, coordinated by a dedicated adviser and delivered by practitioners whom they trust. Consultation with young parents highlights some of the problems they anticipated, and experienced, in their contact with maternity (Price and Mitchell, 2009) and other services. These included practitioners' judgemental attitudes and sometimes disregard for young parents' concerns about their children's health; a wariness of the overlap with social services; and an anxiety that, if they ask for advice, practitioners will think they can't cope, which may result in their children being taken into care (Scottish Government, 2016). Trusted, easily accessible services, positive and supportive attitudes of individual practitioners and removal of practical barriers, for example in returning to education, are key to early and sustained engagement (Department of Children, Schools and Families and Department of Health, 2007). This is particularly important for young people who have been in local authority care.

The lessons of what works in providing holistic support for young parents are drawn from a number of initiatives implemented during the course of the strategy: the evaluations of two main programmes, the Sure Start Plus pilot and the Family Nurse Partnership Programme, and research into the education of school-age parents, the Care to Learn childcare funding scheme and the Supported Housing pilot. Important findings and recommendations from Ofsted's report *Ages of Concern* (2011) further reinforce the need for focused support for young parents.

6.3.2 Sure Start Plus

Sure Start Plus was a new programme designed to provide intensive support for pregnant young women and teenage mothers with the aims of improving their social and emotional wellbeing, health and learning, and strengthening their families and communities. The programme was built around the core role of a dedicated personal adviser who provided coordinated, one-to-one support for young parents, starting in the antenatal period, and drawing in specialist support tailored to the young parent's individual needs. Two-thirds of the programmes focused on young women very early in the pregnancy, with pregnancy testing, counselling on pregnancy choices and support through the chosen pregnancy option of abortion or maternity. The remainder targeted young women after they had made their decision to continue the pregnancy.

The strategy action was to pilot and evaluate Sure Start Plus in 35 local government areas and use the findings to inform future policy on young parent support, including reshaping existing services to make them more user friendly. Management of the programme began in the government's Sure Start Unit, but was moved to the TPU in 2003 (Wiggins *et al.*, 2005).

As the intention of the programme was to be innovative and explore different ways of delivering services, Sure Start Plus was characterised by diversity, with a range of models developed in the pilot areas. This posed some challenges for the national evaluation to distil the learning, as did the difficulty of differentiating the impact of the programme from other support initiatives in both the pilot and the matched areas. However, compared with matched local authorities without Sure Start Plus, the programme did demonstrate success in a number of areas.

Significantly more pregnant teenagers and young mothers in Sure Start Plus areas received help from services in relation to emotional problems, and reported that it had made a difference to their lives. They had been helped in negotiating relationships with their families and subsequently reported more supportive relationships with them. They had received support with partner relationships and reported reduced levels of domestic violence, and had received housing advice and more help in getting and retaining accommodation.

Overall, Sure Start Plus showed no significant difference in rates of participation in education, employment or training. However, positive impact was found after more detailed analysis. In Sure Start Plus areas, younger mothers (15 and under) were significantly more likely to be in education (83 vs 60 per cent). In pilot areas with a more specific focus and target-driven approach to participation, 16- to 18-year-olds' engagement in education or training was 51 per cent, compared with 35 per cent in matched areas and 30 per cent in other Sure Start Plus models. When the personal adviser was based in the education sector or in the Connexions Service,[3] where information about options may have been more easily accessible, participation rates were also higher and led to better attainment of qualifications.

On health objectives – reducing smoking, increasing breastfeeding and delaying subsequent pregnancies – the evaluation found no significant impact. Measurement of progress was hampered by the poor quality of monitoring data returned by programmes, but many Sure Start Plus advisers found the health objectives difficult to address when crisis support on emotional, relationship and housing issues was a priority. Improving breastfeeding also appeared difficult without substantial resources and specialist expertise – for example from midwives. However, some Sure Start Plus areas, which prioritised smoking cessation, did develop promising innovative initiatives, although numbers were too small to include in the formal evaluation (Department for Children, Schools and Families and Department of Health, 2007).

Measurement of the programme's influence on the learning and play experiences of the children showed no impact. In part this may be because these objectives were not prioritised over the support for young parents, but also because the average age of the children at follow-up was only 9 months. The evaluation also found no significant impact on young fathers, possibly due to the fact that, during the first two years of the programme, few areas did any specific work with young fathers. Although by the third year two-thirds of the programmes had a specific strategy, work with young fathers in most areas remained a secondary priority. However, although not significant, a higher proportion of young fathers in Sure Start Plus areas were receiving information about health, smoking cessation, help with domestic violence and support with housing. In areas with a specific strategy to focus on fathers, partner agencies were significantly more likely to report adequate emotional support for young fathers.

The evaluation concluded that Sure Start Plus had been successful in addressing the crisis needs of young parents, both emotional and practical, and laying the foundations for their futures. By targeting the most vulnerable young women, the programme had contributed towards reducing inequalities and combating social exclusion – the key aims of the Teenage Pregnancy Strategy and wider government programmes. Suggestions for the reasons behind the lack of direct impact on health outcomes were the difficulty in data collection, entrenched factors that were beyond the scope of the programme, and insufficient time and resources to influence health behaviours in such a vulnerable and disadvantaged group.

6.3.3 The essential role of a trusted adviser

The essential ingredient of the programme appeared to be the role of the adviser who acted as a 'critical friend' to the young parent, building their confidence and aspirations, and providing a specific point of contact and coordination for other agencies. The role provided help earlier and for longer, acting as a bridge between crisis support and future development. The evaluation cited this as a unique aspect of the programme, as other services tended to provide either crisis management, or ongoing support, but seldom both.

> The one-to-one (work Sure Start Plus advisers do) is absolutely fundamental and crucial . . . (The young women) have individual needs and issues that need to be addressed . . . One-to-one (work) keeps them on track, without it there's no way we'd keep a young person in education or get them into it, because quality time wouldn't be given to them to find out if everything's all right (at home).
>
> (Professional from Connexions)

> Young parents and colleagues from partner agencies, including those in potentially overlapping roles, such as midwives and health visitors, all perceived the adviser role as beneficial.
>
> (Sure Start Plus National Evaluation: Final Report)

Asked to say what they liked about the one-to-one support, young mothers cited friendliness and having an individual relationship with one worker who never pushed them away, and never gave up on them. Confidential support with personal issues; practical help and advice with, for example, benefits and housing; help in accessing groups and other activities; home visits; accompanying them to appointments; and liaising with agencies on their behalf all contributed to a strong sense of reliable consistent support. The only things they disliked related to lack of funding for the programme. This included being discharged from the support earlier than they wanted, and the personal advisers being overstretched.

I liked having a key person – she can remember you, your child, your names, a personal service . . . You can contact them in an emergency, you have their mobile.

(Pregnant young woman aged 18)

I liked not just support – you get trips, (Sure Start Plus) organise parents' groups. They contact people for you – education, Connexions, housing childcare. So they help organise many things. They ask what you need of them and then try and organise what you want.

(Pregnant young woman aged 17)

The other cornerstone of the programme was the strong links Sure Start Plus forged with other partner agencies. Without these, the referral system did not work and the support plan for young parents could not be effectively implemented. Key to successful joint working was having a strong Sure Start Plus partnership board and active forums for service providers to keep in regular contact and share problems and solutions.

6.3.4 The key recommendations from Sure Start Plus

The primary recommendation from the pilot evaluation was that young parents should receive targeted support and that this should be funded in all areas through the role of a teenage pregnancy dedicated adviser, mirroring the role of Sure Start Plus. The advisers should target services at the most vulnerable and socially excluded pregnant teenagers and young parents and expect to work intensively with them during pregnancy and throughout the child's first year. There should be separate advisers for young women and young men to ensure the needs of young fathers are not subsumed by the more obvious support needs of young mothers. For young parents with continuing multiple needs there should be an option for further one-to-one work until the child's fourth birthday. Support for young parents with less critical needs should be provided through short-term, one-to-one interventions and group work combined with support to access other services. A caseload of between 25 and 50 was recommended to enable the essential intensive work to be carried out effectively. As partnerships with local service providers are necessary for the role to work, the evaluation recommended formal strategic links with the local accountable body for children's and young people's outcomes, supported at an operational level by active service forums.

6.3.5 The Family Nurse Partnership

The Family Nurse Partnership (FNP) was not part of the strategy action plan, but was introduced in 2007 as part of government's ongoing quest for effective interventions to reduce social exclusion. It was initially piloted in 10 local authority areas, increasing to around 130 areas by 2015. FNP is a licensed programme, developed in the USA in the 1970s at the University of Colorado, where it is known as the Nurse Family Partnership (NFP). It is a voluntary programme, providing intensive support for first-time young mothers, through structured home visits from a specialist trained family nurse, from early pregnancy (before 28 weeks) until the child's second birthday. The programme has a maximum of sixty-four visits: fourteen during pregnancy, twenty-eight in infancy during the first 12 months, and twenty-two during the toddler phase between 13 and 24 months.

FNP has three aims: to improve pregnancy outcomes, child health and development and parents' economic self-sufficiency. The methods are based on theories of human ecology, self-efficacy and attachment, with much of the work focused on building strong relationships between the client and family nurse to facilitate behaviour change, and attempting to tackle the emotional problems that prevent some mothers and fathers caring well for their child.

Evaluation of the Nurse Family Partnership over the past thirty-five years, in the USA and elsewhere, has shown significant benefits for vulnerable young families in the short, medium and long term, across a wide range of outcomes (Olds et al., 2014). To test the impact of FNP in the UK, the Department of Health commissioned a three-year formative evaluation, followed by a large-scale randomised control trial (RCT). The formative evaluation found the programme could be delivered successfully in England and showed encouraging signs of positive impact. Families valued the programme, with young mothers less likely to smoke in pregnancy and more likely to breastfeed. By the end of the programme mothers were very positive about their parenting capability, reporting high levels of warm parenting and low levels of harsh discipline. A significant achievement was a narrowing of inequalities, with young parents reporting levels of parenting stress similar to those in the general population, and FNP children also developing in line with the general child population (Barnes et al., 2012).

The RCT chose to look at four primary outcomes in mothers receiving FNP: maternal smoking, birth weight, timing of second pregnancy and children's attendance at Accident and Emergency departments. A number of secondary outcomes were also monitored: breastfeeding, child language development, maternal education and employment, caregiving quality, maternal mental health, domestic abuse, child immunisations and child injuries (Robling et al., 2015).

The results showed that FNP appeared to improve some of the secondary outcomes relating to child development, particularly early language development at 24 months. Better protection for children from serious injury, abuse and neglect was also indicated, with earlier identification of safeguarding risks. This was most likely due to the greater level of family nurse contact and the trusted relationship, which may have enabled the young parent to disclose problems earlier. There was also some small improvement in mothers' social support, relationship quality and self-efficacy, which may provide longer-term benefits for the child.

However, the RCT showed no impact across the primary outcomes, even when looked at by sub-group or by variation in programme implementation. Compared with matched sites, young parents' participation in education, employment or training and other secondary outcomes also did not appear to be influenced positively by FNP. The evaluation suggested the lack of impact demonstrated in England may be due to the target group not being as disadvantaged as those in the US cohort. The relatively high levels of universal and specialist support received by young parents in the control group may have also made it more difficult to distil the 'added value' of FNP. As with Sure Start Plus, there were some examples within individual programmes of effective support on smoking and breastfeeding, illustrated by the case study below, but numbers were too small to be picked up in the national evaluation. A limitation of the RCT was being able to measure only the short-term impact of a programme which has strong international evidence of long-term benefits. A follow-up study is currently under way to monitor the children's outcomes up to the age of 6, with a particular focus on the impact on child maltreatment. The trial will report in 2018 and help steer further development of the programme.

CASE STUDY 6.1:
Challenging barriers to sustained breastfeeding

N joined her local Family Nurse Partnership at 17. With the help of her Family Nurse and through the use of a range of FNP 'Facilitators' (specifically designed tools) – such as 'Babies First Feed' – she successfully began breastfeeding her baby. Having stopped attending college while she was pregnant, N returned to resume her studies soon after giving birth, putting her baby in the attached nursery, with the intention of continuing to breastfeed. Despite initial success, the arrangement became difficult when staff at the college started to criticise N for leaving classes to breastfeed and actively encouraged her to have someone bottle-feed her baby when her workload increased.

N discussed this with her Family Nurse, articulating both how proud she was at being able to breastfeed her baby and her shock at the negative response of the college. Through exploring N's feelings with her, the Family Nurse was able to use the opportunity to reinforce the positive decision N had made and highlight the continued benefits of breastfeeding for both her and her baby. She encouraged and supported N to challenge the college, which she did successfully, leading ultimately to the college developing a new breastfeeding-friendly approach. In addition to helping N to breastfeed, the long-term positive, therapeutic relationship between her and her Family Nurse helped to improved N's self-confidence and self-efficacy, which was crucial in her feeling empowered to raise the issue with her college.

The study did confirm two important findings similar to the Sure Start Plus evaluation. First, that a large proportion of the young parents was particularly vulnerable and had entered parenthood with significant disadvantages. Notably, only 14 per cent reported that they had planned the pregnancy. Second, the programme was very popular with the young parents. The Family Nurses had developed respectful and trusting relationships with their clients and uptake of the visits was good. Importantly, they had succeeded in engaging with a group who, because of their prior experiences, are sometimes reluctant to access services and trust professionals.

> Having a baby young was really hard, people judged me and questioned me as a mum. It felt like nobody believed in me!
>
> When I met my family nurse she didn't judge or question me. She believed in me and helped me believe in myself. She didn't patronise me or 'baby' me. I got treated like an adult and as though what I thought mattered. We had a really rough few months with my little girl and I really don't know what I'd have done without my family nurse. Over time she has become someone I can trust, turn to and rely on. She became my friend.
>
> (FNP client, Telford)

6.3.6 Family Nurse Partnership next steps

Although the England study showed mixed results, the Early Intervention Foundation[4] has taken into account the significant impact shown in RCTs in the USA and the Netherlands and has maintained a high evidence rating for FNP (Early Intervention Foundation, 2015). The results of the trial are informing further development of the programme.

FNP Next Steps, a programme of change begun in 2016 and led by the FNP National Unit, aims to improve and adapt the FNP programme in England by testing a series of innovations and improvements to strengthen outcomes, increase value for money, ensure greater flexibility and share learning with other services.

This includes a range of swiftly implemented changes, such as an extension of the eligibility criteria up to age 24 for parents with additional vulnerabilities, – to help address the poorer outcomes experienced by some young parents aged 20–24 (Action for Children, 2017) – as well as provision of improved data reporting to explore any impact of the programme locally and nationally on, for example, safeguarding and child development.

More complex changes to the programme are currently being put through rapid-cycle testing in 11 FNP areas through ADAPT (Accelerated Design and Programme Testing), a co-development project led by the FNP National Unit and involving FNP nurses and supervisors, commissioners, academic experts and Dartington Social Research Unit. The ADAPT project aims to test innovations relating to specific issues, such as smoking cessation, breastfeeding and perinatal mental health, as well as a series of modifications to better 'personalise' the programme to meet individual client needs based on a clear and consistent assessment framework by, for example, offering early graduation from the programme or varying the intensity of visits (Family Nurse Partnership, 2017).

Lastly, in response to growing demand from commissioners, the FNP National Unit has developed a knowledge and skills exchange programme built on the evidence-based methods used in FNP. The aim is to involve FNP teams in workforce development across health and social care to help ensure specialist FNP expertise can benefit a wider local population beyond just those clients who are eligible for the programme.

CASE STUDY 6.2:
Adapting FNP to local need

FNP in Ealing has successfully adapted its eligibility criteria for clients, now offering support to first-time mothers up to the age of 24, and broadening the spectrum of client presenting factors it considers to be vulnerabilities. The primary drivers for the adaptation were a request for greater flexibility and responsiveness to local need from Ealing's service commissioner and the closure of a local maternity unit, hitherto the primary source of client referrals, which placed increased onus on the FNP team to be proactive in its local outreach.

Before embarking on the adaptation, Ealing's Family Nurse Supervisor led an open and transparent consultation with relevant local stakeholders – including all those providing mental health services, social services, Ealing Council, London North West Healthcare NHS Trust, Ealing Primary Care Trust, a local children's centre manager and Family Nurses themselves – to fully understand the specific context and need. The FNP team then developed a draft revision to client eligibility criteria, consulting on this again with the same stakeholders, before taking the revision to the Ealing Family Nurse Partnership Board for finalisation and rollout. This consultative approach – itself rooted in strong existing working relationships between FNP and other community-based services, cultivated sensitively and intensively over a long period of time – ensured that all key local players were aware of and bought into the adaptation, and was crucial to its subsequent success.

6.3.7 Support for school-age mothers to continue with education

In 1999, as part of the strategy's aim to increase the proportion of young parents in education, employment or training, a new Standards Fund Teenage Pregnancy Grant was introduced for 48 local government areas with high conception rates to help reintegrate and support school-age mothers into education. Qualitative research was commissioned in ten areas, some receiving the Standards Fund, some not, to explore the educational experiences of pregnant teenagers and young mothers, and identify what factors and forms of provision influenced success in returning to or continuing in education (Dawson and Hosie, 2005). The ten areas had a range of education support provision, different levels of conception and deprivation, varying levels of ethnic minority and a mix of urban and rural settings.

The study found that the young women who had a positive experience of education before they became pregnant were more likely to get a supportive response from their school when disclosing their pregnancy, and continued to have a good record of attendance and achievement whether attending main-stream school or alternative provision.

However, for many of the young women, pre-existing disengagement from school was a dominant theme in their experience of education. Less than half were attending school regularly at the time they became pregnant. Difficulty with schoolwork, bullying and a sense of failure were all cited as reasons for truancy and increasing levels of non-attendance. The study reported these young women benefited hugely from attending specialist units and non-school education provision. Attendance was greatly improved during and after pregnancy and they were more likely to continue their education post-16. The key success ingredients of specialist provision, as cited by young mothers, included on-site childcare, one-to-one teaching and a flexible timetable, and personalised support with practical and emotional issues as well as with schoolwork.

Areas receiving the Standards Fund appointed Reintegration Officers who had a specific remit of supporting school-age mothers. Whether they were in mainstream school or in specialist provision, young mothers living in areas with a Reintegration Officer felt better supported in choosing and following the best option for their circumstances. Importantly, Reintegration Officers had a particularly positive impact on young mothers who had previously been missing school – the most vulnerable cohort – suggesting that a dedicated role contributes to narrowing inequalities in education and future life chances.

The study concluded that school-age pregnancy in young women who are already enjoying school and coping well should not lead to disengagement. Nor is disengagement inevitable for the most vulnerable. With the right provision, and sufficient resources to provide specialist support, pregnancy can provide the opportunity to re-motivate young women to return to learning and build their confidence and aspirations. Recommendations from the study included the provision of specialist education support in all areas, especially for young women with prior negative experiences of education and poor school attendance; the appointment in all areas of Reintegration Officers, or an equivalent dedicated role, to provide the considerable attention needed to support the most vulnerable young women; and for mainstream schools to take on the lessons from specialist units, particularly in relation to developing a non-judgemental and supportive ethos for pupils disclosing pregnancy. Strong links with other agencies, including midwifery, were also important to ensure early referrals. So too were the improved links with transport and childcare provision – both potential barriers to young mothers continuing or returning to education.

CASE STUDY 6.3:
Specialist education support for young parents

In Bristol, the Meriton specialist school has provided education support for school-age mothers since 1975, but expanded in 2000 to enable students to attend post-16 and significantly improve their transition into further education, training and work.

The multi-agency team of teachers, nursery nurses and support staff work to an ethos of encouraging the young women to believe in themselves, aim high and reach their potential. This has been achieved through high-quality teaching, a broad and balanced curriculum and a safe and secure environment with high-quality nursery provision and a parenting course offered to all students, including young fathers. Regular visits from the midwife, health visitor and sexual health nurse ensure wider needs, including contraception, are met. The holistic approach aims to instil a love of learning and support to become confident in their role as a parent. Key success ingredients reported by the students include the nursery, which enables them to concentrate on learning, knowing their children are receiving exceptional care just down the corridor, the non-judgemental attitudes of the staff, and a clear acknowledgement by the school that their opinions count.

A wide range of academic and vocational subjects is offered to respond to individual needs, with work experience provided through partnerships with local organisations and businesses. Collaboration with the Law Department at Bristol University offers lectures covering real-life cases, helping students to develop their debating skills and empathy, while introducing them to Higher Education.

By ensuring a safe and trusted environment, students are able to explore sensitive issues such as bullying, relationships, contraception and sexual health, substance misuse and domestic violence. Students have contributed to school SRE and PSHE programmes, talking about their experiences of being a young parent, and through participation in a radio and DVD project have challenged the perceived stigma of teenage motherhood.

Students report that the Meriton has transformed their lives, broadened their horizons and improved their relationships and home situations. Ofsted inspections are consistently highly rated, with particular praise for the overwhelming sense of community, the support with managing the dual demands of education and parenthood and the preparation students received to prepare them for the next stage of their lives.

The legacy of the Meriton for Bristol is the number of young parents who are now employed, including teachers, social workers, midwives, policewomen, hairdressers, retail staff, all contributing to the economy and success of Bristol, raising their children's aspirations and reducing risk factors for teenage pregnancy rates in future generations.

6.3.8 Care to Learn childcare funding

Helping young parents with childcare so they could return to education was a specific action of the strategy. Following a pilot of subsidised childcare in the Sure Start Plus areas, the national Care to Learn funding programme was launched to support all young parents.

Care to Learn provides financial support to teenage parents who want to continue their education or training, and need help with the cost of childcare and any associated travel. [Care to Learning funding provides a maximum £160 a week (£175 in London boroughs) for each child (2017).] Childcare payments are made directly to the childcare provider and travel payments are made to the learning provider.

The qualifying criteria for Care to Learn funding are that the young person must: be under 20 on the date they start their course or learning programme; be the main carer for their child(ren); be living and studying in England; and meet the residency criteria. The course or learning programme must have some public funding and the childcare must be registered with Ofsted or the Care Quality Commission.

Evaluation of the programme surveyed 1,728 young parents funded by Care to Learn, which represented 22 per cent of all young parents receiving Care to Learn. Responses were weighted so as to be representative of the overall population.

6.3.9 The benefits of childcare funding

The study found Care to Learn played a vital role in increasing the proportion of young parents in education or training. Three in four teenage parents said they could not have gone into any learning without Care to Learn; three in four who received Care to Learn gained a qualification or partial qualification; only one in four who received Care to Learn were not participating in education or training after their course, compared with two in three before the course; and participation was sustained forty months after Care to Learn was originally received. The study concluded that the success rate for those funded by Care to Learn was comparable to the national average for all learners. 'This represents a significant achievement given that young parents are combining learning with childcare responsibilities' (Vaid *et al.*, 2009).

However, despite the overall positive impact, aspects of Care to Learn have created barriers to young parents' engagement. In areas where costs of childcare and transport are particularly high, the weekly amount is insufficient to provide for more than part-time participation. Restrictions of the programme also currently prevent it being used by young parents in apprenticeships, even though apprenticeship income is low, or for volunteering, which can be a valuable stepping-stone back into education or training.

6.3.10 Housing for young parents

A specific aim of the strategy was to ensure that all lone young parents who couldn't live at home were given housing with support. This was to address the social isolation, and the sometimes cumulative challenges young parents experienced from living on their own in independent tenancies. The aim was included in government housing policy led by the Office of the Deputy Prime Minister, later the Department of Communities and Local Government, with resources drawn from relevant funding streams. By 2007, the numbers of lone young parents living independently without support had dropped by over 75 per cent. However, around 1,000 young parents remained unsupported. Research conducted by one of the regional teenage pregnancy coordinators highlighted significant concerns, including placements in accommodation far from family and support networks, the very poor conditions in some private rented accommodation and the hidden homelessness of young parents 'sofa surfing' in accommodation of friends (Quail, 2007). Insecure and poor-quality accommodation was also cited as a key risk factor in some of the serious case reviews reported by Ofsted (Ofsted, 2011). In 2009, as part of the government's child poverty strategy, seven local government areas were funded to pilot different models of supported housing for young parents.

The pilot areas were asked to design support services to meet local need rather than apply one model. As a result, the structure and focus of each pilot area varied, but the elements tested across the seven pilots included: high-support residential project with on-site staff; intensive floating support and key work services; initiatives to facilitate access to the private rented sector; courses for preparing young parents for independent living; a paid peer mentor scheme; a volunteer adult mentoring initiative; peer education programmes; life coaching; family and relationship counselling; financial incentives; group work; and e-learning. Specialist support workers, often commissioned through an NGO, delivered the services. Multi-agency working was a core principle, with effective working relationships developed in all areas between housing, health, social care and education. An independent evaluation drew together lessons from the pilots' cumulative experience, with recommendations for future policy and commissioning developments (Quilgars *et al.*, 2011).

6.3.11 How supported housing can help

The evaluation found almost 1,000 young parents were referred for support, with 80 per cent accepting. The average age was 18 and the vast majority were pregnant young women or young mothers. Some programmes proactively recruited young fathers, but numbers were low. Participants reported few health problems, but a significant minority (22 per cent) suffered from anxiety, depression or other aspects of poor mental health.

Of the 199 young parents surveyed at the end of the pilot, 72 per cent said the support had made a big difference or some difference to their lives, attributing the benefits to having understanding staff and someone to talk to, help with housing and building confidence and self-esteem. Almost 60 per cent reported a big, or some, difference to their children, due to improved social interaction with other children and adults, feeling better equipped as parents and having access to better accommodation. The key success of the pilots was supporting young parents into independent living. On leaving the service, 67 per cent were living independently compared with 41 per cent at referral, with almost nine in ten preferring the new accommodation to their previous housing. There was less impact on continuing or re-engaging in education or training, possibly because a majority had their babies during the pilot phase so were not yet ready to participate fully. However, many were engaged in some training and development and aspirations for future employment were high.

The lack of a comparison group means the benefits cannot necessarily be attributed directly to the work of the pilot projects. However, the study concluded that the available evidence suggests that enhanced support packages can be advantageous in helping vulnerable young parents. Six lessons were highlighted for further policy and practice.

First, young parents need support through a wide variety of housing provision, tailored to their individual need. This should include supported housing with on-site staff, which was a very valuable option for young parents with high support needs and/or weak family and support networks. Independent tenancies with floating support, near existing networks, should also be in place. All types of provision should include courses on developing skills and confidence for independent living, which were highly valued by young parents.

Second, the support model needs to be delivered flexibly, enabling support workers to provide young parents with help in all areas of their lives, referring on to specialist services when necessary. Pilot initiatives such as life coaching, relationship counselling and parenting support delivered by other agencies were less well liked by young parents, who preferred to get the support from the worker they trusted.

Third, expectations for returning to education and training needed to be realistic, and include long-term goals as well as short-term planning. This was particularly important for new parents and those with previously negative experiences of school. Splitting courses into 'bankable' modules made re-engagement less overwhelming and more manageable with a young baby.

Fourth, the quality of frontline staff was paramount. Young parents greatly valued, and gained substantial confidence from, their relationship with support staff if they trusted them and felt able to ask for help without being patronised. The support worker was also critical as a 'hand-holder' along the path to independent living, including accompanying young parents to other services and appointments.

Fifth, further development is needed in the support for young fathers, both in providing one-to-one advice on different aspects of their lives and in commissioning models of housing support that enable couples to live together.

Finally, the evaluation recommended gathering improved evidence to inform cost–benefit analyses of supported housing models.

> If I didn't have . . .these guys I think I'd probably be on the streets. They've helped me get my flat, helped me get my money . . . I started off with nothing. I had nobody. It started my life for me at the end of the day. I didn't know where to go to get a house, where to get milk, where to get clothes . . . and these guys came along and made it so much easier.
>
> (Teenage parent, Housing Support Pilot)

> I think it would be very hard for a young parent to fall through the net at the moment in (name of area), whereas it never used to be like that. So I think that something I can say, from working with teenage pregnancy from years ago to now, is that very few young mums would slip through the net now.
>
> (Stakeholder, Housing Support Pilot)

6.3.12 The importance of supporting young fathers

Young fathers are generally defined as being under 25. In the latest data for England and Wales, 84 per cent of fathers of babies born to young women under 20 are under 25, 33 per cent under 20 and 51 per cent between 20 and 24 (Office for National Statistics, 2016).

International and UK research strongly suggests that everything a young father does has an impact on the young mother and the child and that many young fathers have vulnerabilities and face challenges in fulfilling both their parenting and educational aspirations (Fatherhood Institute, 2013). However, all too often, they remain invisible to services and fail to get the support they need (Lau Clayton, 2017).

The vast majority of young fathers want to be involved. Among the birth registrations of babies born to mothers under 20, 5 per cent are in marriage or civil partnership, 75 per cent are jointly registered with the father (39 per cent at the same address and 36 per cent at different addresses) and only

20 per cent are sole registrations (Office for National Statistics, Fig. 4, 2016). Supportive involvement is associated with better outcomes. Young fathers have a strong influence over young mothers' attitudes and decisions about smoking and breastfeeding, so can contribute to reducing the risk of infant mortality, sudden unexpected infant death (SUDI) and childhood asthma. A good relationship with the baby's father and supportive behaviour by him is a protective factor for postnatal depression. Having highly involved fathers (even if the couple don't remain together) is associated with better outcomes for the child – emotional, behavioural and educational (Fatherhood Institute, 2013) – with the quality of the relationship during pregnancy the most important predictor of postnatal involvement (Quinton et al., 2002). Importantly, fatherhood can be a catalyst for young men to redefine their aspirations (Florsheim and Ngu, 2003) and re-engage with education and training, which, with the right support, helps reduce the longer-term risk of adult and child poverty.

Early and sustained support for young fathers is key to improving outcomes for them, the mother and their child. In their report on serious case reviews, Ofsted concluded that young fathers need support to become good parents and that their role is too often marginalised (Ofsted, 2011). Similarly to young mothers, young fathers who have never had a trusted adult in their lives may fear judgemental staff attitudes and the overlap with social services, and be reluctant to disclose they are a parent or to ask for advice. But their apprehensions are often compounded by practitioners' assumptions that young fathers are not central to the care of young mothers, a lack of awareness of the importance of their involvement and a lack of confidence and training for services and staff in positive engagement with young fathers (Quinton et al., 2002).

6.3.13 How services respond to young fathers

The *Following Young Fathers* research, which tracked 31 young fathers for three years through their entry into parenthood to see how it affected different aspects of their lives, identified three broad categories of how services responded to young fathers: surveillance, sidelining and support. The following quotes illustrate these experiences (Neale and Davies, 2015).

Surveillance appeared to stem from the assumption that young fathers are irresponsible and a potential risk to themselves or to their children. While safeguarding assessments and actions are critically important, surveillance without the support in place to address their needs undermined young fathers' confidence and potential for change.

> I feel like I've got to act perfect . . . do what they say and if I don't then summat bad is gonna happen.

Sidelining may stem from the same negative perception of young fathers, or from the dominant focus of support services on women, or a combination of both. It can occur in the direct contact with practitioners and at organisational level with services not publicising support for young fathers or, for example, schools and colleges refusing fathers time off to attend maternity appointments. Either way, sidelining, especially if accompanied by judgemental staff attitudes, fosters mistrust and can cement young fathers' disengagement from services.

> It was like I wasn't there. They didn't speak to me. They didn't involve me . . . I said (to the midwife), 'how come you never address me? When you've got something to say about my son you never tell me' . . . and she just said 'it's easier and she's mum after all . . .'

An ethos of support stems from the recognition of the potential contribution young men can make to their children's lives, and the value parenthood can have for them. The benefits of support, and the critical role it can play in transforming the lives of some young fathers, were most apparent in those receiving help from a specialist worker.

> [It was] the best support you can have really. . . . I didn't have a clue what I was doing, like, I was skiving school . . . but he got me referred onto college, and that got me back into education, right. . . . Well I'd have been lost [without him].

> The support I got from college was to help me financially. But he's helped me a lot emotionally . . . cause I didn't sort of have emotional boundaries, that – I couldn't care less about anything. So to get things off my chest with him . . . like someone I could talk to as a friend, but wasn't a friend 'cos he was a professional. It helped me sort of stabilise myself.

Dedicated support was clearly valued by young fathers. However, the simple friendly, inclusive and cost-free behaviours of practitioners in universal services, such as maternity and children's centres, can also engage young fathers, and build their trust and confidence.

> [The hospital staff] involved both of us . . . There was a lot of laughing and joking. The staff and scans . . . they was all fantastic . . . They explained what the pregnancy's going to be like and giving birth. . . . It was really good.

A separate small study in Lincolnshire further illustrates the impact of simple, no-cost actions. The health visiting team increased the participation of fathers in the Primary Birth Visit from 20 to 70 per cent simply by changing the wording of their 'invitation letter'. Instead of addressing the family as 'Dear Parent', they wrote 'Dear new Mum and Dad' and made it clear that they wanted to arrange 'an appointment that is convenient for you both' (Institute of Health Visiting, 2014).

The *Following Young Fathers* research highlighted important policy and practice implications for different aspects of the young fathers' lives, including education and training, housing, shared parenting, with specific recommendations for supporting those, including young fathers, who were involved in the criminal justice system (University of Leeds, 2015). The recommendations reflect some overarching principles for rethinking support for young fathers:

- Moving from a presumption that young fathers are a problem, to a starting point in all services that young fathers' involvement is beneficial to the young mother, their child and the young man himself.
- Ensuring the small minority of serious safeguarding cases are not perceived as the norm.
- Identifying and including young fathers in all early-help assessments and providing tailored support to meet their individual needs.
- Using dedicated practitioners to provide specialist support for young fathers but also to model effective working for non-specialist practitioners to develop a supportive ethos in universal as well as targeted services.

To share their experiences and needs, young fathers involved in the research also developed three booklets to raise awareness of practitioners and share their stories with other young fathers-to-be (Lau Clayton, 2015a, 2015b, 2015c). Some also became part of the following case study – Young Dads Collective – led by Leeds City Council's Teenage Pregnancy and Parenthood team.

CASE STUDY 6.4:
Involving young fathers

Young Dads Collective (YDC) North is the development of a successful partnership between Leeds City Council's Teenage Pregnancy and Parenthood team and YDC London. Modelled on the London-based project, YDC North's key aim is to promote and campaign for support for young dads in the North of England.

The young fathers recruited were between 18 and 25 years old, with children aged between 4 and 7. All the fathers involved in the project had previously worked with the Teenage Pregnancy and Parenthood team, so had a strong, established relationship with the workers. Workers re-established contact with these young fathers through social media and old contact numbers.

Since its development in May 2016 the young men have delivered three events and two workshops to over 300 professionals from a range of services and organisations. They also have representation on the Leeds Teenage Pregnancy and Partnership Board, offering advice and guidance to inform strategic plans.

The work of YDC is showing benefits for professionals and young fathers – helping to raise practitioners' awareness and understanding, and building the confidence and self-esteem of the young men.

It has been really useful to hear the other side. I will try and make time to ask the right questions in the future.

(Health Professional)

So powerful, until you hear it said you don't realise how hard it is.

(Teenage Pregnancy Worker)

I was really nervous before I had to present, because of it being a big crowd. It helped with my courage. I felt valued by the people in the room, people who came over and talked to me and said well done, which really gave me a boost. Made me feel confident to do it again.

(Young dad after presenting to 100 professionals)

Buzzing, love being listened to. It's not just the work with the professionals, it's about meeting up with other dads when we do the planning. We all want other dads to have a better experience.

(Young dad)

CASE STUDY 6.5:
Caring Dads – parenting support to address abusive relationships

Caring Dads is a programme run by St Michael's Fellowship, an NGO working with disadvantaged families in London and the South East of England. Run over 17 weeks, the evidence-based parenting programme aims to help fathers improve their relationship with their children, their children's mother and children's extended family members and to end controlling, abusive and neglectful behaviours. It is funded by the Rayne Foundation, a society focused on reducing exclusion and conflict, which recognised the higher level of relationship breakdown in young families and wanted to support a programme that enabled young fathers to have involvement in their children's lives.

St Michael's second Caring Dads programme worked with four young fathers with greater needs for intensive holistic support. The four fathers were aged 20 years or under and came from homes where they had experienced severe neglect and abuse. Their mothers, where present, had done their best in difficult circumstances to provide for their sons, but this had resulted in their sons feeling abandoned and left to fend for themselves; one said – 'the streets raised me'. Their fathers were largely absent and when present were violent, resulting in their sons being taken into care. These young fathers' experiences had left them with unresolved feelings that were displayed through anger, violence, substance misuse and depression.

Their children were known to children's social care; two were on Child Protection Plans, one was on an Interim Care Order and one had secured the sole care of his child under a Supervision Order. At the end of the programme two had been removed from CP plans, for one there was a Joint Guardianship Order and the father with sole care had developed respect for his former partner who was having positive contact with their child and he was enjoying an engineering apprenticeship.

St Michael's has identified the key factors contributing to impact as the intensive support provided to each participant, the trust that develops from that relationship and the bond that the fathers develop from the group process. The support of other professionals has also been essential in enabling the parents to achieve these outcomes. However, because of their extreme vulnerability the young fathers will continue to receive support.

6.4 Targeted support and a coordinated care pathway

6.4.1 Positive and supportive services: everybody's business

Clearly there is no simple intervention that can transform the lives of young parents and their children. This is unsurprising given the complex mix of individual and circumstantial challenges many teenage mothers and young fathers face, some of which are rooted in causes beyond the scope of individual interventions. However, evidence from all the evaluated programmes strongly suggests the most effective model of care: dedicated, strengths-based, one-to-one support, provided by a lead professional, with the skills to build a trusted relationship, who identifies problems early and draws in specialist services as required, and coordinates a care pathway, which starts early in pregnancy and is sustained until the young parents are on a stable footing. Key to engagement is a positive and supportive ethos from all services and individual practitioners. The programme evaluations and consultations with young parents all highlight that unwelcome services and judgemental staff attitudes may drive young parents away from the support they need.

This model also reflects recommendations in Ofsted's serious case reviews report, mentioned earlier. Pre-birth assessments, dedicated, trusted support for both teenage mothers and young fathers, and careful transfer of care between services were all considered crucial for effective support. Essential, too, was a joined-up multi-agency approach, with every agency understanding their role and the importance of working collaboratively (Ofsted, 2011).

6.4.2 New guidance for supporting young parents

In 2007, TPU developed new guidance for local areas, informed by the evaluation of the support programmes in the first phase of the strategy and a consultation with young parents commissioned from two NGOs. *Teenage Parents Next Steps* was jointly published by the Department for Children, Schools and Families and Department of Health (2007), and set out the actions local partnerships should take to deliver more responsive services. Rather than expecting the creation of new programmes of support, the guidance asked local areas to develop joined-up care pathways for young parents by integrating the lessons from Sure Start Plus into mainstream services, with support from different agencies brokered through dedicated advisers, based either as part of statutory services or commissioned through an NGO.

The principle of integrating improved support for young parents into mainstream services was underpinned by the holistic approach of the government's Every Child Matters Programme (Department for Education and Skills, 2004a), the National Service Framework for Children, Young People and Maternity (Department of Health, 2004) and the Children's Centres Practice Guidance (Department for Education and Skills and Department of Health, 2006b). Ensuring services were informed by the needs and experiences of teenage mothers and young fathers was a key principle underpinning the policy approach, prompting many areas to establish young parent participation groups.

CASE STUDY 6.6:
Involving young parents

Leicestershire County Council prioritised young parents' voices in shaping their local strategy.

Supported by Coventry University, young parents shared their stories and developed these into training materials for practitioners. The young parents then co-delivered training for midwives, health visitors, youth workers and Connexions advisors. In 2007, a Young Parents Forum was established. This forum collated stories from their peers and developed two books, *Dear Me – Letters to my pregnant self* and *The good, the bad and the unforgettable* (GBU). These brought together thoughts, feelings, experiences and lessons learned, and were distributed to pregnant teenagers. 'GBU' was also developed into a training pack for use in schools with pregnant teenagers or young parents, to raise awareness among health professionals and school staff and develop positive strategies for engaging young parents.

Other resources developed with the forum included a Young Parents Support Directory outlining sources of information and support during pregnancy and into parenthood, a Breastfeeding On the Go booklet promoting positive messages around feeding options to be distributed during pregnancy, and Post-Natal

Contraception Information to share clear messages about the need to make decisions about contraception choices during pregnancy or very early postnatally, to prevent subsequent unplanned pregnancies. Most recently the forum has helped develop Baby Boxes, based on the Finnish model. The boxes are given to young mothers-to-be at a one-to-one intervention at around 24 weeks, which offers an opportunity to discuss their pregnancy and find out about local services. The scheme has also helped increase practitioners' knowledge about all young parents in the area and ensure early help for any concerns (www.parentsunder20.co.uk).

To ensure young fathers feel heard and supported, a group of young fathers developed the idea, content and implementation of a short film and website. Becoming Dad shares their experiences and provides information about local services and resources – as well as helping to raise practitioners' awareness of young fathers' needs (www.becomingdad.co.uk).

Teenage Parents Next Steps also incorporated a number of additional initiatives TPU had developed to help improve young parents' support. Three guides were published to improve early and sustained uptake of antenatal care. *Teenage parents: who cares?* provided commissioning guidance for local areas on delivering effective maternity services for young parents (Department for Children, Schools and Families, 2008). This included recommending funding specialist teenage pregnancy midwives, a role which encompasses the ingredients of care now recommended for teenage parents by NICE in the guidance on maternity services for socially disadvantaged groups (NICE, 2010).

CASE STUDY 6.7:
Dedicated midwifery support for young mothers

In Brighton and Sussex University hospitals, a specialist teenage pregnancy midwife, also trained in sexual health, provides antenatal and postnatal care to all young mothers under 20, with an average caseload of thirty-five. Referrals are made directly to the midwife from the pregnant teenagers themselves, their families, general practitioners, midwives, sexual and reproductive health services or other practitioners.

The care is provided in two clinics dedicated for young parents, one in an area with a high teenage pregnancy rate, and one in a children's centre, which is easily accessible in the middle of Brighton. To make it as easy as possible for young parents to book early and keep all their antenatal appointments, the midwife also offers home visits in the evening, after college or work. Antenatal classes are held weekly as drop-in sessions, and a tour of the labour ward offered to all young mothers and their partners.

On average the young mothers receive twelve antenatal and six postnatal visits, including a contraception consultation. This is backed up with text message advice available from 8 a.m. to 8 p.m. seven days a week. The *Baby Buddy* phone app is also promoted to provide additional information and support in between visits.

Having a dedicated role, with continuity of care, has helped the young mothers maintain contact throughout the antenatal period, with an associated improvement in outcomes. Between 2007 and 2013, there has been a decline in the percentage of premature births and low-birth-weight babies and an increase in the average weight from 3,319 grams to 3,412 grams. Postnatal readmission rates have also declined.

The continuity of care and a trusted relationship has been particularly important for young mothers with additional vulnerabilities:

> At least half my clients have complex issues requiring a child protection referral and pre-birth assessment, but I haven't found young women won't engage with me after I have made a referral. My policy is to be honest, transparent and up front about any risks, and help link them to specialist support they may need – for example to the perinatal mental health team or to housing and benefit advice.
>
> (Mitch Denny, specialist midwife Brighton and Mid-Sussex)

Originally funded as a part-time post in 2004 by the local teenage pregnancy strategy, the role expanded to full time in 2008. It is now supported by mainstream funding and includes providing advice and support to other non-specialist midwives.

Getting maternity services right for pregnant teenagers and young fathers was aimed at the 'universal' maternity workforce of midwives, maternity assistants, doctors and receptionists, with practical suggestions on making services welcoming and young parent friendly (Department of Health and Department for Children, Schools and Families, 2008, updated 2015).

Multi-agency working to support pregnant teenagers provided guidance on the importance of information sharing between midwives and other agencies to prevent young parents falling through the gaps between services, with examples of local protocols (Department for Children, Schools and Families, 2008).

Other resources commissioned by TPU included a set of posters with positive images of teenage mothers and young fathers, developed in collaboration with a photo-journalist. Designed to help young parents feel more welcome in mainstream services, the posters were sent nationally to all maternity units and were available free for local areas to display in relevant support services. A teenage pregnancy midwifery network, founded by two specialist midwives, was also funded by TPU to strengthen support for midwives working specifically with young parents and to facilitate the sharing of innovation and good practice.

As with the revised prevention guidance published after the mid-course review, *Teenage Parents Next Steps* was accompanied by a self-assessment toolkit to help local partnerships identify and address gaps and monitor improvements. To ensure support for young parents was embedded in local strategies, the two self-assessments were published in one document (Department for Children, Schools and Families and Department of Health, 2009).

6.4.3 The principles of a joined-up care pathway for young parents

(These can be applied to any commissioning context.)

1   Early pregnancy confirmation

- Free and well-publicised pregnancy testing available in easily accessible locations
- Provision and publicity of unbiased information on pregnancy options, with access to counselling if required.

2   Swift referral to maternity services

- Clear referral pathways from pregnancy testing services to maternity services
- Early antenatal booking with information to support healthy pregnancy, including vitamin D and folic acid supplements
- Referral to Family Nurse Partnership or dedicated support service.

3   Early needs assessment

- Sensitive but robust needs assessment in maternity services, undertaken by a practitioner trusted by the young parent, and taking into account the wider relationship and family situation
- Identification of any health, relationship or safeguarding concerns
- Provision of early help for any identified problems, bringing in specialist services as required – e.g. smoking cessation, domestic violence, mental health, housing support.

4   Tailored antenatal care

- Antenatal care and preparation for parenthood for teenage mothers and young fathers
- Delivered in local settings, which are trusted and accessible by young parents in the local area, with easy access to other services, and ideally meeting the *You're Welcome* quality standards.

5   Postnatal contraception choice

- Information about return of fertility after birth, and discussion about postnatal contraception options during antenatal care
- Method of choice provided before leaving maternity care.

6   Referral pathway to postnatal dedicated support

   •   Agreed information sharing protocol and referral pathway between maternity services and dedicated support services, so all young parents are known about
   •   Dedicated adviser providing one-to-one support and coordinating involvement of any specialist services, with more intensive help for the most vulnerable, and inclusive of young fathers
   •   Arrangements for continued dedicated support for young parents if their child is taken into care.

7   Personal development plans – for both parents

   •   Support to continue or re-engage with education and training, including for school-age parents the provision of specialist education units or specialist reintegration support
   •   Education and training support linked to local planning for workforce development and employment, to provide pathways into employment
   •   Free or low-cost childcare to enable return to education, training or employment.

8   Support with contraception and sexual health

   •   Continued information and advice about contraception, condoms and good sexual health for both young parents
   •   Help with accessing specialist contraception and sexual health service if required.

9   Information about all relevant support services

   •   Information for both young parents about all local support services well publicised in relevant settings and proactively offered by all practitioners
   •   Supported transfer for young parents from specialist dedicated support to mainstream services.

6.5 Maintaining the focus beyond 2010

6.5.1 Some good progress, but more to do to improve and sustain support

By 2010, there had been a doubling in the proportion of teenage mothers participating in education, training or employment (Wellings *et al.*, 2016). This indicated significant progress towards the goal of reducing inequalities and social exclusion. Nevertheless, a significant proportion of 16–18-year-old young mothers were not participating, and barriers remained for young parents wanting to re-engage with education (Department for Children, Schools and Families and Department of Health, 2010). There was some improvement on other maternity and child outcomes, notably stillbirth, but it was clear that a continuing concerted focus was needed.

As mentioned in Chapter 4, the coalition government elected in 2010 decided against continuing with a stand-alone teenage pregnancy strategy, but asked local government to continue their efforts to reduce rates and improve outcomes for young parents as part of the drive to narrow health and educational inequalities and reduce child poverty.

The importance of further progress was reflected in the new Public Health Outcomes Framework, which local areas use to assess their performance and focus efforts to reduce inequalities. As well as the under-18 conception rate, one of the three sexual health indicators, the Framework includes around twenty other indicators to which improved support for teenage parents directly contributes; these included infant mortality, children in poverty, maternal smoking, low birth weight, breastfeeding, rates of 16- to 18-year-olds not in education, employment or training and hospital admissions caused by unintentional and deliberate injuries to under-5s.

6.5.2 Making support everybody's business: new government guidance

However, the combination of no longer having a specific strategy, the dismantling of the national and regional support structures and the new commissioning landscape following the Health and Social Care Act posed significant challenges for local areas in maintaining a coordinated support offer for young parents. Following a request for national guidance from several local government areas, Public Health England developed a new *Framework for supporting teenage mothers and young fathers* to help commissioners and service providers review and improve coordinated support arrangements for young parents in their area (PHE and Local Government Association, 2016).

The Framework enshrined the principle of all areas providing young parents with dedicated support, either by the Family Nurse Partnership or other lead professional, starting early in pregnancy and continued through a coordinated care pathway. It also made clear that early help and effective support rely on multi-agency collaboration, with universal services and relevant programmes being aware of the needs of teenage mothers and young fathers and understanding how they can contribute to improving outcomes.

To help engage busy commissioners and service providers, a slide and infographics format was used to highlight the relevance and importance of young parents to the priorities of each individual service, with key actions for tailoring the service to meet their needs, which were designed to be used as an updated self-assessment checklist (Figure 6.1). To accompany the framework Public Health England also developed a *Teenage Parents Data Modelling Tool* designed to help local areas model the impact of certain services; for example, setting up a new stop smoking service for young mothers.

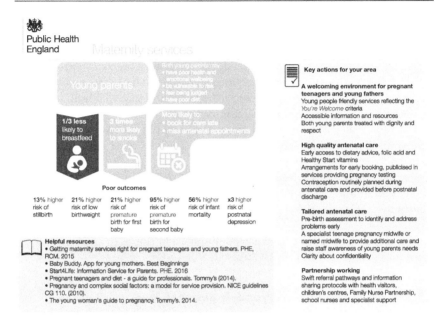

Figure 6.1 Example of Framework infographic slide.

Importantly, the Framework, jointly published with the Local Government Association, helped to signal that support for young parents was an integral part of long-term prevention, and that improved outcomes contributed to benefits at individual, societal and economic level.

> Getting support right for teenage mothers and young fathers can transform the lives of individual young parents and their children, enabling them to fulfill their aspirations and potential. At a strategic level good support:
>
> - is integral to safeguarding, the Early Help agenda and improving life chances;
> - is key to giving every child the best start in life;
> - breaks intergenerational inequalities;
> - reduces future demand on health and social services;
> - contributes to Public Health and NHS Outcomes.
>
> Framework for supporting teenage mothers
> and young fathers, PHE-LGA 2016

6.5.3 Integrating support for young parents into other government priorities

Although the Framework is aimed at integrating support into mainstream services, prioritising support for young parents has also been included in Public

Health England's *Best Start in Life* programme and the government's *Maternity Transformation Plan for England*, both designed to narrow inequalities. Funding for the Care to Learn programme has continued, and data on teenage mothers' participation in education and training continue to be collected.

Further progress will depend on a number of factors. First, all local areas applying the principles of the Framework, with the funding of dedicated support, agreeing a coordinated care pathway and securing the contribution of all relevant agencies. Second, identifying and incorporating further learning from the Family Nurse Partnership follow-up study, which is monitoring children's outcomes up to the age of 6, and from the programme's development of more flexible approaches to vulnerable families. Third, ensuring that local areas' commissioning models of dedicated support other than FNP are helped to evaluate their impact. Fourth, that government continues to monitor outcomes for young parents, including disaggregating data sets by age, and develops indicators for measuring outcomes for young fathers. Fifth, that local areas continue to consult with teenage mothers and young fathers to understand their perspective of support services and identify any barriers. As mentioned at several points in this chapter, unwelcome services, judgemental staff and the challenges of poor housing and limited educational and work opportunities will always undermine policies and strategies designed to improve outcomes for young parents.

Finally, progress will rely on government and local areas continuing to focus on supporting young parents as an integral part of further teenage pregnancy work. With such significant reductions in the under-18 conception rate, it may be tempting to lower the priority. However, as suggested by the Family Nurse Partnership experience, the diminishing numbers may lead to an increasingly vulnerable group of young women and men with even greater need of dedicated support. In short, neglect of young parents now is likely to widen inequalities and subject another generation to unfulfilled life chances.

Notes

1   Except where stated, outcome data compare mothers under 20 with all mothers.
2   Foundation Learning programmes provide a curriculum and personalised learning programme, and are specifically developed to raise participation and attainment in 14–19-year-olds.
3   The Connexions service was established in 2000 in every local government area, to provide information, advice and guidance for young people aged 13–19.
4   The Early Intervention Foundation is an NGO established in 2013 and is one of the UK government's 'What Works Centres'. EIF evaluates evidence and provides advice on effective early intervention to improve outcomes for children and young people.

Chapter 7

Sharing lessons internationally to galvanise action

7.1 The need for scaled-up, effective programmes

7.1.1 Overview

This final chapter discusses the success factors of the England strategy, some of the challenges faced and elements that could have been done differently and sets the lessons learned in the international context of adolescent sexual and reproductive health improvements.

In 1994, the International Conference on Population and Development (ICPD) put adolescent sexual and reproductive health (ASRH) on the global public health agenda and called for the needs of young people to be met and their rights fulfilled. This was further reinforced by the Millennium Development Goals, which were formulated as part of the United Nations Millennium Declaration.

Twenty-three years since the ICPD and seventeen years after the Millennium Declaration, while many countries have developed national policies and strategies on adolescent sexual and reproductive health and on HIV – either as part of population-wide or adolescent-focused normative documents – only a few have ever translated these into adequately funded and implemented strategies. A number of factors – often acting in combination – have contributed to this. First, the focus of policy makers and programme managers in many places has been on childhood and maternal mortality reduction, and less so on adolescent health. Second, the paucity of reliable national data on adolescent health has hindered the identification of clear priorities. Third, lack of know-how on effective interventions, how to measure them and how to cost them has translated into weak plans. Fourth, lukewarm political commitment and poorly defined, and defended, priorities have been unable to attract resources. And finally, limited capacity – especially in government bodies – in managing, implementing and monitoring adolescent health activities and discomfort in dealing with the sensitivities around sexual and reproductive health have meant that little good work was done even when other prerequisites were in place. As a result, in most places there are no concerted and sustained government-led efforts under way. Non-governmental organisations have tried to fill this space, but have neither the mandate nor the human and financial resources to go beyond piecemeal, small-scale and time-limited initiatives (Chandra-Mouli *et al.*, 2013a).

7.1.2 Distilling the key actions for successful, scaled-up programmes

In 2014, the World Health Organization identified the England strategy as one of a small number of countries with a successful nationally led programme to address pregnancy and parenthood in young people. In collaboration with the former head of the Teenage Pregnancy Unit (TPU), now Director of the Teenage Pregnancy Knowledge Exchange, and the research lead on the strategy's Independent Advisory Group, WHO analysed the elements of the strategy that were transferable to other countries and settings (Hadley *et al.*, 2016a, 2016b).

To share and discuss the learning in more detail with other countries, England participated in a global consultation event led by WHO, in collaboration with Implementing Best Practices, USAID, UNFPA, the Evidence to Action Project, Pathfinder International and the Bill and Melinda Gates Foundation. The meeting brought together the first generation of countries that had succeeded in scaling up comprehensive sexuality education (CSE) and/or adolescent-friendly health services over an entire country, or a province/state in the case of large countries, and sustained for at least three years. Fourteen low- and middle-income countries, and four high-income countries,[1] participated. By bringing together government and non-government representatives, United Nations agency and international NGO staff academics and young people, the consultation provided an opportunity to table and share global experiences and to distil the success factors, and the challenges faced, to help inform new developments and sustain the progress of existing programmes. The common elements of success were framed under five key actions:

1   Placing adolescent sexual and reproductive health on the national agenda
2   Planning for scale-up from the start
3   Managing scale-up effectively and efficiently
4   Building support while anticipating and addressing opposition
5   Promoting and safeguarding sustainability.

The chapter starts by analysing the England strategy against the WHO actions, followed by international examples illustrating how the actions applied in other countries' successful programmes. Finally, the chapter summarises the next steps for addressing adolescent sexual and reproductive health in the global context – capitalising on what is described as a 'never before' moment in adolescent health (United Nations, 2015).

7.2 The England strategy: success factors and learning points

7.2.1 Placing adolescent and sexual health on the national agenda

The window of opportunity for the development of the England strategy was the incoming Labour government's focus on reducing social exclusion. Addressing high rates had been a concern of the previous government, with a national target to halve the under-16 conceptions included as one of the policies in a new Health of the Nation strategy focusing on coronary heart disease, cancer, mental illness, accidents and HIV/AIDS and sexual health (Department of Health, 1992). However, although this prompted a welcome investment and growth in youth-friendly contraceptive services, there was no comprehensive action plan to address poor sex and relationships education[2] (SRE) or the wider determinants of teenage pregnancy, and no agreement of local targets or requirement for a local strategy. It also omitted attention to 16- and 17-year-olds, who are more likely to be sexually active and to whom, in England, 80 per cent of conceptions to under-18s occur.

Interestingly, the Health of the Nation policy had been based on WHO's Health for All (World Health Organization, 1997), which promoted a goal of holistic health achieved by collaborative cross-government action, but an assessment of the policy found it was largely regarded as a Department of Health initiative. Notably, it was seen as lacking ownership and commitment from other departments or local government, missing the necessary horizontal and vertical structures for effective partnership working, and failing to spell out the expectations, tasks and responsibilities of different agencies. Importantly, there was no defined budget (Universities of Leeds and Glamorgan and the London School of Hygiene and Tropical Medicine, 1998).

The lack of progress during the 1990s had been kept high on the political agenda through strong advocacy from NGOs and professional organisations, and teenage pregnancy was quickly identified as a priority issue for the new Social Exclusion Unit (SEU). The SEU, established in 1997, was set up specifically to 'help government action to reduce social exclusion by producing joined up solutions to joined up problems' (Office of the Deputy Prime Minister, 2004).

Positioning teenage pregnancy in the SEU not only secured it a place high on the national agenda but also helped ensure the strategy was anchored across government, rather than in its traditional silo of health. The relevance of teenage pregnancy and young parents was made clear to other government departments from the start, with their required contributions set out in the strategy action plan and an inter-department ministerial group established to support implementation.

Notably, the new approach of the strategy addressed the weaknesses highlighted in the Health of the Nation assessment. It also reflected the nine key characteristics of modern policy making identified by the National Audit Office, an independent Parliamentary body with a role of scrutinising public spending (National Audit Office, 2001):

- Be forward thinking
- Be outward looking
- Be innovative and creative
- Use evidence
- Be inclusive
- Be joined up
- Evaluate
- Review
- Learn lessons.

The recognition that teenage pregnancy was a complex issue, which would need a comprehensive multi-factorial solution, helped secure the essential long timescale for the strategy. The ten-year goal, and commitment to sustained resourcing, signalled government's commitment, and made clear there was no quick fix.

The launch of the strategy by the Prime Minister in Downing Street further underlined that teenage pregnancy was a national priority, with progress reliant on the whole of government:

> *This is a comprehensive programme of action which we will put into practice straight away. It will not be easy. It will mean putting aside prejudice and embarrassment to engage in a mature debate. But we owe it to today's and tomorrow's teenagers to get this right at last.*
>
> (Prime Minister Tony Blair, 1999, Foreword to SEU
> Teenage Pregnancy Report)

7.2.2 Planning for scale-up from the start

National scale-up was integral to the strategy's ambition from the start. A national comprehensive multi-agency programme, framed around four themes, was to be delivered in all 150 local government areas, with agreed local targets contributing to the national 50 per cent reduction goal (Social Exclusion Unit, 1999):

Joined-up action with new mechanisms to coordinate action at both national and local levels and ensure the strategy is on track.

Better prevention of teenage pregnancy: improving sex and relationships education (SRE) in and out of school, and access to contraception for all young people, with targeted prevention for at-risk groups and a new focus on reaching young men.

A national campaign involving government, media, non-governmental organisations (NGOs) and others to improve understanding and change behaviour.

Better support for pregnant teenagers and young parents, with a new focus on returning to education and free childcare to enable participation; working to a position where no under-18 lone parent is put in a housing tenancy without support; and pilots around the country providing intensive support for young parents and their children – the Sure Start Plus programme.

Fundamental to the planned scale-up was the establishment of the strategy's national, regional and local vertical and horizontal structures. These provided the architecture for effective implementation of such a complex, multi-agency programme.

The Teenage Pregnancy Unit (TPU), resourced by cross-department funding, provided national leadership and was the 'engine room' of the strategy and essential for delivering such a large programme of work. A lead minister had overall responsibility for the strategy but was supported by an Inter-Departmental Teenage Pregnancy Board, established to reflect the cross-cutting nature of the policy and the shared responsibility for action. A Regional Teenage Pregnancy Coordinator (regional coordinator) was appointed for each of the nine Government Office regions to support local areas, working closely with other relevant regional policy leads to ensure multi-agency engagement. Locally, every local government area (150) and the local health organisation appointed a Teenage Pregnancy Coordinator (local coordinator) and a Teenage Pregnancy Partnership Board (partnership board), with representation from health, education, social services, youth services, housing and relevant non-governmental organisations (NGOs) (Department of Health, 2001a; Teenage Pregnancy Unit, 2002a).

A Local Implementation Grant was provided to each area. The grant allocation was determined by the size of the local population of 15–17-year-old young women and the baseline under-18 conception rate, which indicated the degree of challenge the local area would have in meeting the reduction target. Annual allocations ranged from £150K to £600K, with most areas receiving around 300–400K.

The grant was ring fenced, with conditions on how it was spent. This included appointing a teenage pregnancy coordinator and partnership board, which helped establish the structures across the country. Two years into the strategy, all areas had a coordinator and partnership board, with 50 per cent of the boards meeting at least once every two months, and fewer than one in ten meeting less than three times a year. Importantly, the structures, and accompanying national and local funding, were largely maintained throughout the course of the strategy, providing a secure environment for the strategy to mature and build momentum. That said, there were some challenges in maintaining continuity, notably during periods of organisational change, which affected local structures and sometimes personnel (London School of Hygiene and Tropical Medicine, UCL and BMRB International, 2005).

Recognising that the strategy was going to be implemented over a long period of time, plans for monitoring the progress of national scale-up (described below) were established in the strategy action plan.

7.2.3 What could have been done differently?

The key constraint on national scale-up was government's decision not to make SRE a statutory requirement from the start of the strategy. There is no documentation of government's reason for the decision. However, it was widely believed to stem from fears of a backlash from some sections of the media, anti-choice groups, some faith organisations and from parliamentarians with socially conservative views. As the Labour government was taking office after eighteen years in opposition, these concerns may have been particularly pronounced at the time the strategy was being developed. Although the new administration had secured the support of the popular conservative media, the ongoing relationship was fragile and fostered a risk-averse approach on issues perceived to be 'sensitive', such as SRE.

Government clearly recognised the essential role of high-quality SRE in achieving the goals of the strategy, with the action plan including new guidance for schools, training and accreditation for teachers and inspection of school provision. However, having no statutory lever to raise the priority of SRE in all schools was a significant barrier to scale-up and securing universal provision for all children and young people. How government could have taken a more proactive approach to SRE and other potentially controversial aspects of the strategy is discussed later.

7.2.4 Manage scale-up effectively and efficiently

Effective and efficient scale-up was greatly assisted by the continuity and funding of national, regional and local structures for the duration of the strategy. Having a dedicated national unit was essential to manage the volume of work and maintain highly visible leadership. The regional coordinators provided a vital intermediate role, cascading the national strategy actions to local areas, but also using their knowledge of local challenges to help the Unit provide guidance that was relevant and fit for purpose. The regular network meetings with local areas helped to maintain momentum and morale, and enabled good practice to be quickly shared to minimise duplication of effort. For example, local protocols developed by one area for nurses to provide contraception in education or youth settings, or workforce training programmes, could be easily adapted by others. Seminars and conferences led by the TPU helped to promote local application of national guidance and campaign activities. The guiding principle

CLOSE MONITORING OF PROGRESS: A KEY SUCCESS INGREDIENT

Careful monitoring of progress was essential for effective implementation of the ten-year programme of work. The strategy combined the use of reliable outcome data with systematic arrangements for checking implementation of the strategy actions.

Monitoring progress on outcomes

National and local progress towards the targets was monitored by reliable under-18 conception data, collected from birth registrations and abortion notifications, and published quarterly by the independent Office for National Statistics. The data enabled the comparison of progress between areas, leading to the mid-course review, and the comparison of progress on reducing births and abortions. Conception data for small geographies highlighted high-rate areas and helped monitor progress in reducing inequalities within local government areas.

Monitoring strategy implementation at local level

In the first phase of the strategy, all local areas were required to provide an annual report on how they were implementing their strategy actions, which was reviewed by the national and regional teams. After the mid-course review, all areas were asked to complete a self-assessment against the revised government guidance. The self-assessment toolkit included a recommended indicator set for monitoring implementation of the ten key factors, with a summary of agreed actions signed off by senior leaders. Areas making slow progress were required to provide six-monthly reports to ministers and offered additional support, until a downward trend was established. Progress towards the local reduction target was included as part of government's comprehensive performance reviews with senior leaders of local government and health agencies. Completion of the self-assessment process was recognised as an indicator of the local area's collaboration and commitment to reach their agreed target.

Monitoring strategy implementation at national level

An independent evaluation was commissioned on the first phase of strategy implementation, including routinely collected data, a survey of young people and parents, media coverage of the strategy and local experience of implementation. The evaluation informed the second phase of the strategy. Progress on implementing some of the key strategy actions was monitored by data collected on the numbers of young people specialist clinics, clinic attendance and contraceptive method uptake by age, the numbers of teachers receiving SRE training and the proportion of young mothers in education or training. National progress, and government commitment, was monitored by the Independent Advisory Group. The Group's annual reports and recommendations for action required a published government response.

of partnership working, at national, regional and local level, harnessed commitment and brought in additional resources from other agencies.

Careful monitoring of progress was an essential ingredient of effective implementation. The very accurate conception data published quarterly and annually provided a reliable measure of national and local trends. Local progress was also monitored through assessments of annual reports. Every local area was required, as a condition of the grant, to submit an annual report on their strategy implementation, with assessment and feedback provided by the regional coordinator and the TPU. An independent evaluation was also commissioned to report on the first phase of implementation (1999–2004), which included: a national random-location tracking survey of young people aged 13–21 and parents of 13–17-year-olds to monitor change in knowledge, attitudes and behaviour at an individual level; an area-level analysis of routinely collected data on conceptions, abortion, deprivation scores and intervention- and non-intervention-related activity to explore demographic and strategy-related variation in key outcomes at area level; analysis of regional and national press coverage of the strategy; and a combination of qualitative and quantitative research to evaluate process, such as local coordination of strategy activities and the experience of those involved in implementing them. The evaluation provided important learning for the mid-course review and the second phase of the strategy (London School of Hygiene and Tropical Medicine, UCL and BMRB International, 2005).

To help avoid teenage pregnancy being seen as an isolated issue, as government developed its system for overall performance management of local government and health organisations the teenage pregnancy reduction target was included. This helped to put a spotlight on progress among local senior leaders and added further weight to the review process.

For example, the under-18 conception rate was included as one of the indicators that could be chosen as a priority for Local Area Agreements, three-year agreements between national government and local areas. This prompted local government and their partners to collectively review their progress on teenage pregnancy and make a joint commitment to further action. The indicator was chosen as a priority by 106 out of the 150 local areas, including all those where declines were slow. Local areas were also encouraged to use the strategy's self-assessment toolkit (mentioned below) to review their progress as evidence for the Comprehensive Area Assessment (CAA) annual performance review conducted by the Audit Commission. CAAs, introduced as part of public sector reform, focused on how results could be achieved through part-nership collaboration. Completion of the self-assessment process was recognised by the Audit Commission as an indicator of the local area's collaboration and commitment to reach their agreed target (Department for Children, Schools and Families and Department of Health, 2009).

At a national level, government was held to account by the Advisory Group. The Group's annual reports and recommendations for action required a written government response, which was recorded in parliament and attracted signifi-cant media interest. The reports were also avidly taken up by local coordinators to raise the profile of teenage pregnancy among senior leaders and increase commitment to local implementation.

Critical to success was the regular review of progress and use of the findings to tailor and strengthen the strategy. The mid-course review in 2005, which showed that areas applying all the strategy actions were successfully reducing rates, was followed up with more prescriptive guidance, direct engagement by ministers with poor-performing areas and additional support from the regional coordinators and a new National Support Team (Department of Education and Skills, 2006). The National Support Team combined the influence of ministers, who offered the additional support to the poor-performing areas, with the highly regarded expertise of the team. With a trusted leader who had extensive experience of local implementation, the visits helped to unlock the doors of senior leaders, which provided the necessary catalyst for change.

> By undertaking intensive, 'diagnostic' visits to local areas and meeting with key local leaders the National Support Team provided intelligence, chal-lenge and support to local areas, using a constructive and non-confron-tational support model, which raised the local profile of teenage pregnancy and engaged senior-level partners. In particular it moved teenage preg-nancy much higher up the agenda of councils and enabled very senior sponsorship from chief officers and council leaders.
>
> (Kate Quail, Head of Teenage Pregnancy
> National Support Team)

New guidance for supporting young parents was also published, consoli-dating the learning from the evaluation of the Sure Start Plus programme, which provided dedicated advisers for young parents (Department for Children, Schools and Families and Department of Health, 2007). A self-assessment tool-kit with a recommended indicator set was provided to help local areas review their strategies against actions from both pieces of guidance, and address any gaps (Department for Children, Schools and Families and Department of

Health, 2009). In 2007 data analysis showing that within the overall reduction in conceptions there was a steeper decline in births compared with abortions, made the case for additional funding to increase young people's knowledge of, and access to, effective contraception.

To ensure equity in the strategy's implementation, a close eye was kept on reducing inequalities, with the mid-course review and the first phase independent evaluation both highlighting the need for additional support for young people most at risk. Data and qualitative research were regularly reviewed to identify potential risk factors for early pregnancy, or poor outcomes for young parents and their children. Summaries were provided to local areas to inform targeted work, and strategy actions integrated nationally into relevant government programmes aimed at improving health and educational outcomes for the most disadvantaged young people. For example, as part of the Targeted Youth Support (TYS) programme, which aimed to address the underlying risk factors that can result in a range of poor outcomes, TYS practitioners were given guidance on providing young people with the knowledge and skills they need to experience positive relationships and good sexual health, and to support them to access contraception when they need it. Guidance on establishing on-site contraception and sexual health services was also provided to the Extended Schools programme, prioritised in areas of deprivation, and to Further Education Colleges. The joint health and education department guidance highlighted the mutual benefits of collaboration. Reductions in pregnancy would contribute to local health targets but would also help improve student wellbeing and learning progression, and prevent young women dropping out of education due to pregnancy.

7.2.5 What could have been done differently?

A weakness in the effective and efficient scale-up was, once again, not having statutory SRE. Although the impact of statutory status would have taken time to reach all young people, it would likely have contributed to more rapid progress. Government's decision in 2008 to introduce statutory SRE came too late to secure the necessary legislation. With the benefit of hindsight, four other measures might also have strengthened national scale-up and accelerated progress.

First, providing more prescriptive guidance for local areas from the start of the strategy. While the original guidance for developing local strategies set out a clear framework for what needed to be in place, the 'must do' actions required of each agency and relevant senior leaders were not sufficiently clear. This resulted in some inconsistencies in local implementation, and presented a challenge in monitoring progress across the breadth of the strategy actions.

Second, establishing more sustained collaboration with general practice.[3] Although a leading GP was a member of the Advisory Group, and some proactive work was done with general practice in the first phase of the strategy on confidentiality and young-people-friendly services, there was not a sufficiently strategic approach to maximise its contribution. Given that general practice is a universal service, open all week and visited by young people at least once a year, there is huge untapped potential to increase young people's knowledge and early uptake of contraceptive advice, make links with local schools, colleges and youth services and provide early help for young parents.

Third, having a stronger focus on contraception from the start in the national campaign messages. While the rationale for focusing on condoms was clear – to convey an integrated message on prevention of pregnancy and sexually transmitted infections (STIs) to both young men and young women – progress was slow in improving young people's knowledge about the range of effective contraception available. That said, there remains a challenge, still to be resolved, in how to effectively convey strong messages about contraception *and* condoms in one campaign.

Fourth, monitoring how the strategy actions were reaching young people. Some data were collected through the tracking survey, included in the first phase evaluation of the strategy, but was not continued beyond 2004. An annual national survey of young people, including young parents, to monitor improvements in SRE, access to contraception, confidence in asking for advice and the quality of support services would have provided some helpful proxy indicators of progress. The same survey could have been made available for local areas to help review the impact of local strategy actions.

7.2.6 Build support while anticipating and addressing opposition

The strategy was strongly endorsed by NGOs and professional organisations – confirmed by the finding in the first phase evaluation that there was 'near universal support' for its aims. Some had been advocating for specific action on teenage pregnancy prior to the strategy. Others welcomed it as a catalyst for improving SRE, making services and the workforce young people friendly, addressing the long-term neglect of young parents' needs and embedding children's rights. The SEU's thorough review of the evidence, and clear statements on the ineffectiveness of approaches such as abstinence-only programmes or benefit conditionality, strengthened the credibility of the strategy.

Stakeholder trust in the integrity of the strategy was also enhanced by the appointment of experts to support implementation. The TPU combined the skills of civil servants with external specialists drawn from the statutory sector and from NGOs, and the regional and local coordinators had relevant experience in adolescent health, youth work or social care. The appointment of experts to the Advisory Group, spanning the different aspects of the strategy, provided reassurance that the monitoring of the strategy, and the recommendations to government, were informed by evidence and specialist knowledge. The Advisory Group's gravitas and expertise were particularly influential with local senior leaders, as was the advice provided by the National Support Team. The national NGO and inter-faith forums provided a two-way exchange with stakeholders, keeping them informed about the strategy implementation and also providing a channel to voice concerns or point to barriers.

> The Advisory Group played a key role in holding the confidence of both NGOs and ministers. We held firmly to the principle of young people's rights to information and reproductive choices but were able to reassure government that the strategy's actions were grounded in evidence. The independence of the Group was the vital ingredient.
>
> (Gill Frances, Chair Teenage Pregnancy
> Independent Advisory Group)

The co-badging of guidance and publications with relevant organisations was particularly helpful in illustrating support for the strategy and influencing their own members; for example, delivering the campaign messages to parents through the largest parenting NGO, publishing guidance for midwifery services with the Royal College of Midwives and providing briefing for elected councillors with the Local Government Association.

7.2.7 What could have been done differently?

Convincing government of the support for statutory SRE proved the biggest challenge. Despite surveys showing parental support and repeated recommendations from the Advisory Group, there was persistent opposition from a very small but vocal minority, particularly regarding SRE for younger children, with unfounded claims that it encouraged sexual activity and robbed children of their innocence. This was fanned by misleading and ill-informed media coverage suggesting 'sex lessons for 5-year-olds', which not only misinformed and alarmed parents, but also created the distorted impression of majority opposition, and deterred government action on statutory status until the end of the strategy. Some other aspects of the strategy, such as providing contraception in school health clinics, were also criticised by the same minority groups and received similar media coverage, despite surveys showing parental support for confidential services for under-16s. This made some local areas nervous about applying the strategy actions. It also gave young people very confusing messages about whether or not they should be asking for advice.

Although government issued reactive comments to the media reports, the strategy would have benefited from a planned proactive media campaign from the start – working with selected supportive journalists to explain SRE and other potentially controversial strategy actions and highlight the consensus between young people, parents, professional organisations and NGOs. Two other experiences during the strategy suggest that this might have had a beneficial effect. First, the finding that as local teenage pregnancy coordinators became more engaged and confident with the media, local and regional reporting of the strategy became increasingly positive: from 34 per cent positive articles in year 1 to 50 per cent in year 4. Second, during the preparation for statutory SRE after government made its decision in 2008, it was clear that once parents understood the content of SRE at different ages and had any concerns over any negative impact allayed, they strongly supported SRE for its protective benefits. A well-planned, proactive media strategy would not have guaranteed a smooth run, but led by ministers, with spokespeople from young people, parents and stakeholder organisations, it would have placed government on the front foot and in a much better position to establish the narrative and lead a calm and well-informed discussion. The later case study from Pakistan (see p. 187) is an interesting example of how to harness the positive support of the media.

At times, the strategy was criticised for stigmatising teenage parents. Although the vast majority of NGOs working with young parents endorsed the aim to improve support for teenage mothers and young fathers, there was some challenge that the focus itself created a stigma. This was fuelled by a number of factors. First, although the headline goal of the strategy was to halve the under-18 conception rate, this was sometimes misinterpreted as a goal to eradicate teenage pregnancy, and was seen as taking away, rather than increasing, choice for young people. Second, the prevention actions of the strategy, such as SRE and increasing access to contraception, attracted significant media attention, whereas the strategy's considerable support programme for young parents was much less reported, so was less visible. Third, while the conception data allowed close monitoring of progress in reducing early pregnancy and fuelled regular media reports, there were no comparably robust data to monitor improvements in young parents' lives. That said, there is always a challenge in levering action to increase young people's knowledge and skills to delay early pregnancy, without highlighting the negative aspects of young parenthood. However, while having a specific focus on teenage pregnancy was a key asset for the strategy, particularly in engaging collaboration from non-health agencies, different terminology might have been preferable. The term used for the new Scottish Government's strategy – *Pregnancy and Parenthood in Young People* – may be perceived as less judgemental, and reflect a better balance between prevention and support (Scottish Government, 2016).

7.2.8 Promote and safeguard sustainability

The strategy had to respond to two challenges: sustaining momentum throughout the long implementation period, and sustaining progress after the strategy had ended, in the context of a new government and diminishing resources.

7.2.9 Sustaining momentum throughout implementation

Although the strategy had a very clear focus and action plan, it was never intended to be delivered in isolation. Throughout the implementation, much effort was put into linking teenage pregnancy to other government priorities and integrating the strategy actions into relevant programmes. This was a key role of the TPU, and one that needed proactive and determined commitment to gain the attention of other busy programmes, and help them understand the relevance of teenage pregnancy to their own priorities.

Including the target in the national Public Service Agreements and local performance indicators for local government and health partners secured ongoing monitoring of progress and performance management. New legislation, which put a legal duty on local areas to cooperate with partner agencies and promote a holistic approach to improving outcomes for children and young people, built on and strengthened the strategy's core principle of joint working. Including SRE as a key criterion for achieving the *Healthy Schools Programme* accreditation and translating the best practice guidance on contraceptive services into the national *You're Welcome* standards (Department of Health, 2005, 2007, 2011) helped extend the reach of the strategy actions into mainstream programmes. Issuing guidance for non-health practitioners in touch with young people most at risk, such as youth workers, social workers and targeted support practitioners, stitched the strategy actions into the wider workforce.

Strong leadership was a critical factor in sustaining momentum. Nationally, having an accountable lead minister, with nominated ministerial leads in all government departments, signalled that teenage pregnancy was a multi-factorial issue relevant to, and reliant on action from, the whole of government. Resourcing a national Unit throughout the ten years was essential both to provide leadership and to manage the large programme of work. At a local level, the prioritisation of teenage pregnancy increased as senior leaders understood the link with poor intergenerational outcomes, and recognised their actions could make a difference. Towards the end of the ten-year period, over two-thirds of areas had chosen the under-18 conception rate as a priority indicator for monitoring overall progress. National and local leadership was particularly important when early progress was slow and some media commentators were claiming the strategy had failed. The Advisory Group also provided helpful independent expert challenge to media criticism and reassured ministers that it takes time to address complex social phenomena.

> Sensational, polarised media stories simply do not reflect public opinion. The vast majority of parents and young people agree that sex and relationships education, within personal, social and health education (PSHE), should be provided in schools and that confidential contraception and support services should be available. Further, inaccurate stories in the media

reporting 'rising teenage pregnancy rates' are not only misleading but fuel the belief that nothing can be done. We know it can.

(Gill Frances, Chair Teenage Pregnancy
Independent Advisory Group, 2006)

7.2.10 Sustaining progress beyond the strategy

The year 2010 marked the calendar year for the end of the strategy. It also marked a change of government, ending the thirteen years of Labour administration with the first coalition government in the UK since the Second World War. The challenge was how to maintain progress without a defined strategy or target, in a new context of devolved decision making and changes to the commissioning landscape (Health and Social Care Act, 2012), with no structures for supporting implementation and significant public funding cuts.

This posed many difficulties, but the strategy had some strong assets, which gave it an advantage. It had established a high level of awareness of the importance of teenage pregnancy among a wide range of stakeholders at national and local level, and notably the recognition that high rates were not inevitable. Its implementation was seen as the vanguard of effective multi-agency partnership working, and there continued to be robust and reliable data to monitor progress. It also retained committed and experienced 'champions' at national and local level who were determined not to let progress stop in the maelstrom of change. All four factors helped to make the case for a continued focus.

The need for further progress was signalled in the Department of Health's new sexual health policy, with a specific ambition to reduce under-18 and under-16 conception rates (Department of Health, 2013a), and by inclusion of the under-18 conception rate indicator in the Public Health Outcomes Framework (Department of Health, 2013b).

Using the same principle as the strategy of highlighting to other relevant programmes the relevance of teenage pregnancy and the economic benefits of progress, the need for prevention and support for young parents was included in new government priorities and guidance documents. To reiterate the importance of continued local action, the Local Government Association published *Good progress, more to do*, a briefing for locally elected leaders, making the case for why, and how, to maintain momentum (Local Government Association and Public Health England, 2016, updated 2017). In the same vein, meeting the contraception and sexual health needs of young people was included in new commissioning guidance, published by Public Health England, to help local areas manage the new and complex landscape (Public Health England, 2014, revised 2015).

The call for national leadership also came from local areas, which requested government guidance to restate the evidence and consolidate the principles of effective implementation. Developed in collaboration with local areas, two frameworks were published: *A Framework for supporting teenage mothers and young fathers* (Public Health England and Local Government Association, 2016) and *A Framework to support young people to develop healthy relationships and prevent unplanned pregnancy* (Public Health England and Local Government Association, 2017). Both highlighted the case for further action, and the importance of continuing to apply the ten key factors for an effective strategy to the current and future landscape of commissioning and service provision. Local areas were also able to access expert advice, albeit limited, from Public Health England to help them maintain or accelerate progress.

Conception data at national and local level continue to be published quarterly and Public Health England provide detailed teenage pregnancy profiles for each local government area to inform local needs assessments and commissioning. A new PHE *Maternal and Child Health* data set now provides outcomes by age of mother, which will enable closer monitoring of the impact of improved support for young parents.

As discussed in Chapter 4, the start of the accelerated downward trend in 2008 continued beyond 2010, with a 39 per cent reduction between 2010 and 2015. This is an encouraging sign that the momentum has been sustained, with an ongoing focus and continued work of local areas, some of which is illustrated in previous chapters. However, the key challenge for local areas has been, and will continue to be, the significant reduction in funding to local government. This has impacted not only on the provision of contraception and sexual health services, but also on youth services and NGOs which played a key role in reaching more marginalised young people. The cuts make it very difficult for local areas to retain a strategic coordinator function, which is essential for securing and monitoring multi-agency collaboration. There is also significantly reduced capacity for supporting specific strategy actions, such as the SRE/PSHE advisory role to support school SRE improvements.

To sustain progress in the long term in this challenging context, three game-changing actions are needed. First, SRE needs to be made statutory in all schools to ensure universal provision for children and young people, with delivery adhering to internationally recognised effectiveness factors. Second, all services, including support for young parents, should be young people friendly, reflecting the *You're Welcome* quality criteria and WHO global standards (WHO and UNAIDS, 2015). This would create a 'no wrong door' approach, widening access to trustworthy and non-judgemental advice, and reducing the need for dedicated young people's services. And third, discussion about sexual health and relationships needs to be normalised, removing the barriers of embarrassment or stigma, so young people feel that asking for advice is the right and responsible thing to do.

These changes would lay the foundations for equipping all children and young people to make safe, well-informed decisions about relationships, pregnancy and sexual health – a fundamental aspect of children's rights. By fully embedding the actions of the strategy into universal provision, it would allow local areas to use their diminishing resources to focus on targeted support and early help for those most in need.

All three changes are the focus of lobbying and strong advocacy from a wide range of NGO and professional stakeholders. In separate inquiries, five parliamentary all-party select committees recommended statutory SRE in all schools at primary and secondary level, to address not just teenage pregnancy and sexual health, but the wider issue of keeping children and young people safe – from sexual exploitation and abuse, sexual harassment, violence against women and girls and homophobic bullying – in an increasingly complex twenty-first-century world of the internet and social media. Universal SRE, delivered by trained educators, was also the recommendation of three independent reviews into child sexual exploitation in local areas. The UK Youth Parliament, which was so influential in persuading ministers to take the decision for statutory SRE in 2008, chose 'Life Lessons' (including SRE) as a priority issue for 2016, and NGOs such as Brook continue to promote the 'sex positive' campaign described in the previous chapter. Securing these changes will enshrine the key principles and actions of the strategy and sustain its impact for the long term.

In March 2017, the intensive lobbying for statutory SRE finally had the desired impact! The Conservative government announced its intention to introduce legislation for compulsory relationships education in all schools for children aged 4–11 and compulsory relationships and sex education for children aged 11–16. The government acknowledged their decision was influenced by the convincing evidence presented by the parliamentary select committees, the strong support from parents' groups and the powerful case made by young people. Notably, the decision recognised that the internet has eclipsed any previous, albeit illusory concept of children's innocence, and that government has the responsibility to equip young people to look after themselves in the twenty-first century.

> The Secretary of State for Education confirms the Government's ambition to support all young people to stay safe and prepare for life in modern Britain by making Relationships Education (Primary), Relationships and Sex Education (RSE – Secondary) . . . statutory in all schools.
>
> Given the increasing concerns around child sexual abuse and exploitation and the growing risks associated with growing up in a digital world, there is a particularly compelling case to act in relation to pupil safety.
>
> (Department for Education, 2017)

The decision was widely welcomed by the vast majority of stakeholders, including the Church of England and the Catholic Education Service (Church of England, 2017; Catholic Education Service, 2017), with very little opposition reported in the media. NGOs voiced some reservations about the distinction between relationships education and sex and relationships education, the proposal to continue the right of parents to withdraw their children from SRE and the flexibility given to faith schools to reflect their beliefs, but the announcement was nevertheless overwhelmingly celebrated as a huge step forward. The legislation is now in place and will come into effect in September 2019. The challenge now is to ensure it translates into reality for all children and young people. This will depend on the details of the regulations, the new guidance for schools, investment in the training and ongoing support of educators, and the monitoring of the quality of school programmes. Advocacy from NGOs and professional organisations will remain critical.

> Uncertainty in schools about exactly what SRE they should provide has been a factor in its patchy provision across the country. All schools want clear, unequivocal backing from the government to give them confidence to meet the challenges of training staff, gathering parental support and protecting curriculum time. Over the course of the strategy the Sex Education Forum has campaigned for statutory status, with our diverse membership of education, sexual health and faith organisations, making a powerful case to government. At last, in spring 2017, the change we have all fought for is in sight. But while we celebrate the achievement, the priority now is to help government and schools turn policy into action, so that all children and young people receive high-quality SRE throughout their school career.
>
> (Jane Lees, Chair, Sex Education Forum, 2008–17)

7.3 Applying the lessons internationally

The following case studies illustrate how the five key actions from the global consultation can be applied in widely differing countries. Nigeria provides an example of how to place adolescent sexual and reproductive health on the national agenda; India describes how to plan for scale-up from the start; Mozambique shows how to manage scale-up effectively and efficiently; Pakistan, how to build support while anticipating and addressing opposition; and Moldova illustrates how to promote and safeguard sustainability.

7.3.1 Placing ASRH scale-up on the national public health agenda

In some countries, a major shift opened up the window of opportunity. For example, independence provided the Estonia Sexual Health Association a 'never before' opportunity to initiate sexuality education and youth-friendly clinics with support from individuals and organisations in neighbouring countries such as Sweden. In other countries, a national policy decision to put in place school-based adolescent education created an opening for the Centre for Development and Population Activities, the Indian chapter of a US-based NGO, to engage with the Jharkhand state government to initiate a programme in that state. In some, political commitment had to be created through concerted lobbying by a coalition of advocates from the country with support from the outside. Nigeria is a case in point (Huaynoca et al., 2013).

With support from international NGOs such as the International Women's Health Coalition, UN agencies such as UNFPA and funders such as the MacArthur and Ford Foundations, Action Health Incorporated (AHI) led the advocacy for access to Comprehensive Sexuality Education in Nigeria. At that time, Nigeria was in a military era and efforts were more directed at getting key policy makers in Lagos State and the Federal Ministry of Education to appreciate the sexual and reproductive health, including HIV/AIDS, challenges of young people and how effective sexuality education implementation will help prevent and reduce these challenges. AHI worked with allies, including Girls' Power Initiative, National Parent–Teacher Association of Nigeria, Society for Women and AIDS in Africa (Nigerian Chapter), Adolescent Health and Information Project (Nigeria), Nigerian Medical Association, National Association of Nigerian Nurses and Midwives, Christian Health Association of Nigeria, Women's Health and Action Research Centre, and Association for Reproductive and Family Health, to advance advocacy for sexuality education in Nigeria. They knew that sexuality education was desperately needed on the one hand, and that there was a strong and vocal constituency opposed to it on the other.

In 1995, AHI identified a number of advocates and experts from allied disciplines and institutions across the country and constituted them into members of the CSE National Guidelines Task Force to adapt the US Guidelines published by Sexuality Information and Education Council of the United States (SIECUS). Thereafter the draft guidelines were distributed to over 140 organisations across the country for review and endorsements. The Federal Ministry of Education, with technical support from AHI, submitted a memo for the integration of sexuality education into the school curriculum to the National Council for Education (NCE), and the NCE made and announced its decision to integrate sexuality education in the school curriculum in 1999. In 2001, the Nigerian Education Research and Development Council, in collaboration with the Federal Ministry of Education and AHI, developed The National Sexuality Education Curriculum. The curriculum was welcomed by many but was opposed by some influential religious leaders and media from a section of the country. Under their pressure, the name of the curriculum was changed from CSE to Family Life and HIV Education, and some content that was objectionable to them was deleted. These negotiations were slow and painstaking, with the process – not surprisingly – accompanied by opposition in some quarters. An enormous amount of time and effort was devoted to forging a common understanding among different stakeholders and articulating a national policy, as summarised in Table 7.1.

A major challenge in formulating the policy was that people were often in positions of authority for short time periods. There was no guarantee that those who replaced them would uphold the positions that their predecessors did, or follow up on prior decisions. Establishing rapport and building support needed to be done and redone. This was only possible because there was continuous advocacy that ensured that sexuality education remained a priority response in assuring the health and wellbeing of adolescents and young people.

Table 7.1 Timeline from policy formation to implementation of FLHE.

Year	Activity
1995	Formation of a nationwide coalition on sexuality education
1996	Development of guidelines on CSE by a task force emerging from the coalition
1999	Decision by the National Council on Education to integrate sexuality education into the school curricula, at the First National Conference on Adolescent Reproductive Health
2000	Development of the national CSE curriculum by the National Education Research Council and Action Health Incorporated
2002	Name of curriculum was changed to FLHE due to conservative political-religious pressure. The curriculum was adopted by the FMoE with the decision to scale up
2003	Initiation of scaling up at the state level

7.3.2 Planning for scale-up from the start

Common elements feature in all the countries that have successfully scaled up ASRH programmes. First, they institutionalised ASRH scale-up in national policies and strategies. This took considerable time in some places, for example Nigeria, but was quicker in others such as Mozambique. Second, they clearly identified the interventions that were to be scaled up and defined exactly what each would consist of. For example, the Family Life and HIV Education (FLHE) programme in Nigeria precisely defined who would be reached (students in junior secondary school), by whom ('carrier' teachers, e.g. science teachers who would carry out FLHE in addition to the subjects they were responsible for), with what content (a detailed curriculum with learning materials for teachers and students was distributed to each school and teachers were trained in their use), when (an incremental year-by-year curriculum was clearly spelled out in the curriculum) and where (in school). Third, they identified the government institution that would oversee the scale-up effort. In Nigeria this was the Federal Ministry of Education, and in Moldova, described below, the Ministry of Health. Finally, they made difficult operational choices on issues such as:

1 Whether the scale-up process should be phased or not.
2 Whether it would be guided by a central institution, or by provincial/state-level institutions.
3 What would be the extent of involvement of other stakeholders, e.g. academic institutions and NGOs.
4 How the scale-up effort would be integrated into existing systems, e.g. for developing educational materials or for building the capacities of educators and health workers; and how these systems would be strengthened.

5   How the scale-up effort would be integrated into existing monitoring and health/education information systems; and how these systems would be strengthened.

One common area of weakness was that most countries did not develop costed plans. In retrospect they realised this was a weakness. Another area of weakness was that while, in some countries, the scale-up of sexuality education was combined with efforts to make health service provision adolescent friendly, in some others this was not done.

Mozambique provides an excellent example of a cleverly and strategically planned programme (Chandra-Mouli et al., 2015). The objectives of the programme – later branded Geracao Biz (Busy Generation) – were: 'To improve Adolescent Sexual and Reproductive Health, including a reduction in the incidence of early and unintended pregnancy, Sexually Transmitted Infections and Human Immuno-Deficiency Virus infections, through activities that equip young people with the knowledge, skills and services needed for positive behaviour change.' From the outset, Geracao Biz was a truly multi-sectoral programme involving three sectors. The Ministries of Health, Education, and Youth and Sport were the key implementers of this initiative. Government staff from each of these sectors worked with community-based organisations, including youth organisations, and young people to deliver three complementary interventions entwined with each other – youth-friendly clinical services, school-based education and community-based outreach.

To facilitate collaboration, a strong coordination mechanism was put in place – at the national, provincial and district levels, as shown in Figure 7.1. Young people were active members of coordination committees at all three levels.

The initiative was launched in 1999 in two pilot sites. Over the next ten years, it was scaled up to cover all the provinces of the country. In addition to expanding activities into additional provinces, there was expansion within provinces so as to reach large numbers of adolescents.

> The vitality of the youth movement that has been nurtured under Geracao Biz is an integral part of the program. Young people not only participate in the program design, implementation, and evaluation, but they also identify new areas that are of importance and advocate for the policy makers to respond to these needs, demonstrating that they can be leaders in solving their own issues. Beginning with the end in mind is fundamental to design a program that will be scalable. It is also crucial to nurture a new generation.
>
> Julio Pacca, Senior Advisor, Pathfinder International

7.3.3 Managing scale-up effectively and efficiently

Good management was the hallmark of countries that scaled up their ASRH programmes. This included, first, efforts to ensure that players with the required

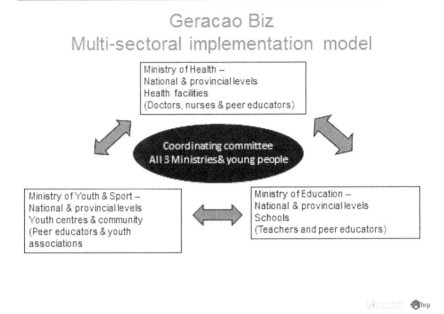

Figure 7.1 Geracao Biz – Implementation model and coordination mechanism.

attributes were engaged to contribute to the evolving effort; second, that resources needed for programme scale-up were secured; third, that there was a shared understanding of the level of quality to be achieved and sustained, and a system was put in place to do this; fourth, that there was a similar commitment and system to assure equity; and finally, that data were gathered and used to make well-informed programmatic decisions.

A number of players contributed technically to the scale-up effort. In all countries, one or more government ministries led the effort. Indigenous NGOs and academics played key roles in some, but not all places, and youth organisations and networks were involved but not widely tapped into. External players included international NGOs, UN agencies, bilateral agencies, and foundations. One challenge was coordination. Where coordination mechanisms were functional (as in Mozambique), they helped to facilitate joint work. Where they were not (as in India), dogged efforts kept the lead government ministry/ministries engaged and involved. A second challenge was to bring new players on board as the scale-up effort evolved. In Colombia, for example, to address the problem of lack of sense of ownership of health facilities and their poor uptake by young people, especially by those from indigenous communities, a more active effort was made to work with local government departments and civil society bodies to set up community oversight committees.

Ensuring adequate resources over an extended period, including staff, materials to provide CSE/SE and adolescent-friendly health services and funds, was central to the scale-up effort. Internal resources came primarily from national governments; external ones came from governmental and non-governmental funders and UN agencies. Government funding ranged from substantial and consistent, for example in Argentina, to limited in Pakistan. Donor funding, too, ranged from substantial and long term as in Mozambique, or limited and in two-year cycles initially in Moldova. In all places, governments contributed in kind through the use of staff and facilities (clinics and schools). All countries devoted considerable efforts to maintain support through the scale-up effort. This included financial support, further discussed in section 7.3.7 on promoting and sustaining sustainability, and in securing the deployment of human resources to deliver CSE/SE and adolescent-friendly health services and/or to manage this effort.

Countries were well aware that with scale-up, quality was likely to decline, especially if the pace of scale-up was rapid. To address this, many countries defined national quality standards. Using these standards and criteria, they supported quality assessments, for example for sexuality education in Argentina and Nigeria and for adolescent-friendly health services in Moldova and Malawi. These assessments were followed by quality improvements by formal and informal teams. Despite the efforts that many countries made, quality declined with scale-up.

Countries were also well aware that without deliberate efforts, marginalised groups of adolescents could be bypassed in the scale-up effort. To prevent this, some countries – but not all of them – put in place deliberate strategies to expand equitable coverage. For example, the adolescent education programme in Pakistan was directed at both boys and girls, and operated in private, public and religious schools, and the multi-component Mozambique programme reached out to young people in and out of school. In Argentina and Nigeria, there was a dedicated effort to advocate for the scale-up effort in more conservative provinces of the country. Despite these efforts, there was clear recognition that much more needed to be done.

Many of the countries assessed the outcomes of their scale-up efforts. They assessed and could point to changes in knowledge and understanding, and to changes in behaviours, for example sexual behaviour and contraceptive use and/or condom use. Only some tracked, and could point to, changes in health outcomes. Countries used these data to advocate for continued investment, as discussed in section 7.3.7 on promoting and safeguarding sustainability. They also used them to reshape their efforts. For example, the positive outcomes of SE efforts in Lagos State fed into the development of an implementation guide for use elsewhere in the country.

7.3.4 Scaling up a school-based adolescent education programme in India

The scale-up of Udaan, a school-based adolescent education programme, in Jharkhand State, India, illustrates how each of these five issues has been addressed (Chandra-Mouli *et al.*, 2016). In a number of Indian states, school-based adolescent health education programmes have been halted because of opposition from some groups in the community, or have slowly run into the ground. The Udaan programme is an exception; it has been scaled up state-wide in Jharkhand, India, between 2006 and 2016. The programme began reaching students in classes 9–11 and has now been extended to students in classes 6–8. Exploring this in more detail highlights the ingredients of success.

First, the Udaan programme is owned and managed by the state government and the NGO, the Centre for Catalysing Change (C3), has provided the state government with technical support throughout the scale-up effort. Second, the state government provides all the human resources and infrastructure for delivering the programme in schools through trained and supported teachers, and for supervising the effort through dedicated functionaries at state and district level. It also covers the cost of producing and disseminating the educational materials for teachers and students. The Packard Foundation supports C3's technical support effort. Third, quality assurance of classroom teaching is a key area of Udaan's focus. To achieve this, C3 works to ensure the quality of teacher training (including in-service and pre-service training), to conduct retraining and to carry out periodic monitoring visits in schools. This is complemented with periodic external evaluations. Between 2007 and 2010, five external evaluations were conducted. Each examined the quality of the classroom teaching and the factors that contributed to this, in addition to effects on students. Lessons learned on factors that helped and hindered the scale-up effort fed into strengthening the effort. Fourth, efforts were made to improve equitable coverage. C3 worked with the government to include all the schools in the scale-up effort, including the residential Kasturba Gandhi Balika Vidyalayas, which are part of the state government's efforts to enrol girls from the poorest families and communities. Finally, based on needs assessment studies, C3 secured the approval of the state government to extend education programmes from children in classes 9 to 11 to younger pupils in classes 6 to 8. In short, the sustained scale-up of Udaan was helped by a number of factors, but key to this was the shared commitment of C3 and the state government to oversee the implementation, and to continually improve it.

7.3.5 Building support while anticipating and addressing opposition

In most of the countries, scale-up of sexuality and reproductive health programmes faced resistance because of the sensitivities – especially but not only religious – associated with adolescent sexuality. In some places, this resistance was strong, persistent or recurring, and came from a variety of community sources. Building support and dealing with resistance at all stages of the scale-up effort was a key element of the work of these countries.

On the one hand, the countries engaged proactively and strategically with different stakeholders to build alliances and champions, thereby making progress even in difficult circumstances. The drivers of Argentina's sexuality education programme pressed for support, referring to guiding principles in foundational documents such as the national constitution. Nigeria's proactive and energetic advocacy efforts began early and extended from national to state and local levels as scale-up progressed. Government and non-government players who led the effort in Senegal actively engaged with influential community leaders and members to dispel myths and to find common denominators on issues of shared concern.

On the other hand, the countries anticipated and responded promptly and effectively to opposition from civil society groups and to negative media coverage. A key challenge many faced was pressure to dilute the content of the intervention, for example pressure to leave out discussion on contraceptives in comprehensive sexuality education, and to limit the provision of contraceptives and condoms to married adolescents only.

7.3.6 Effective strategic advocacy in Pakistan

The efforts by a coalition of NGOs in Pakistan, to strategically choose issues to address in their adolescent education work, to carefully frame these issues, to build community support for their work and to stand up to attacks, is particularly impressive.

First, in Pakistan as in many other countries, initiatives providing sexual and reproductive health education face a lot of resistance. The widespread belief that adolescents – especially girls – are not meant to be sexually active before marriage is a particular obstacle to teaching these topics. Recognising these deep-seated barriers, two leading NGOs working in this area – Aahung and Rutgers WPF – adapted World Health Organization guidelines for life skills-based education (LSBE) to the local context. LSBE aims to inform students about health while equipping them with skills to better manage their own lives and make healthier decisions. Language matters, so both organisations describe their work as LSBE instead of sex education, which is a highly controversial term in Pakistan. Second, having consulted local communities, Aahung recognised it would be culturally inappropriate to directly address sensitive topics such as pre-marital sexual activity by providing information on contraceptives. Instead, the organisation targets related problems identified by communities, including child marriage and gender-based violence. Aahung simultaneously serves these community interests while adhering to internationally established recommendations by focusing on common intermediate outcomes, such as knowledge of sexual and reproductive health and rights, comfort with one's own body, communication skills, confidence and decision-making abilities.

Third, Aahung carried out a 'power mapping' exercise to identify influential community members. It then worked to gain support – from local organisations, such as religious groups and school associations, up to the Department of Education – by organising a series of communication-focused activities, learning forums, sharing briefing notes and holding face-to-face meetings. Realising that the support of parents and the wider community was also crucial for reaching adolescents, Aahung supported them with counselling by school administrators and teachers. It also conducted public theatre performances and discussion sessions to demystify LSBE and win people over to its way of working. Rutgers WPF created a Parents Involvement Strategy in 2011 to contribute to the same objective.

Fourth, both organisations encountered occasional resistance to their work. In 2011 and 2012, Rutgers WPF was criticised, for 'breaking the moral fabric of Pakistan' and corrupting the minds of pupils, by conservative media outlets linked to a religious political party, Jamat-ul-Islami. Following discussions in parliament, the organisation's work in Punjab was stopped, and in Sindh, it was advised to get the content vetted by religious scholars. Rutgers WPF linked up with the media to respond to this backlash. It reached out to a small group of respected and well-known journalists from print, radio and television to help facilitate a dialogue with mass media personnel in the affected provinces. This stimulated public discussion of the vulnerabilities of adolescents and how LBSE could address them. Additionally, school visits demonstrated to media personnel how the programme increased the confidence and performance of its students and teachers. They saw for themselves that the accusations about Rutgers WPF – for example that it was teaching 11-year-old children how to have sex – were false. The participating journalists went on to produce a number of stories about what they learned.

Rutgers WPF also arranged for progressive religious scholars to review the content of the LBSE curriculum and to supplement its content with messages from the Koran. This work fed into a series of meetings with parliamentarians, policy makers, religious scholars and media personnel that culminated in permission to resume LSBE in schools in Sindh. While Aahung also had its content reviewed by a technical committee of teachers, Department of Education administrators and religious scholars, it chose not to mix religious content into the curriculum. Instead, it used a human-rights-based approach to bring legitimacy to its work. Both Aahung and Rutgers WPF recognise that it's not enough to run effective education programmes if they are not accepted locally or by society at large. Even so, they realise that backlash from misguided individuals and organisations, including the media, will occur from time to time. A two-pronged approach, whereby they communicate with communities while working with the media, secures both organisations' local support as well as a network of journalists ready to champion their cause in the face of heated opposition (Svanemyr *et al.*, 2015; Jahangir and Mankani, 2016).

7.3.7 Promoting and safeguarding sustainability

Countries that have sustained their scale-up efforts worked on three complementary fronts. First, they worked hard to sustain engagement and ownership
by government officials at national and subnational levels. This was a challenge
in many cases because retirements, transfers and reshuffles meant that officials
with no previous knowledge or appreciation of the decisions made, or the work
done, were now in positions to make decisions about continued support for
the scale-up effort. In some cases, decisions about government policy, for example whether to provide dedicated services to adolescents in Ecuador or to
do so within the context of an overall response, changed radically. In the
context of the state-wide scale-up of sexuality education in Jharkhand State,
India, the Centre for Catalysing Change addressed this by keeping Education
Department government officials at the state and district levels informed about
progress in the scale-up of the adolescent education programme. By pointing
to small and big successes and recognition by national authorities, the organisation consolidated the support of the authorities.

Second, countries such as Argentina sought to create 'demand' for continued
sexuality education from civil society groups and the community at large, as
a means of securing popular support for the effort in cash and in kind, and to
provide a bulwark of support and safety in case government support faltered.

Third, countries such as Estonia and Moldova reduced the reliance of the
scale-up effort on external sources by incorporating some of the costs into
national health insurance, although they still required some top-up funding.
Others such as Mozambique and Pakistan tried hard to diversify their funding sources so that they were not entirely reliant on one or a small number of
donors. Two overall lessons emerged from the experiences of the countries:
(1) ensuring the sustainability of the scale-up effort requires a combination of
approaches and should be an ongoing effort; and (2) despite these efforts, even
well-established scale-up programmes can run into the ground or collapse if
they lose political support, as Ecuador did, or financial support as South
Africa did.

7.3.8 Scaling up and sustaining youth-friendly health centres in Moldova

Moldova's experience is illustrative. In 2001, the government of Moldova
responded to the health needs of young people, as part of a multifaceted effort,
by beginning to invest in youth-friendly health centres (YFHC). In 2002–2003,
it set up three pilot YFHCs with support from UNICEF. This evolved to a
network of twelve centres by 2005, with continuing support from UNICEF,
the International Development Agency, the World Bank and the Swiss Agency
for Development and Cooperation. In 2007, YFHCs that had been operating
as distinct projects became sub-divisions of existing primary health facilities,

and, from 2008, the National Health Insurance Company started to finance them.

In 2009, the Ministry of Health approved Quality Standards of Youth Friendly Health Services (YFHS), developed with WHO's support. This provided the basis to plan and implement actions at the national and subnational levels for quality improvement and to advocate for national-wide scaling-up (Chandra-Mouli *et al.*, 2013b). A systematic process of scaling up the YFHS was initiated by the Ministry of Health in 2011 with the support of the project 'Healthy Generation – scaling up of YFHS in Republic of Moldova' implemented by 'Health for Youth', an NGO in partnership with UNICEF, with funding from the Swiss Agency for Development and Cooperation. In the process of YFHS scale-up, a pre-service education component was integrated into the medical education curriculum. In 2014, the scale-up process was externally evaluated (Carai *et al.*, 2015) and a costing exercise conducted (Kempers *et al.*, 2014). These exercises validated the scale-up effort and further consolidated the place of YFHS in the National Health Insurance Company's list. By 2016, thirty-nine YFHSs were delivering the required package of health services according to defined quality standards in thirty-five districts and two municipalities across the country. Indigenous funds cover 70 per cent of the costs of the scale-up effort, but top-up funding is still required (Lesco, 2016).

In summary, the main factors that contribute to the sustainability of YFHS in Moldova are: strong governmental commitment; a supportive normative framework; National Health Insurance Company financing of the YFHS, which was grounded in quality assessments and economic evaluations; continued technical and financial support of UN organisations and international donors; and the dedication of a core team of professionals passionately committed to moving the adolescent health agenda forward (Lesco, 2016).

7.4 Moving forward: harnessing experience, political leadership and collective commitment!

The England strategy and the other country case studies in this chapter illustrate the wealth of expertise and understanding of how to develop and implement scaled-up national programmes to improve adolescent sexual and reproductive health. The good news is that we now have the political commitment, the technical consensus and the resources to build on this experience.

In 2010, Mr. Ban Ki-moon, the United Nations Secretary-General, launched a Global Strategy for Women's and Children's Health (2010, updated 2015). The Strategy was aimed at stepping up global efforts to reduce childhood and maternal mortality, two key Millennium Development Goals. In the call for action the Secretary-General said: 'Every year, millions of women and children die from preventable causes. They are not mere statistics. They are people with names and faces. Their suffering is unacceptable in the twenty-first century.' The global community responded to his call for action. The 2015 Millennium

Development Goals Report announced that between 1990 and 2015, the global under-5 mortality rate declined by more than half from 90 to 43 deaths per 1000 births, and the maternal mortality ratio was cut nearly in half from 580 to 210 deaths per 100,000 live births in women aged 15–49, with much of the progress occurring in the years leading up to the target date.

However, the Report noted that while there has been impressive progress, this has not been equitable – between and within countries and communities. To address this 'unfinished business', Secretary-General Ban Ki-moon launched a revised Global Strategy for Women's, Children's and Adolescents' Health. A significant departure from the previous strategy is its strong focus on adolescence. In his call for action in 2015, the Secretary-General said: 'The updated Global Strategy includes adolescents because they are central to everything we want to achieve, and to the overall success of the 2030 Agenda.' The Secretary-General's statement reflects the growing acceptance of the health, economic and human rights rationale for investing in the health and development of adolescents. A concrete expression of the increased consensus on the need to invest in adolescents' health and development is that four of the seventeen Sustainable Development Goals include explicit targets related to adolescent health.

Funding agencies are committing substantial resources to address health conditions such as HIV infection and social problems such as early and forced marriage, and to expand the delivery of interventions such as the Human Papilloma Virus vaccine, contraceptives and menstrual care products. Technical agencies are speaking with one voice about what interventions need to be delivered and how this needs to be done. And there is a growing experience base to build upon. As Laski and colleagues noted, this is a 'never before' moment in adolescent health, which we must put to full use (2015).

Key to success will be the collective passion of individuals in many countries who are committed to improving the choices and life chances of young people. Individuals in NGOs, professions and academia, who gather evidence to build consensus and challenge the denial of young people's rights, believe that change is possible and never give up! Those individuals drove the success of the England strategy and were also the catalysts for change in the other country case studies. It will be this commitment combined with political leadership and the sharing of expertise that will help all countries make progress – whether they are at the start of the journey or, like England, building on success to secure improvements for future generations.

Notes

1   Africa: Ethiopia, Malawi, Mozambique, Nigeria, Senegal and South Africa. Central and Eastern Europe: Belarus, Estonia and Moldova. Latin America: Argentina, Columbia and Ecuador. Asia: India and Pakistan. High-income countries: England, Finland, Netherlands and Colorado in the USA.

2   Sex and relationships education (SRE) or Relationships and Sex Education (RSE) are the terms used in the UK, so are referred to in the discussion of the England strategy. The international terms of Comprehensive sexuality education (CSE) and Sexuality Education (SE) are used in the case studies from other countries.

3   In the UK, general practitioners are medical professionals who treat acute and chronic illnesses and provide preventive care and are the first and most commonly used first contact with the NHS. The vast majority of the population is registered with a general practitioner.

Epilogue

This book has focused much on the policy aspects of teenage pregnancy – how the strategy was developed, the complexities of implementation and transferable lessons for other countries. But as I mentioned in my introduction, the teenage pregnancy strategy was all about making a difference to young people's lives, so I wanted to end with the voices of some young people, and those who were involved in translating the strategy into action.

There is of course much more to do, globally and in England, to ensure children and young people's rights to high-quality information and reproductive choices, to narrow inequalities and ensure all young parents are able to fulfil their ambitions without stigma or judgement.

However, eighteen years since the strategy was launched, it feels important to reflect on how much has changed for the better. In 1999, I edited a book – *Tough Choices: young women talk about pregnancy* – in which young women, in their own words, described their experiences of getting pregnant, making the decision whether or not to continue the pregnancy, and their journey through abortion or into motherhood. Reading their stories again, I was struck by how isolated they were and how little support they received.

Today, reading the many comments from young people gathered by local areas, I'm instead struck by how much the landscape of support has changed and how the strategy actions have touched and influenced young people's lives. This selection is a tiny fraction of the positive feedback, but gives a flavour of what a difference good prevention and support services can make.

> They came into school and our class talked about sex and stuff – it was really easy to ask questions and I didn't feel stupid. My boyfriend wanted us to have sex, but I didn't want to as I was scared about getting pregnant. They talked about us being ready and it being a big decision, and then if we wanted to, to make sure we were protected against infections and pregnancy. I went to the drop-in and saw someone that talked to me about different contraception. They made me an appointment and also gave me condoms. I go back now to say hi and see the nurse when I need to.
>
> (Young woman, aged 15)

I came first for the full (STI) screening. I was scared but the staff were really helpful and now I come on a regular basis. I come in for condoms and stay for an hour or so to discuss other things, or just to chit-chat.

(Young man, aged 17)

I have really bad anxiety so coming to 'Young Mums' helps a lot with that because I've made great friends here and we talk about things. . . . it's a great support because the kids learn in the crèche and so do we. It's good to get back into education because it's difficult with young children and I didn't really like school. This is different and it's relaxed, but we learn.

(Young mother attending Young Mums Will
Achieve support group)

[It was] the best support you can have really. . . . I didn't have a clue what I was doing, like, I was skiving school . . . but he got me referred onto college, and that got me back into education, right. . . . Well I'd have been lost [without him].

(Young father, attending a specialist mentoring
scheme)

And this is how the changes felt to some of the local teenage pregnancy champions who were involved throughout the strategy:

Working on the teenage pregnancy strategy was about more than reducing the conception rate. It was the opportunity to change the lives of a generation of young people for the better, through good education and skill development so they can make positive health choices and cope with the challenges they may experience in life. We have achieved a big reduction in the conception rate, but it is the feedback from young people that tells the real story. Improvements in the quality of their sex and relationships education, easier access to advice in young people services, and a youth-friendly workforce so whoever they turn to for advice is confident to help.

(Gail Teasdale, Hull)

If you get it right for young people you can see amazing changes. The teenage pregnancy strategy has brought together some great people to learn, share, make mistakes and tackle things differently. When I hear young people say 'it's so easy in Brighton to know where to get condoms and have a chlamydia test', or that they've already chosen which contraception method they want to use, it makes me smile because it really wasn't the case at the beginning. Over the course of the strategy the culture changed.

(Kerry Clarke, Brighton and Hove)

I look back on my time as a teenage pregnancy coordinator as one of the most fulfilling periods in my working life. All the elements needed to make something work were there. This was a government priority but it wasn't just a priority written on paper. It had strategic support, infrastructure, clear guidance and funding. We knew what we wanted to achieve and had a clear plan of how we would get there. The work was always rewarding. This wasn't a punitive approach to early sexual activity or teenage parenthood but an opportunity to support young people to celebrate their sexuality and make informed choices about their relationships and their sexual health. Over the ten years, the improvements in SRE and the development of services like the school-based health clinics became embedded as part of young people's lives. How lucky am I to have been part of something that made such a difference. My fear now is that initiatives that were part of our success are starting to be eroded by funding cuts. As our rates have dropped it becomes harder to maintain the funding!

(Anne Colquhoun, Bristol)

This last small note of caution about disinvestment is an important reminder that the strategy's success was not magic! It resulted from good policy, extraordinary collaboration between national and local government, health partners, NGOs and professional organisations – and sustained resources. Cultures have changed, with high teenage pregnancy rates no longer seen as inevitable if young people are given choices. Much of the strategy's innovation has become normal practice, and government's announcement of statutory relationships and sex education, from 2019, should embed the foundations of knowledge and skills in all schools. But the principles of the strategy, on both prevention and supporting young parents, need to continue to be applied. Much will continue to be achieved through advocacy and committed individuals. But passion will need to be accompanied by adequate resources so successive generations of young people are equipped to make well-informed choices and to ensure the amazing progress made doesn't start to unravel.

The journey continues!

References

Action for Children (2017). *The Next Chapter: Young People and Parenthood*. London.

Advocates for Youth. (2007). *The History of Federal Abstinence-Only Funding*. Washington, DC: Advocates for Youth. http://www.advocatesforyouth.org/storage/advfy/documents/fshistoryabonly.pdf.

Arai, L. (2009). *Teenage Pregnancy: The Making and Unmaking of a Problem*. Bristol: The Policy Press.

Aspinall, P.J. and Hashem, F. (2010). Are our data on teenage pregnancy across ethnic groups in England fit for the purpose of policy formulation, implementation, and monitoring? *Critical Public Health*, 20(1), 47–70.

Barnes, J., Ball, M. and Meadows, P. (2012). *Nurse Family Partnership Implementation Evaluation*. London: Birkbeck University of London.

Bates, L. (2015). *Everyday Sexism*. London: Simon & Schuster.

Bates, L. (2016). *Girl Up*. London: Simon & Schuster.

Berrington, A.M., Diamond, I., Ingham, R. and Stevenson, J. (2005a). *Consequences of Teenage Parenthood: Pathways Which Minimise the Long Term Negative Impacts of Teenage Childbearing*. Final report submitted to the Department of Health, Social Sciences and Demography, University of Southampton.

Berrington, A.M., Cobos Hernandez, M.I., Ingham, R. and Stevenson, J. (2005b). *Antecedents and Outcomes of Young Fatherhood: Longitudinal Evidence from the 1970 British Birth Cohort Study*. S3RI Applications and Policy Working Papers, A05/09: University of Southampton, UK.

Bozon, M. and Kontula, O. (1998). Sexual initiation and gender in Europe: a cross-cultural analysis of trends in the twentieth century, in Hubert, M., Bajos, N. and Sandfort, T. (eds) *Sexual Behaviour and HIV/AIDS in Europe*. London: UCL Press, pp. 37–67.

Breuner, C.C., Mattson, G., AAP Committee on Adolescence and AAP Committee on Psychosocial Aspects of Child and Family Health. (2016). Sexuality education for children and adolescents, *Pediatrics*, 138(2), e20161348.

British Association for Sexual Health and HIV (BASHH) and Brook. (2014). *Spotting the Signs: A National Proforma for Identifying Risk of Child Sexual Exploitation in Sexual Health Services*. London: BASHH and Brook.

Broadhurst, K., Bachar, A., Yeem, E., Harwin, J., Shaw, M., Pilling, M., Mason, C. and Kershaw, S. (2015). Connecting events in time to identify a hidden population: Birth mothers and their children in recurrent care proceedings in England. *British Journal of Social Work*, 45(8), 2241–2260.

Brook. (1998). *Someone with a Smile Would Be Your Best Bet*. London: Brook.

Brook. (2008a). *Sexual Health Outreach: Why, What and How*. London: Brook.

Brook. (2008b, updated 2014). *C-Card Condom Distribution Schemes: Why, What and How*. London: Brook.

Brook. (2010). *Young Men, Sex and Pregnancy: Practical Guidance on Effective Approaches*. London: Brook.

Brook. (2013). *Sexual Behaviours Traffic Light Tool*. London: Brook.

Brook. (2014). *Teenage Conceptions: Statistics and Trends*. London: Brook.

Brook. (2017). *Privacy and Confidentiality*. London: Brook.

Brook, PSHE Association and Sex Education Forum. (2014). *Sex and Relationships Education (SRE) for the 21st Century: Supplementary advice to the SRE guidance DfEE (0116/2000)*. London: Brook, PSHE Association and Brook.

Burchett, H. and Seeley, A. (2003). *Good Enough to Eat: The Diet of Pregnant Teenagers*. London: Maternity Alliance and the Food Commission.

Carai, S., Bivol, S. and Chandra-Mouli, V. (2015). Assessing youth-friendly-health-services and supporting planning in the Republic of Moldova. *Reproductive Health*, 12, 98.

Chan, D.L. and Sullivan, E.A. (2008). Teenage smoking in pregnancy and birthweight: A population study, 2001–2004. *Medical Journal of Australia*, 188(7), 392–396.

Chandra-Mouli, V., Bloem, P. and Ferguson, J. (2013a). The World Health Organisation's work on adolescent sexual and reproductive health. *Bundesgesundheitsbl*, 5, 256–261.

Chandra-Mouli, V., Baltag, V. and Ogbaselassie, L. (2013b). Strategies to scale up and sustain youth friendly health services in the Republic of Moldova. *BioMedCentral Public Health*, 13, 284.

Chandra-Mouli, V., Gibbs, S., Badiani, R., Quinhas, F. and Svanemyr, J. (2015). Programa Geracao Biz, Mozambique: How did this adolescent health initiative grow from a pilot to a national programme, and what did it achieve? *Reproductive Health*, 12, 12.

Chandra-Mouli, V., Plesons, M., Barua, A., Patnaik, A., Gogoi, A., Katoch, M., Ziauddin, M., Mishra, R. and Sinha, A. (2016). What did it take to scale up and sustain Udaan, a school-based adolescent education programme in Jharkhand, India? Submitted.

Connolly, A., Pietri, G., Yu, J. and Humphreys, S. (2014). Association between long-acting reversible contraceptive use, teenage pregnancy, and abortion rates in England. *International Journal of Women's Health*, 6, 961–974.

Crawford, C., Cribb, J. and Kelly, E. (2013). *Teenage Pregnancy in England*. CAYT Impact Study, report number 6. London: Centre for Analysis of Youth Transitions, NatCen, IoE, IFS.

Cresswell, J., Yu, G., Heatherall, B., *et al.* (2013). Predictors and timing of initiation of antenatal care in an ethnically diverse urban cohort in the UK. *BMC Pregnancy and Childbirth*, 12, 103.

Darroch, J.E., Singh, S., Frost, J.J. and the Study Team. (2001). Differences in teenage pregnancy rates among five developed countries: The roles of sexual activity and contraceptive use. *Family Planning Perspectives*, 33(6), 244–281.

Davidson, N. (2003). *Building Bridges: Integrating School SRE and Contraceptive Services for Young Men*. London: Working with Men.

Dawson, N. and Hosie, A. (2005). *The Education of Pregnant Young Women and Young Mothers in England*. Bristol, UK: University of Bristol.

Department for Children, Schools and Families. (2006). *Extended Schools: Improving Access to Sexual Health Services*. London: DCSF.

Department for Children, Schools and Families. (2008). *Teenage Parents: Who Cares? A Guide to Commissioning and Delivering Maternity Services for Young Parents*. London: DCSF.

Department for Children, Schools and Families. (2008a). *Government Response to the 4th Annual Report of the Teenage Pregnancy Independent Advisory Group*. London: DCSF.

Department for Children, Schools and Families. (2008b). *Review of Sex and Relationships Education (SRE) in Schools. A Report by the External Steering Group. Issues*. London: DCSF.

Department for Children, Schools and Families. (2008c). *Government Response to the Report by the Sex and Relationships Education (SRE) Review Steering Group*. London: DCSF.

Department for Children, Schools and Families. (2009). *Government Response to the 5th Annual Report of the Teenage Pregnancy Independent Advisory Group*. London: DCSF.

Department for Children, Schools and Families and Department of Health. (2007). *Teenage Parents, Next Steps. Guidance for Local Authorities and Primary Care Trusts*. London: DCSF.

Department for Children, Schools and Families and Department of Health. (2009). *Teenage Pregnancy Prevention and Support: A Self-Assessment Toolkit for Local Performance Management*. London: DCSF and Department of Health.

Department for Children, Schools and Families and Department of Health. (2010). *Teenage Pregnancy Strategy: Beyond 2010*. London: DCSF and Department of Health.

Department for Education. (2010). *The Importance of Teaching. The Schools White Paper 2010*. London: DfE.

Department for Education. (2012). *New Learning from Serious Case Reviews: A Two Year Report for 2009–11*. London: DfE.

Department for Education. (2016). *Keeping Children Safe in Education: Statutory Guidance for Schools and Colleges*. London: DfE.

Department for Education. (2017). *Policy Statement: Relationships Education, Relationships and Sex Education and Personal, Social, Health and Economic Education*. London: DfE.

Department for Education and Employment. (2000). *Sex and Relationship Guidance*. Ref DfEE 0116/2000. London: DfEE.

Department for Education and Skills. (2004a). *Every Child Matters: Change for Children*. London: DfES.

Department for Education and Skills. (2004b). *Enabling Young People to Access Contraception and Sexual Health Information and Advice: Legal and Policy Framework for Social Workers, Residential Social Workers, Foster Carers and Other Social Care Practitioners*. London: DfES.

Department for Education and Skills. (2005). *Enabling Young People to Access Contraceptive and Sexual Health Advice: Guidance for Youth Support Workers*. London: DfES.

Department for Education and Skills. (2006a). *Teenage Pregnancy: Accelerating the strategy to 2010*. London: DfES.

Department for Education and Skills. (2006b). *Teenage Pregnancy Next Steps: Guidance for Local Authorities and Primary Care Trusts on Effective Delivery of Local Strategies*. London: DfES.

Department for Education and Skills. (2007). *Targeted Youth Support: A Guide*. London: DfES.

Department for Education and Skills and Department of Health. (2006a). *Teenage Pregnancy: Working Towards 2010. Good Practice and Self-Assessment Toolkit*. London: DfES and DH.

Department for Education and Skills and Department of Health. (2006b). *Sure Start Children's Centres Practice Guidance*. London: DfES and DH.

Department for Education and Skills, Department of Health and Association of Colleges. (2007). *Improving Access to Sexual Health Services for Young People in Further Education Settings*. London: DfES.

Department for Work and Pensions. (2006). *Proportion of Teenage Mothers in Education, Training or Employment in England, 2004–06 from Labour Force Survey Households Spring Datasets*. London: DWP.

Department of Health. (1992). *Health of the Nation: A Strategy for Health in England*. London: HMSO.

Department of Health. (2000). *Best Practice Guidance on the Provision of Effective Contraceptive and Advice Services for Young People*. London: Department of Health.

Department of Health. (2000, updated 2004). *Best Practice Guidance for Doctors and Other Health Professionals on the Provision of Advice and Treatment to Young People under 16 on Contraception, Sexual and Reproductive Health*. London: Department of Health.

Department of Health. (2001a). *Independent Advisory Group on Teenage Pregnancy. First annual report*. London: Department of Health.

Department of Health. (2001b). *The National Strategy for Sexual Health and HIV*. London: Department of Health.

Department of Health. (2004a). *Choosing Health: Making Healthy Choices Easier*. London: Department of Health.

Department of Health. (2004b). *National Service Framework for Children, Young People and Maternity*. London: Department of Health.

Department of Health. (2005, updated 2007 and 2011). *You're Welcome: Quality Criteria for Young People Friendly Health Services*. London: Department of Health.

Department of Health. (2011). *Teenage Pregnancy National Support Team: Evaluation of Impact*. London: Department of Health.

Department of Health. (2013a). *A Framework for Sexual Health Improvement in England*. London: Department of Health.

Department of Health. (2013b). *Public Health Outcomes Framework 2013–2016*. London: Department of Health.

Department of Health. (2016). *Abortion Statistics England and Wales: 2015*. London. Department of Health.

Department of Health and Department for Children Schools and Families. (2008, updated 2015). *Getting Maternity Services Right for Pregnant Teenagers and Young Fathers*. London: Public Health England, Department of Health and Royal College of Midwives.

Department of Health and Department for Education and Employment. (2001). *National Healthy School Standard: Sex and relationships education*. London: Department of Health and DfEE.

Department of Health and Department for Education and Skills. (2004). *National Service Framework for Children, Young People and Maternity Services*. London: Department of Health.

Department of Health and Department for Children, Schools and Families. (2009). *Teenage Pregnancy and Sexual Health Marketing Strategy.* London: Department of Health and DCSF.

Department of Health (Teenage Pregnancy Unit). (2001). *Guidance for Field Social Workers, Residential Social Workers and Foster Carers on Providing Information and Referring Young People to Contraceptive and Sexual Health Services.* London: Department of Health.

Department of Health and Teenage Pregnancy Unit. (2001). *Guidance for Youth Workers on Providing Information and Referring Young People to Contraceptive and Sexual Health Services.* London: Department of Health.

Diamond, I., Clements, S., Stone, N. and Ingham, R. (1999). Spatial variation in teenage conceptions in south and west England. *Journal of the Royal Statistical Society Series A (Statistics in Society)*, 162(3), 273–289.

Duncan, S., Edwards, R. and Alexander, C. (eds) (2010). *Teenage Parenthood: What's the Problem?* London: Tufnell Press.

Early Intervention Foundation. (2015). *Early Intervention Foundation Guidebook.* London: EIF.

Eborall, C. and Garmeson, K. (2000). *Teenage Pregnancy in England: Desk Research to Inform the National Campaign.* London: Teenage Pregnancy Unit.

Education for Choice. (2004). *Abortion: Rights, Responsibilities and Reason – A Cross Curricula Resource.* London: Education for Choice.

Ermisch, J. and Pevalin, D.J. (2003). *Does a 'Teen-birth' Have Longer-Term Impacts on the Mother? Evidence from the 1970 British Cohort Study.* ISER Working Papers, Number 2003–28.1. Colchester, UK: Institute for Social and Economic Research, University of Essex.

Faculty of Sexual and Reproductive Health Clinical Effectiveness Unit and Royal Colleges of Midwives, Nursing and General Practitioners. (2017). *FSRH Guideline: Contraception After Pregnancy.* London: FSRH.

Fallon, D. and Broadhurst, K. (2015). *Preventing Unplanned Pregnancy and Improving Preparation for Parenthood for Care-Experienced Young People: A Comprehensive Review of the Literature and Critical Appraisal of Intervention Studies.* Universities of Manchester and Lancaster, on behalf of Coram.

Family Nurse Partnership. (2017). *FNP: Next Steps.* http://fnp.nhs.uk/evidence/fnp-next-steps.

Family Planning Association and Brook. (2014). *Decision Making Support Within the Integrated Care Pathway for Women Considering or Seeking Abortion. Guidance for Commissioners for Improving Access and Outcomes for Women.* London: fpa and Brook.

Fatherhood Institute. (2013). *Research Summary: Young Fathers.* London: Fatherhood Institute.

Ferguson, R.M., Vanwesenbeeck, I. and Knijn, T. (2008). A matter of facts . . . and more: An exploratory analysis of the content of sexuality education in the Netherlands. *Sex Education: Sexuality, Society and Learning*, 8(1), 93–106.

Fine, M. and McClelland, S.I. (2006). Sexuality education and desire: Still missing after all these years. *Harvard Educational Review*, 76(3), 297–338.

Florsheim, P. and Ngu, I.Q. (2003). *Differential Outcomes Among Adolescent Fathers: Understanding Fatherhood as a Transformative Process.* Paper presented at the Rocco C. and Marion S. Siciliano Forum Mini Conference, 18 October.

Food Standards Agency. (2000). *National Diet and Nutrition Survey: Young People Aged 4–18 Years.* London: TSO.

Ford, K., Butler, N., Hughes, K., Quigg, Z. and Bellis, M.A. (2016). *Adverse Childhood Experiences (ACEs) in Hertfordshire, Luton and Northamptonshire*. Liverpool, UK: Centre for Public Health, Liverpool John Moores University. www.cph.org.uk/wp-content/uploads/2016/05/Adverse-Childhood-Experiences-in-Hertfordshire-Luton-and-Northamptonshire-FINAL_compressed.pdf.

fpa. (2016). *Under-16s: Consent and Confidentiality in Sexual Health Services*. Factsheet. London: fpa.

Golding, J., Pembrey, M., Jones, R. and the ALSPAC Study Team. (2001). ALSPAC – The Avon Longitudinal Study of Parents and Children. *Pediatric and Perinatal Epidemiology*, 15(1), 74–87.

Haberland, N. and Rogow, D. (2015). Sexuality education: Emerging trends in evidence and practice. *Journal of Adolescent Health*, 56(1), pp. S15–S21.

Hadley, A., Ingham, R. and Chandra-Mouli, V. (2016). Implementing the United Kingdom's ten-year teenage pregnancy strategy for England (1999–2010): How was this done and what did it achieve? *Reproductive Health*, 13, 139.

Hadley, A., Chandra-Mouli, V., Ingham, R. (2016) Implementing the United Kingdom government's 10-year teenage pregnancy strategy for England (1999-2010): Applicable lessons for other countries. *Journal of Adolescent Health*. May 2016.

Hansard (2010). Children, Schools and Families Bill. Clause 11: PSHE in maintained schools, Column 1589. 7 April. www.publications.parliament.uk/pa/ld200910/ldhansrd/text/100407-0018.htm.

Hardman I. (2016). *The Spectator*, 24 May. https://blogs.spectator.co.uk/2016/05/how-good-government-often-goes-unnoticed-and-unrewarded/.

Hawkes, D. (2010). Just what difference does teenage motherhood make? Evidence from the Millennium Cohort Study, in Duncan, S., Edwards, R. and Alexander, C. (eds) *Teenage Parenthood: What's the Problem?* London: Tufnell Press, pp. 69–84.

Health and Social Care Act. (2012). c.7 www.legislation.gov.uk/ukpga/2012/7/contents/enacted.

Hirst, J. (2012). 'It's got to be about enjoying yourself': Young people, sexual pleasure and sex and relationships education. *Sex Education: Sexuality, Society and Learning*, 13(4), 423–436.

HM Government. (2011). *Positive for Youth: A New Approach to Cross-Government Policy for Young People Aged 13–19*. London: TSO.

HM Government. *Child Poverty Strategy: 2014–17*. Presented to Parliament by the Secretary of State for Work and Pensions, pursuant to Section 9 of the Child Poverty Act 2010. London: TSO.

Hoggart, L., Newton, V. and Dickson, J. (2013). *Understanding Long-Acting Reversible Contraception: An In-Depth Investigation into Sub-Dermal Contraceptive Implant Removal Amongst Young Women in London*. A report for the London Sexual Health Commissioning Programme. London: University of Greenwich School of Health and Social Care.

Horta, B., Bahl, R., Martines, J.C. and Victoria, C. (2007). *Evidence on the Long Term Effects of Breastfeeding: Systematic Review and Meta-Analyses*. Geneva: World Health Organization.

Huaynoca, S., Chandra-Mouli, V., Yaqub, N., Jr and Denno, D.M. (2013). Scaling up comprehensive sexuality education in Nigeria: From national policy to nationwide application. *Sex Education: Sexuality, Society and Learning*, 14(2), 191–209.

Image in Action. (2010). *Going Further, Getting Started. Sex and Relationships Education for Learners with Additional Needs at Colleges of Further Education.* High Wycombe: Image in Action.

Ingham, R. (1998). *Exploring Interactional Competence: Comparative Data from the United Kingdom and the Netherlands on Young People's Sexual Development.* Paper presented at the 24th Meeting of the International Academy of Sex Research, 3–6 June, Sirmione, Italy.

Ingham, R. (2007). Variations across countries: The international perspective, in Baker, P., Guthrie, K., Hutchinson, C., Kane, R. and Wellings, K. (eds) *Teenage Pregnancy and Reproductive Health.* London: Royal College of Obstetricians and Gynaecologists, pp. 17–29.

Ingham, R. and van Zessen, G. (1997). From individual properties to interactional processes, in Van Campenhoudt, L., Cohen, M., Guizzardi, G. and Hausser, D. (eds) *Sexual Interactions and HIV Risk: New conceptual perspectives in European research.* London: Taylor & Francis, pp. 83–99.

Ingham, R., Clements, S. and Gillibrand, R. (2001). *Factors Affecting Changes in Rates of Teenage Conceptions.* Unpublished report submitted to Department of Health. Southampton, UK: Centre for Sexual Health Research, University of Southampton.

Institute of Health Visiting. (2014). *Good Practice Points for Health Visitors: Engaging with Fathers.* London: Institute of Health Visiting.

Jahangir, M. and Mankani, N. (2016). *Aahung – Empowering Adolescents in Pakistan through Life Skills-Based Education.* New York: United Nations Girls' Education Initiative.

Jones E.F., Forrest J.D., Goldman, N., Henshaw, S.K., Lincoln, R., Rosoff, J.I., Westoff, C.F. and Wulf, D. (1985). Teenage pregnancy in developed countries: Determinants and policy implications. *Family Planning Perspectives*, 17(2), 53–63.

Jones, E.L. and Alan Guttmacher Institute Study Team. (1986). *Teenage Pregnancy in Industrialized Countries.* New Haven, CT: Yale University Press.

Kane, R. and Wellings, K. (2007). *Teenage Pregnancy: The views of young mothers.* Ch. 19 in *Teenage Pregnancy and Reproductive Health.* London: Royal College of Obstetricians and Gynaecologists, pp. 219–227.

Kempers, J., Ketting, E. and Lesco, G. (2014). Cost analysis and exploratory cost-effectiveness of youth-friendly sexual and reproductive health services in the Republic of Moldova. *BMC Health Services Research*, 14, 316.

Khashan, A., Baker, P. and Kenny, L. (2010). Preterm birth and reduced birthweight in first and second teenage pregnancies: A register-based cohort study. *BMC Pregnancy and Childbirth*, 10, 36.

Kiernan, K. (1997). Becoming a young parent: A longitudinal study of associated factors. *British Journal of Sociology*, 48, 406–428.

King-Hill, S. (2016). *Implementing the Brook Sexual Behaviours Traffic Light Tool in Cornwall: An Evaluation.* Commissioned by Brook and Cornwall Council and carried out by the University of Worcester, UK. University of Worcester.

Kirby, D (2007). *Emerging Answers 2007: Research Findings on Programs to Reduce Teen Pregnancy and Sexually Transmitted Diseases.* Washington, DC: National Campaign to Prevent Teen and Unplanned Pregnancy.

Kirby, D (2008). The impact of abstinence and comprehensive sex and STD/HIV education programmes on adolescent sexual behaviour. *Sexuality Research and Social Policy*, 5(3), 18–27.

Kohler, P.K., Manhart, L.E. and Lafferty, W.E. (2008). Abstinence-only and comprehensive sex education and the initiation of sexual activity and teen pregnancy. *Journal of Adolescent Health*, 42, 344–351.

Laski, L. (2015). For the Expert Consultative Group for Every Woman Every Child on Adolescent Health. Realising the health and wellbeing of adolescents. *BMJ* 2015, 351 Suppl.

Lau Clayton, C. (2017). Young Fathers and their Perspective of Health and Well-Being, in Portier, F. (ed.) *Population Health Perspective*. Abingdon, UK: Routledge.

Lau Clayton, C. (2015a). *Becoming a Young Father*. Leeds, UK: University of Leeds.

Lau Clayton, C. (2015b). *Being a Young Father*. Leeds, UK: University of Leeds.

Lau Clayton, C. (2015c). *Reflections on Young Fatherhood*. Leeds, UK: University of Leeds.

Lee, E., Clements, S., Ingham, R. and Stone, N. (2004). *A Matter of Choice? Explaining National Variation in Teenage Abortion and Motherhood*. York: Joseph Rowntree Foundation.

Lesco, G. (2016). Youth Friendly Health Services (YFHS) scaling up in the Republic of Moldova. Achievements and lessons learned. *Buletin Perinatologie*, 3(71), 4–14.

Lindberg, L. and Maddow-Zimet, I. (2012). Consequences of sex education on teen and young adult sexual behaviors and outcomes. *Journal of Adolescent Health*, 51, 332–338.

Lindberg, L., Santelli, J. and Desai, S. (2016). Understanding the decline in adolescent fertility in the United States, 2007–2012. *Journal of Adolescent Health*, 59, 577–583.

Local Government Association and Public Health England. (2016, updated 2017). *Teenage Pregnancy and Young Parents. Good Progress But More to Do*. London: LGA & PHE.

Local Government Association, Public Health England, Sex Education Forum and RSE Hub. (2017). *Relationships and Sex Education: Contribution to the safeguarding, Sexual and Reproductive Health and Wellbeing of Children and Young People*. London: LGA, PHE, SEF and RSE Hub.

London School of Hygiene and Tropical Medicine, UCL and BMRB International. (2005). *Teenage Pregnancy Strategy Evaluation. Final Report Synthesis*. Wellings, K., Wilkinson, P., Grundy, C., Kane, R., Lachowycz, K., Jacklin, P., Stevens, M. and Gerressu, M. (LSHTM), Stephenson, J., French, R. and Kingori, P. (UCL), London: LSHTM.

Macdowall, W., Jones, K.G., Tanton, C., Clifton, S., Copas, A.J., Mercer, C.H., Palmer, M.J., Lewis, R., Datta, J., Mitchell, K.R., Field, N., Sonnenberg, P., Johnson, A.M. and Wellings, K. (2015). Associations between source of information about sex and sexual health outcomes in Britain: Findings from the third National Survey of Sexual Attitudes and Lifestyles (NATSAL-3). *BMJ Open*, 5:e007837.

Madden, H., Eckley, L., Hughes, L., Lavin, R. and Timpson, H. (2014). *Long Acting Reversible Contraception: Young Women and Social Norms*. Liverpool, UK: Centre for Public Health, Liverpool John Moores University.

Marmot, M. (2010). *Fair Society, Healthy Lives: The Marmot Review*. London: The Marmot Review.

Martins, C. and Gaffen, E.A. (2002). Effects of early maternal depression on patterns of infant mother attachment: A meta analysis investigation. *Journal of Child Psychology and Psychiatry*, 41, 737–46.

Mason-Jones, A.J., Sinclair, D., Mathews, C., Kagee, A., Hillman, A. and Lombard, C. (2016). School-based interventions for preventing HIV, sexually transmitted infections and pregnancy in adolescents (Review). *Cochrane Database of Systematic Reviews*, Issue 11, Art. No. CD006417.

McGinn, L., Stone, N., Ingham, R. and Bengry-Howell, A. (2016). Parental interpretations of 'childhood innocence': Implications for early sexuality education. *Health Education*, 166(6), 580–594.

McKee, A. (2007). Positive and negative effects of pornography as attributed by consumers. *Australian Journal of Communication*, 34(1), 87–104.

Morinis, J., Carson, C. and Quigley, M.A. (2013). Effect of teenage motherhood on cognitive outcomes in children: A population-based cohort study. *Archives of Disease in Childhood*, 98, 959–964.

National Audit Office. (2001). *Modern Policy Making: Ensuring Policies Deliver Value for Money*. Report by the Comptroller and Auditor General. HC 289 Session 2001–02. London: NAO.

National Children's Bureau and fpa. (2003). *Let's Make It Happen: Training on Sex, Relationships, Pregnancy and Parenthood for Those Working With Looked After Children and Young People*. London: National Children's Bureau.

National Children's Bureau. (2006). *Involving Young People in Teenage Pregnancy and Sexual Health Work: A Practical Guide*. London: NCB.

National Institute for Care and Health Excellence (NICE). (2008). *Antenatal Care for Uncomplicated Pregnancies*. Clinical guidance (CG62). London: NICE.

National Institute for Care and Health Excellence (NICE). (2010). *Pregnancy and Complex Social Factors: A Model for Service Provision for Pregnant Women with Complex Social Factors*. Clinical guideline (CG110). London: NICE.

Neale, B. and Davies, L. (2015). *Rethinking Support for Young Fathers*. Following Young Fathers Briefing Paper 6. University of Leeds, UK.

NHS and Parentline Plus. (2010). *Talking to Your Teenager about Sex and Relationships*. London: NHS.

NICE. (2014). *Contraceptive Services for Under 25s: Public Health Guidance 51*. London: NICE.

NICE. (2016). *Contraception*. Quality standard (QS129). London: NICE.

NICE. (2017). *STIs and Condom Distribution Schemes: Public Health Guidance*. London: NICE.

Nichols, J. (2011). *Reducing Teenage Pregnancy Rates in England Post-2010: The Challenge of Changing Time*. MSc Dissertation, University of Bradford, UK.

Office of the Deputy Prime Minister. (2004). *The Social Exclusion Unit*. London: Office of the Deputy Prime Minister.

Office for National Statistics. (2014). *Link Between Deprivation and Teenage Conceptions in England*. London: ONS.

Office for National Statistics. (2016). *Table 1. Statistical Bulletin: Births by Parents' Characteristics in England and Wales, 2015*. London: ONS.

Office for National Statistics, 2017a). *Conception Statistics, England and Wales, 2015*. London: ONS.

Office for National Statistics. (2017b). *Childhood Mortality Statistics, 2015*. Table 4 and Table 10. London: ONS.

Office for National Statistics. (2017c). *Pregnancy and Ethnic Factors Influencing Births and Infant Mortality, 2014*. Table 4. London: ONS.

Office for Standards in Education, Children's Services and Skills (Ofsted). (2007). *Time for Change? Personal, Social and Health Education*. London: Ofsted.

Ofsted. (2011). *Ages of Concern: Learning Lessons From Serious Case Reviews. A Thematic Report of Ofsted's Evaluation of Serious Case Reviews From 1 April 2007 to 31 March 2011*. Manchester, UK: Ofsted.

Olds, D.L., Kitzman, H., Knudtson, M.D., Anson, E., Smith, J.A. and Cole, R. (2014). Effect of home visiting by nurses on maternal and child mortality: Results of a 2-decade follow-up of a randomized clinical trial. *JAMA Pediatrics*, 168(9), 800–806.

Parkes, A., Strange, V., Wight, D., Bonell, C., Copas, A., Henderson, M., Buston, K., Stephenson, J., Johnson, A., Allen, E. and Hart, G. (2011). Comparison of teenagers' early same-sex and heterosexual behavior: UK data from the SHARE and RIPPLE studies. *Journal of Adolescent Health*, 48, 27–35.

Price, S. and Mitchell, M. (2009). *Teenagers' Experiences of the Maternity Services*. London: Royal College of Midwives.

Public Health England. (2014). *Using Conception Data to Monitor Progress on Teenage Pregnancy*. London: PHE.

Public Health England. (2016). *National Drug Treatment Monitoring System (NDTMS) Data for 2014/15*. London: PHE.

Public Health England. (2017). *National Public Health Profiles*. London: PHE.

Public Health England and Local Government Association. (2016). *A Framework for Supporting Teenage Mothers and Young Fathers*. London: PHE & LGA.

Public Health England and Local Government Association. (2017). *A Framework to Support Young People to Prevent Unplanned Pregnancy and Develop Healthy Relationships*. London: PHE & LGA.

Public Health England, Local Government Association, Association of Directors of Public Health and NHS England. (2014, revised 2015). *Making It Work: A Guide To Whole System Commissioning for Sexual Health, Reproductive Health and HIV*. London: PHE, LGA, ADPH and NHSE.

Public Health England, Royal Society for the Prevention of Accidents and Child Accident Prevention Trust. (2014). *Reducing Unintentional Injuries in and around the Home among Children under Five Years*. London: PHE.

Quail, K. (2007). Housing difficulties for teenage parents and their children: An East Midlands study. Ch. 18 in *Teenage Pregnancy and Reproductive Health*. London: Royal College of Obstetricians and Gynaecologists (RCOG Press).

Quilgars, D., Johnson, S., Pleace, N., Beecham, J. and Bonin, E. (2011). *Supporting Independence? Evaluation of the Teenage Parent Supported Housing Pilot – Final Report*. Centre for Housing Policy, University of York, UK.

Quinton, D., Pollock, S. and Golding, J. (2002). *The Transition to Fatherhood in Young Men: Influences on Commitment*. Bristol, UK: Economic Social Research Council.

Rademakers, J. (1991). Contraception and interaction among Dutch boys and girls. *Planned Parenthood in Europe (Planning familial en Europe)*, 19(3), 7–8.

Reddington, S. (2007). Education and childcare for young mothers: How do we ensure they do not miss out? In *Teenage Pregnancy and Reproductive Health*. London: Royal College of Obstetricians and Gynaecologists (RCOG Press).

Robling M., Bekkers M.J., Bell K., Butler C.C., Cannings-John R., Channon S., Corbacho Martin B., Gregory J.W., Hood K., Kemp A., Kenkre J., Montgomery A.A., Moody G., Owen-Jones E., Pickett K., Richardson G., Roberts Z.E.S.,

Ronaldson S., Sanders J., Stamuli E. and Torgerson D. (2015). Effectiveness of a nurse-led intensive home-visitation programme for first-time teenage mothers (Building Blocks): A pragmatic randomised controlled trial. *Lancet*, 387, 146–155.

Royal College of General Practitioners. (2017). *RCGPLearning: Contraception*. London: RCGP.

Royal College of General Practitioners, British Medical Association, General Practitioners Committee, Royal College of Nursing and Medical Defence Union. (2001, revised 2016). *Confidentiality and Young People Toolkit*. London: RCGP.

Royal College of General Practitioners and Royal College of Nursing. (2002). *Getting It Right for Young People in Your Practice*. London: RCGP.

Royal College of Obstetricians and Gynaecologists and Royal College of Midwives. (2010). *Pregnancy and Complex Social Factors: A Model for Service Provision for Pregnant Women with Complex Social Factors*. National Collaborating Centre for Women's and Children's Health. Commissioned by NICE. London: RCOG and RCM.

Royal College of Paediatrics and Child Health. (2015). *Adolescent Health e-learning*. London: RCPCH.

Royal College of Paediatrics and Child Health. (2017). *The State of Child Health: Conception, Pregnancy and Infancy Indicators*. London: RCPCH.

Sabates, R. and Dex, S. (2012). *Multiple Risk Factors in Young Children's Development*. CLS Working Paper 2012/1. London: IoE Centre for Longitudinal Studies.

Santelli, J.S., Lindberg, L.D., Finer, L.B. and Singh, S. (2007). Explaining recent declines in adolescent pregnancy in the United States: The contribution of abstinence and improved contraceptive use. *American Journal of Public Health*, 97(1), 150–156.

Santelli, J. (2008). Medical accuracy in sexuality education: Ideology and the scientific process. *American Journal of Public Health*, 98(10), 1786–1792.

Santelli, J., Ott, M.A., Lyon, M., Rogers, J., Summers, D. and Schleifer, R. (2006). Abstinence and abstinence-only education: A review of U.S. policies and programs. *Journal of Adolescent Health*, 38, 72–81.

Schalet, A. (2000). Raging hormones, regulated love: Adolescent sexuality and the constitution of the modern individual in the United States and the Netherlands. *Body & Society*, 6(1), 75–105.

Schalet, A. (2011). *Not Under My Roof: Parents, Teens and the Culture of Sex*. Chicago, IL: Chicago University Press.

Scottish Government. (2016a). *Pregnancy and Parenthood in Young People Strategy: 2016–2026*. Crown Copyright.

Scottish Government. (2016b). *Pregnancy and Parenthood in Young People Strategy: Engagement with Young People Feedback Report*. Crown Copyright.

Sex Education Forum. (2003). *Secondary Schools and Sexual Health Services: Forging the Links*. London: National Children's Bureau.

Sex Education Forum. (2006). *Beyond Biology*. London: National Children's Bureau.

Sex Education Forum. (2008a). *Are You Getting It Right? A Toolkit for Consulting Young People on Sex and Relationships Education*. London: National Children's Bureau.

Sex Education Forum. (2008b). *National Mapping of On-Site Sexual Health Services in Education Settings: Provision in Schools and Pupil Referral Units in England*. London: National Children's Bureau.

Sex Education Forum. (2008c). *National Mapping Survey of On-Site Sexual Health Services in Education Settings: Provision in FE and Sixth Form Colleges*. London: National Children's Bureau.

Sex Education Forum (2015). *SRE – The Evidence*, London: Sex Education Forum and National Children's Bureau.

Singh, S. and Darroch, J.E. (2000). Adolescent pregnancy and childbearing: Levels and trends in developed countries. *Family Planning Perspectives*, 32(1), 14–23.

Skinner, R. and Marina, J. (2016). England's teenage pregnancy strategy: A hard-won success. *Lancet Comment*, 23 May.

Smith, N.S.P. (2015). *Health Equity Audit of Booking for Antenatal Care in London*. London: NHS.

Smith, D.M. and Elander, J. (2006). Effects of area and family deprivation on risk factors for teenage pregnancy among 13–15-year-old girls. *Psychology, Health and Medicine*, 11(4), 399–410.

Smith, T. (1993). Influence of socio-economic factors on attaining targets for reducing teenage pregnancies. *British Medical Journal*, 306, 1232–1235.

Social Exclusion Unit. (1999). *Teenage Pregnancy*. London: SEU, Cmnd 4342.

Steiner, R.J., Liddon, N., Swartzendruber, A.L., Rasberry, C.N. and Sales, J.M. (2016). Long-acting reversible contraception and condom use among female US high school students: Implications for sexually transmitted infection prevention. *JAMA Pediatrics*, 170(5), 428–434.

Stephenson, J., Strange, V., Allen, E., Copas, A., Johnson, A., Bonell, C., Babiker, A., Oakley, A. and the RIPPLE Study Team. (2008). The long-term effects of a peer-led sex education programme (RIPPLE): A cluster randomised trial in schools in England. *PLoS Medicine*, 5, 1579–1590.

Stephenson, J.M., Strange, V., Forrest, S., Oakley, A., Copas, A., Allen, E., Babiker, A., Black, S., Ali, M., Monteiro, H., Johnson, A.M., and the RIPPLE study team. (2004). Pupil-led sex education in England (RIPPLE study): Cluster-randomised intervention trial. *Lancet*, 364, 338–346.

Stone, N., Ingham, R. and Gibbins, K. (2012). 'Where do babies come from?' Barriers to early sexuality communication between parents and young children. *Sex Education: Sexuality, Society and Learning*, 13(2), 228–240.

Svanemyr, J., Baig, Q. and Chandra-Mouli, V. (2015). Scaling up life skilled based sexuality education in Pakistan: A case study. *Sex Education: Sexuality, Society and Learning*, 15(3), 249–262.

Tanton, C., Jones, K.G., Macdowall, W., Clifton, S., Mitchell, K.R., Datta, J., Lewis, R., Field, N., Sonnenberg, P., Stevens, A., Wellings, K., Johnson, A.M. and Mercer, C.H. (2015). Patterns and trends in sources of information about sex among young people in Britain: Evidence from three National Surveys of Sexual Attitudes and Lifestyles. *BMJ Open*, 5:e007834.

Teenage Pregnancy Independent Advisory Group. (2009). *Parliamentary Briefing: Why We Need Sustained Action to Accelerate Reductions in Teenage Pregnancy*. London: TPIAG.

Teenage Pregnancy Independent Advisory Group. (2010). *Teenage Pregnancy: Past Successes – Future Challenges*. Final report. London: TPIAG.

Teenage Pregnancy Unit. (2000a). *Guidance for Developing Contraception and Sexual Health Advice Services to Reach Boys and Young Men*. London: Teenage Pregnancy Unit.

Teenage Pregnancy Unit. (2000b). *Guidance for Developing Contraception and Sexual Health Advice Services to Reach Young People from Black and Minority Ethnic Communities*. London: Teenage Pregnancy Unit.

Teenage Pregnancy Unit. (2002a). *Government Response to the First Annual Report of the Independent Advisory Group on Teenage Pregnancy*. London: Teenage Pregnancy Unit.

Teenage Pregnancy Unit. (2002b). *Involving Young People in Peer Education: A Guide for Establishing Sex and Relationships Peer Education Projects*. London: Teenage Pregnancy Unit.

Teenage Pregnancy Unit. (2002c). *Diverse Communities: Identity and Teenage Pregnancy*. London: Teenage Pregnancy Unit.

Teenage Pregnancy Unit. (2002d). *A Guide to Involving Young People in Teenage Pregnancy Work*. London: Teenage Pregnancy Unit.

Teenage Pregnancy Unit. (2004–07). *Teenage Pregnancy Research Briefings 1–8*. London: Department of Health.

Teenage Pregnancy Unit. (2006, updated 2009). *Teenage Pregnancy: Working Towards 2010. Good Practice and Self-Assessment Toolkit*. London: Teenage Pregnancy Unit.

Teenage Pregnancy Unit and Department of Health. (2004). *Long Term Consequences of Teenage Births for Parents and Their Children*. Teenage Pregnancy Unit Research Programme Briefing. London: TPU and Department of Health.

The Catholic Education Service. (2017). *Press Statement from Archbishop Malcolm McMahon OP KC★HS, Chairman of the Catholic Education Service*. London: CES.

The Church of England. (2017). *The Bishop of Ely, the Rt Revd Stephen Conway, the Church of England's Lead Bishop on Education. Blog: Equipping Children for the World in Which They Live*. http://cofecomms.tumblr.com/post/157857761432/equipping-children-for-the-world-in-which-they.

The Health and Social Care Information Centre. (2012). *Infant Feeding Survey 2010*. London: HSCIC.

Trivedi, D., Bunn, F., Graham, M. and Wentz, R. (2007). *Update on Review of Reviews on Teenage Pregnancy and Parenthood*. Submitted as an addendum to the first evidence briefing 2003. Hertfordshire: Centre for Research in Primary and Community Care, University of Hertfordshire, on behalf of National Institute for Health and Clinical Excellence.

UK Youth Parliament. (2007). *SRE: Are You Getting It?* A report by the UK Youth Parliament. London: UKYP.

UN. (2014). *Special Rapporteur on Violence Against Women Finalizes Country Mission to the United Kingdom and Calls for Urgent Action to Address the Accountability Deficit and also the Adverse Impacts of Changes in Funding and Services*. www.ohchr.org/EN/NewsEvents/Pages/DisplayNews.aspx?NewsID=14514&LangID=E.

UNESCO. (2016). *Review of the evidence on sexuality education*. Report to inform the update of the UNESCO International Technical Guidance on Sexuality Education; prepared by Paul Montgomery and Wendy Knerr, University of Oxford Centre for Evidence-Based Intervention. Paris, UNESCO.

UNESCO. (2017). *International Technical Guidance on Sexuality Education. An evidence-informed approach*. Revised edition. Paris, UNESCO. (In press).

UNFPA. (2013a). *Adolescent Pregnancy: A review of the evidence*. New York: UNFPA.

UNFPA. (2013b). *Motherhood in Childhood: Facing the challenge of adolescent pregnancy*. New York: UNFPA.

UNFPA. (2015). *Girlhood, Not Motherhood: Preventing Adolescent Pregnancy*. New York: UNFPA.

UNICEF. (2001). *A League Table of Teenage Births in Rich Nations*. Innocenti Report Card No. 3. Florence, Italy: UNICEF Innocenti Research Centre.

United Nations. (2015). *The Global Strategy for Women's, Children's and Adolescents' Health*. New York: UN.

University of Leeds, School of Sociology and Social Policy. (2015). *Following Young Fathers*. Briefing Papers 1–8. University of Leeds, UK.

Universities of Leeds and Glamorgan and the London School of Hygiene and Tropical Medicine. (1998). *Health of the Nation: A Policy Assessed*. London: Department of Health.

Vaid, L., Mavra, L. and Sims, L. (2009). *The Impact of Care to Learn: Tracking the Destinations of Young Parents Funded in 2006/07 and 2007/08*. London: Centre for Economic and Social Inclusion and Learning and Skills Council.

Wellings, K. and Kane, R. (1999). Trends in teenage pregnancy in England and Wales: How can we explain them? *Journal of the Royal Society of Medicine*, 92(6), 277–282.

Wellings, K.G., Mercer, C.H., Tanton, C., Clifton, S., Datta, A.J., Erens, B., Gibson, L.J., Macdowall, W., Sonnenberg, P., Phelps, A. and Johnson, A.M. (2013). The prevalence of unplanned pregnancy and associated factors in Britain: Findings from the third National Survey of Sexual Attitudes and Lifestyles (NATSAL-3). *Lancet*, 382(9907), 1807–1816.

Wellings, K., Palmer, M.J., Geary, R.S., Gibson, L.J., Copas, A., Datta, J., Glasier, A., Scott, R.H., Mercer, C.H., Erens, B., Macdowall, W., French, R.S., Jones, K., Johnson, A.M., Tanton, C. and Wilkinson, P. (2016). Changes in conceptions in women younger than 18 years and the circumstances of young mothers in England in 2000–12: An observational study, *Lancet* 388(10044), 586–595.

WHO and UNAIDS. (2015). *Global Standards for Quality Health-Care Services for Adolescents: A Guide to Implement a Standards-Driven Approach to Improve the Quality of Health Care Services for Adolescents*. Volume 1: Standards and criteria, Volume 2: Implementation guide, Volume 3: Tools to conduct quality and coverage measurement surveys to collect data. WHO. Geneva.

WHO. (1998). *The World Health Report 1998. Life in the 21st Century. A Vision for All*. Report of the Director-General. Geneva: WHO.

Wiggins, M., Rosato, M., Austerberry, H., Sawtell, M. and Oliver, S. (2005). *Sure Start Plus*. National Evaluation: Final report. London: Social Science Research Unit, Institute of Education, University of London.

Wight, D. (2011). The effectiveness of school based sex education: What do rigorous evaluations in Britain tell us? *Education and Health*, 29, 67–73.

World Health Organization. (2012). *Making Health Services Adolescent Friendly. Developing National Quality Standards for Adolescent-Friendly Health Services*. Geneva: Department of Maternal, Newborn, Child and Adolescent Health.

World Health Organization. (1977). *Global Strategy for Health for All by the Year 2000*. Geneva: WHO.

Index

Note: bold indicates tables; italics indicate figures; 'n' indicates chapter notes.